International Law

INTERNATIONAL LAW

122159

BY

GEORGE GRAFTON WILSON, Ph.D.

PROFESSOR IN BROWN UNIVERSITY

AND

GEORGE FOX TUCKER, Ph.D.

LATELY REPORTER OF DECISIONS OF THE SUPREME JUDICIAL
COURT OF MASSACHUSETTS

SECOND EDITION

SILVER, BURDETT AND COMPANY

NEW YORK   BOSTON   CHICAGO

PREFACE TO THE SECOND EDITION

THE authors have in this new edition introduced changes made necessary by the development of international relations. The wars of recent years and the results of the Hague Conference have greatly modified earlier practice. Appendix X contains the Convention for the Pacific Settlement of International Disputes. Appendix XI contains the Convention with Respect to the Laws and Customs of War on Land. The other codes and rules printed in the Appendices in a measure supplement this Convention and give an opportunity for valuable comparison.

The authors express their appreciation of the reception which the first edition has received.

G. G. W.

G. F. T.

SEPTEMBER, 1902.

PREFACE

THE authors have freely used the substantive material as found in cases, codes, etc., which involve the principles of International Law. Owing to the increasing importance of international negotiation, relatively more attention than usual has been given to matters connected with diplomacy. The appendices contain material which the authors have found advantageous to have easily accessible to each student. •The study of this book should in all cases be supplemented by reference to a considerable number of the books mentioned in the bibliography.

G. G. W

G. F. T.

SEPTEMBER, 1901.

CONTENTS

PART I

GENERAL AND HISTORICAL

CHAPTER I

  1. DEFINITION.
      (a) Philosophical: what ought to be.
      (b) Scientific: what is.
  2. DIVISIONS.
      (a) Public.
      (b) Private.
  3. SCOPE.

CHAPTER II

  4. EARLY TERMINOLOGY.
      (a) Jus naturale.
      (b) Jus gentium.
      (c) Other terms.
  5. HISTORICAL BASES.
  6. ETHICAL BASES.
  7. JURAL BASES.
      (a) Roman law.
      (b) Canon law.
      (c) Common law.
      (d) Equity.
      (e) Admiralty law.

v

PART II

PERSONS IN INTERNATIONAL LAW

CHAPTER V

CHAPTER VI

PART III

INTERNATIONAL LAW OF PEACE

CHAPTER VII

CHAPTER VIII

CHAPTER IX

CHAPTER X

CHAPTER XI

PART IV

INTERNATIONAL LAW OF WAR

CHAPTER XVI

CHAPTER XVII

CHAPTER XVIII

CHAPTER XIX

CHAPTER XX

CHAPTER XXI

PART V

INTERNATIONAL LAW OF NEUTRALITY

CHAPTER XXII

CHAPTER XXIII

CHAPTER XXIV

BIBLIOGRAPHY

THIS list contains the titles of books most frequently cited in the following pages : —

BLUNTSCHLI, J. C. Le droit international. (Lardy), 1886.

BONFILS. Droit International Public. (Fauchille), 1898.

CALVO, CH. Droit International. 5ᵉ ed. 6 vols. 1896.

COBBETT, PITT. Leading Cases and Opinions on International Law. 2d ed. 1892.

DAHLGREN, J. A. Maritime International Law. 1877.

DAVIS, G. B. The Elements of International Law. 1901.

DESPAGNET. Droit International Public. 2d ed. 1899.

FIELD, D. D. Outline of an International Code. 1876.

GLASS, H. Marine International Law. 1884.

GLENN, E. F. Hand Book of International Law. 1895.

GROTIUS, H. De Jure Belli ac Pacis. 3 vols. Whewell. 1853.

HALL, W. E. International Law. 4th ed. 1895.

HALLECK, H. W. Elements of International Law. 3d ed. Baker. 1893.

HEFFTER, A. G. Droit International. 4th ed. Geffcken. 1883.

HERTSLET, E. Map of Europe by Treaty, 1815–1891. 4 vols. 1875–1891.

HOLLS, F. W. The Peace Conference at the Hague. 1900.

HOSACK, J. Rise and Growth of the Law of Nations. 1882.

KENT, J. Commentaries on American Law. 14th ed.

LAWRENCE, T. J. Principles of International Law. 3d ed. 1900.

LEHR, E. Manuel des Agents Diplomatiques et Consulaires. 1888.

MAINE, H. International Law. 1888.

MOORE, J. B. Extradition and Interstate Rendition. 2 vols. 1891.
—— International Arbitrations. 6 vols. 1898.

ORTOLAN, T. Diplomatie de la Mer. 4th ed. 2 vols. 1864.

PERELS, F. Manuel de Droit Maritime International par Arendt.
  1884.

PHILLIMORE, R. International Law. 3d ed.

POMEROY, J. N. International Law in Times of Peace. 1886.

PRADIER-FODÉRÉ, P. Trait de Droit International Public Européen
  et Americain. 7 vols. 1885–1897.

RIVIER, A. Principes du Droit des Gens. 2 vols. 1896.

SNOW, F. Cases and Opinions on International Law. 1893.
—— American Diplomacy. 1894.
—— International Law. Naval War College. Prepared by Stock-
  ton. 2d ed. 1898.

TAKAHASHI, S. Cases on International Law, Chino-Japanese. 1896.

TAYLOR, H. International Public Law. 1901.

TREATIES AND CONVENTIONS between the United States and Other
  Powers, 1776–1887. 1887.

TREATIES IN FORCE, Compilation of United States. 1899.

VATTEL, E. Law of Nations. Trans. Ingraham. 1876.

WALKER, T. A. Science of International Law. 1893.
—— Manual of Public International Law. 1895.
—— History of the Law of Nations, vol. 1. 1899.

WESTLAKE, J. Chapters on Principles of International Law. 1894.

WHARTON, F. Digest of International Law. 3 vols. 2d ed. 1887.

WHEATON, H. Elements of International Law. 1836.
—— Edited by Lawrence, W. B. 1863.
—— Edited by Dana, R. H. 1865.
—— Edited by Boyd, A. C. 2d ed.

WOOLSEY, T. D. International Law. 6th ed. 1891.

ABBREVIATIONS OF CITATIONS

The following are the important abbreviations of citations: —

Ann. Cycl. . . . . . . Appleton's Annual Cyclopædia.

Br. & For. St. Pap. . . British and Foreign State Papers.

C. Rob. . . . . Chr. Robinson's English Admiralty Reports.

Brussels Code . . . . Conference at Brussels, 1874, on Military Warfare.

Cr. . . . . Cranch's United States Reports.

Fed. Rep. . . . . . Federal Reporter.

Gould & Tucker . . . Gould and Tucker's Notes on the United States Statutes.

Hall . . . . Hall's International Law (4th ed.).

Hertslet . . . . . . Hertslet Map of Europe by Treaty.

How. . . . . Howard United States Reports.

Instr. U. S. Armies . . Instructions for the Government of Armies of the United States in the Field.

Kent's Com. . . . . Kent's Commentaries (14th ed.).

Lawrence . . . . . Lawrence's Principles of International Law.

Oxford Manual . . . Manual of the Laws of War on Land, Oxford, 1880.

Pet. . . . . Peters's United States Reports.

Schuyler . . . . . . Schuyler's American Diplomacy.

Takahashi . . . . . Takahashi's Cases during the Chino-Japanese War.

Treaties of U. S. . . . Treaties and Conventions of the United States, 1776–1887.

U. S. For. Rel. . . . United States Foreign Relations.

TABLE OF CASES CITED

PART I

GENERAL AND HISTORICAL

INTERNATIONAL LAW

CHAPTER I

DEFINITION AND GENERAL SCOPE

1. **DEFINITION.**
    (*a*) Philosophical: what ought to be.
    (*b*) Scientific: what is.

2. **DIVISIONS.**
    (*a*) Public.
    (*b*) Private.

3. **SCOPE.**

§ 1. Definition

International law may be considered from two points of view, viz. : —

(*a*) **From the philosophical point of view,** as setting forth the rules and principles which *ought to be observed* in interstate relations.

(*b*) **From the scientific point of view,** as setting forth the rules and principles which *are* generally observed in interstate relations.

Wheaton, D., 23: "International law, as understood among civilized nations, may be defined as consisting of those rules of conduct which reason deduces, as consonant to justice, from the nature of the society existing among independent nations; with such definitions and modifications as may be established by general consent." See also I. Pradier-Fodéré, pp. 8, 41.

Early writers treated especially of those principles which *ought to be* observed in interstate action, and the wealth of quotation and testimony introduced to establish the validity of principles now considered almost axiomatic, is overwhelming. In the days of Ayala, Brunus, Gentilis, Grotius, and Pufendorf, all the argument possible was needed to bring states to submit to these principles. The conditions and relations of states have so changed that at the present time a body of fairly established rules and principles *are* observed in interstate action, and form the subject-matter of international law.[1]

§ 2. Divisions

International law is usually divided into : —

(*a*) **Public international law**, which treats of the rules and principles which are generally observed in interstate action, and

(*b*) **Private international law**, which treats of the rules and principles which are observed in cases of conflict of jurisdiction in regard to private rights. These cases are not properly international, and a better term for this branch of knowledge is that given by Judge Story, " The Conflict of Laws." [2]

International law, in the true sense, deals only with state affairs.

§ 3. Scope

International law is generally observed by civilized states; even some of those states not fully open to

[1] Hall, Introductory chapter.

[2] Dicey, " Conflict of Laws," English, with notes of American cases, by J. B. Moore.

western civilization profess to observe its rules.[1] The expansion of commerce and trade, the introduction of new and rapid means of communication, the diffusion of knowledge through books and travel, the establishment of permanent embassies, the making of many treaties containing the same general provisions, and the whole movement of modern civilization toward unifying the interests of states, has rapidly enlarged the range of international action and the scope of international law. Civilized states, so far as possible, observe the rules of international law in their dealings with uncivilized communities which have not yet attained to statehood. International law covers all the relations into which civilized states may come, both peaceful and hostile. In general, it should not extend its scope so as to interfere with domestic affairs or to limit domestic jurisdiction, though it does often limit the economic and commercial action of a given state, and determine to some extent its policy.

[1] Wheaton's "International Law," translated and made a textbook for Chinese officials in 1864.

CHAPTER II

NATURE

§ 4. Early Terminology

The conception of those rules and principles of which international law treats has varied greatly with periods, with conditions, and with writers.

The early terminology indicates the vagueness of the conceptions of the principles governing conduct of man toward his fellows.

(a) **Jus naturale** is defined broadly by Ulpian[1] as "the law which nature has taught all living creatures,

---

[1] "Inst.," I., 1, 1.

6

so as to be common to men and beasts." Grotius also uses this term, defining it as "the dictate of right reason, indicating that any act from its agreement or disagreement with rational nature has in it moral turpitude or moral necessity, and consequently such act is either forbidden or enjoined by God, the author of nature."[1] Lieber says, "The law of nature, or natural law . . . is the law, the body of rights, which we deduce from the essential nature of man."[2] The discussion of *jus naturale* has been carried on from an early period,[3] covering many portions of the field of modern international law, and making possible the broadening and strengthening of its foundation.

(*b*) **Jus gentium**, according to Justinian, is "that which natural reason has established among all men, that which all peoples uniformly regard."[4] "*Jus gentium* is common to the whole human kind."[5] This idea of a body of law common to all men assumed a different meaning when states multiplied and writer after writer redefined and qualified its meaning. *Jus gentium* became the subject of many controversies.[6] Among the qualifying terms were "internal," "necessary," "natural," "positive."

(*c*) **Other terms** were used to name the field or portions of the field of modern international law. *Jus fetiale* applied particularly to the declaration of war and sanction of treaties.[7] *Jus inter gentes* was used by

---

[1] "De Jure Belli," Bk. I., Ch. I., § 10.
[2] I. "Political Ethics," 2d ed., p. 68.
[3] Maine, "Ancient Law," Ch. IV.
[4] "Inst.," I., 2, 1.   [5] "Inst.," I., 2, 2.
[6] Heffter, "Völkerrecht," § 2.
[7] Cicero, "De Republica," 2. 17.

Zouch in 1650 to name the real field of international law. *Law of nations* was the term commonly used in England till the days of Bentham; since that time the term *international law*, which he adopted, has steadily grown in favor, till almost universal in the English language.[1]

The change in terminology shows in a measure the growth in demarking the field of international law.

§ 5. Historical Bases

International law in its beginning may have been largely determined by abstract reasoning upon what *ought to be* the principles and rules governing interstate relations; but in its later development, as it has become more and more recognized as a safe guide for the conduct of states in their relations with other states, not abstract reasoning as to what *ought to be*, but direct investigation of what *is*, has determined the character of the rules and principles. What *is* state practice in a given case can only be determined by reference to history. From the history of cases and practice, the general rule and principle is derived, and modern international law thus comes to rest largely upon historical bases.

§ 6. Ethical Bases

While international law now looks to history as one of its most important bases, it must nevertheless accord somewhat closely with the ethical standards of the time, and will tend to approximate to them. The growth of the body of law upon slavery has rested on both ethical

[1] *Droit international* is the French term, subsequently adopted.

and historical bases. International law is principally an output of civilized nations having certain ethical standards. Such ancient practices as the giving of hostages for the fulfillment of treaty stipulations have disappeared, and ethical bases are generally recognized in determining practice.[1] While these ethical bases should be recognized, international law cannot be deduced from the subtle reasoning upon the abstract ideas of what it *ought to be*. Modern international law treats mainly of what *is*, but what *is* in international relations is always conditioned by a recognition of what *ought to be*.

§ 7. Jural Bases

The nature of modern international law is in part due to the jural bases upon which it rests.

(*a*) **The Roman law** was the most potent influence in determining the early development, particularly in respect to dominion and acquisition of territory. International law gained a certain dignity and weight from its relation to the Roman law, the most potent legal institution in history.

(*b*) **The canon law,** as the law of the ecclesiastics who were supposed to recognize the broadest principles of human unity, gave an ethical element to early international law. Gregory IX. (1227–1241), the Justinian of the Church, reduced canon law to a code. The abstract reasoning upon its principles among the clergy and counsellors of kings, made it a part of the mental stock of the early text writers, while it strongly influenced state practice. The canon law gave a quasi-

[1] Last hostages given in Europe 1748, by England to France.

religious sanction to its observance, and in so far as international law embodied its principles, gave the same sanction to the observance of international equity. This may be seen in the religious formula in treaties, even to a late date.

(c) **The common law**, itself international as derived from three systems, according to tradition, by Edward the Confessor, and subsequently modified by custom, furnished a practical element in determining the nature of international law.

(d) **Equity** promoted the development of the recognition of principles in international law. In the early days of England cases arose which were not within the cognizance of the common law judges. The petitioner having applied to the king in Parliament or in council for justice, his petition was referred to the chancellor, the keeper of the king's conscience, who, after a hearing, required that what was equitable should be done. Thus the simpler matters came before the common law court, the more difficult before the equity court. Even now a jury largely deals with questions relating to the recovery of money, and their decision is a *verdict*, which is followed by a judgment. In an equity court, the more difficult problems of business and commerce are considered; and the decision of the judge is a *decree*.

(e) **Admiralty law** may be defined as in one sense the law of the sea. Anterior to and during the Middle Ages, the maritime relations of states gave rise to sea laws, many of which are to-day well-recognized principles of international law.

§ 8. International and Statute Law

Statute law proceeds from legislative enactment, and is enforced by the power of the enacting state within its jurisdiction.

International law, on the other hand, is not formally enacted, and has no tribunal for its enforcement. Resort may be had to war in case of infraction of its rules, but the issue may rather depend upon the relative powers of the two states and not upon the justice of the cause.

§ 9. How far is International Law entitled to be called Law?

If law is defined, as by Austin, "A rule laid down for the guidance of an intelligent being by an intelligent being having power over him,"[1] it would not be possible to include under it international law without undue liberality in the interpretation of the language.

In form, however, law is a body of rules and principles in accord with which phenomena take place. If these rules are not followed as enunciated by the state in case of statute law, certain penalties are inflicted. The nature of the penalty must to a great extent depend on the source. International law is the body of rules and principles, in accord with which, interstate phenomena take place. Violations of international law do not meet the same penalties as those of statute law, as they do not have the same source nor an established tribunal for their enforcement. International law is, however, in form law and in practice so regarded.[2]

[1] "Lectures on Jurisprudence," I.

[2] Walker, "Science of International Law," Chs. I. and II., fully discusses Austin's definition.

CHAPTER III

§ 10. Early Period

The history of the development of those rules and principles now considered in international law naturally falls into three periods, early, middle and modern.[1]

The **early period** dates from the time of the development of early European civilization, and extends to the

---

[1] Bluntschli, "Völkerrecht," Introduction; Lawrence, § 20.

(*b*) **Rome.** Rome made many contributions to the principles of international law in the way of the extension of her own laws to wider spheres, and in the attempt to adapt Roman laws to conditions in remote territories. In this early period Rome may be said to have contributed to the field of what is now considered private international law rather than to that of public international law. This is evident in the laws in regard to marriage, contract, property, etc. The dominance of Rome impressed her laws on others, and extended the influence of those principles which, from general practice, or conformity to accepted standards, gained the name *Jus Gentium*.[1]

§ 11. Middle Period

The varied struggles of the middle period —from the beginning of the Christian Era to the middle of the seventeenth century — had a decided influence upon the body and form of international law.

(*a*) **Roman Empire.** The growth of the Roman Empire, as the single world, power and sole source of

religious traditions. This is shown in the oath of the members, " We will not destroy any Amphyctionic town nor cut it off from running water, in war or peace ; if any one shall do this, we will march against him and destroy his city. If any one shall plunder the property of the god, or shall be cognizant thereof, or shall take treacherous counsel against the things in his temple at Delphi, we will punish him with foot and hand and voice, and by every means in our power." They also agreed to make and observe humane rules of warfare. See also Bluntschli, " Völkerrecht," Introduction.

[1] Maine, " Ancient Law," Ch. III. The idea as to what *jus gentium* was, of course varied with times. Under the Empire it lost its old meaning. See Cicero, " De Officiis," III., 17 ; Livy, VI., 17 ; IX., 11 ; I., 14 ; V., 36 ; Sallust, " Bell. Jug.," XXII. ; Tacitus, " Ann.," 1, 42 ; " Quintus Curtius," IV., 11, 17.

political authority, left small need of international standards. The appeal in case of disagreement was not to such standards, but to Cæsar. The idea of one common supremacy was deep-rooted. Political assimilation followed the expansion of political privileges.

(b) **The Church.** A similar unifying influence was found in the growth of the Christian Church which knew no distinction — bond or free, Jew or Gentile. Christianity, called to be the state religion early in the fourth century, modeled its organization on that of the Roman Empire ; and from the sixth century, with the decay of the Empire, the Church became the great power. The belief in the eternity and universality of Roman dominion was strengthened by the Church, although materially changed in its nature.[1] Whatever the inconsistencies in Church and State during the first ten centuries of our era, there had grown up the idea, of great importance for international law, that there could be a ground upon which all might meet, a belief which all might accept, both in regard to political and religious organization. For five hundred years before the days of Boniface VIII. (1294–1303), the holder of the papal office had from time to time acted as an international judge.

The canon law, codified by Gregory IX. (1227–1241), was planned to rival the Corpus Juris Civilis. The Popes, with varying degrees of success, tried to render such international justice as the discordant elements introduced by the growth of cities and rise of nationalities demanded.[2] From the Council of Con-

---

[1] Bryce, "Holy Roman Empire," Ch. VII.
[2] Bryce, "Holy Roman Empire," Chs. VII. and XV. The "Truce

stance (1414–1418), which was a recognition of the fact of nationality, and at which the emperor for the last time appeared as the great international head, the decline of both the Church and the Empire as direct international factors was rapid.

(c) **Feudalism.** By the eleventh century feudalism had enmeshed both the temporal and spiritual authorities. This system, closely related to the possession of land and gradation of classes, discouraged the development of the ideas of equality of state powers necessary for the development of international law, though it did emphasize the doctrine of sovereignty as based on land in distinction from the personal sovereignty of earlier days.

(d) **The Crusades** (1096–1270), uniting Christendom against the Saracen for foreign intervention, awakening Europe to a new civilization, expanding the study and practice of the Roman law which feudal courts had checked, weakening many feudal overlords, enfranchising towns, freeing the third estate, spreading the use of the Latin language, enlarging and diversifying commerce, teaching the possible unity of national interests, led to the apprehension of a broader basis in comity which made the growth of interstate relations more rapid.[1]

(e) **Chivalry.** The code of chivalry and the respect for honor which it enjoined introduced a basis of equable dealing which on account of the

of God " introduced by the clergy (1034) left only about eighty days in a year for fighting and settling feuds.

[1] On effects of Crusades, see Milman, "Latin Christianity," VII., 6 ; Hallam, "Middle Ages," Ch. III., Pt. I. ; Bryce, "Holy Roman Empire," Chs. XI., XIII.

international character of the orders of chivalry reacted upon state practice throughout Christian Europe.

(f) **Commerce and Sea Laws.** The expansion of commerce, especially maritime, emphasized the duties and rights of nations. The old Rhodian laws of commerce, which had in part been incorporated in and expanded by the Roman code during the days before the overthrow of the Empire, formed a basis for maritime intercourse. From the fall of the Empire to the Crusades commerce was attended with great dangers from pirates on the sea and from exactions in the port. The so-called *Amalfitan Tables* seem to have been the sea law of the latter part of the eleventh century. The much more detailed *Consolato del Mare* of doubtful origin between the twelfth and fourteenth centuries derived some of its principles from the eleventh-century code. The *Consolato* was recognized by maritime powers as generally binding, and made possible wide commercial intercourse. Many of its principles have stood to the present day, though touching such questions as the mutual rights of neutrals and belligerents on the sea in time of war.[1] As the *Consolato* formed the code of Southern Europe, the *Laws of Oleron* formed the maritime code for Western Europe, and were compiled the latter part of the twelfth century, whether by Richard I. or by his mother Queen Eleanor is a disputed question. These laws are based in large measure on the other existing systems. The *Laws of Wisby*, dating from about 1288, supplemented the *Laws of Oleron*, and formed the funda-

[1] Hall, § 268, p. 740.

C

mental law of maritime courts of the Baltic nations.[1]
The Hanseatic League in 1591 [2] compiled a system of
marine law, *Jus Hanseaticum Maritimum*, based on the
codes of Western and Northern Europe. The maritime
law of Europe was practically unchanged for nearly a
hundred years, when systematized in 1673 under Louis
XIV. Similar to the maritime codes are the "Customs
of Amsterdam," the "Laws of Antwerp," and the
"Guidon de la Mar."[3]

(*g*) **Consulates.** Closely connected with the development of maritime law during the latter part of
the middle period was the establishment of the office
of consul. The consuls, under the title of *consules
marinariorum et mercatorum*, resident in foreign countries, assisted by advice and information the merchants
of their own countries, and endeavored to secure to
their countrymen such rights and privileges as possible.
These seem to have been sent by Pisa early in the
eleventh century, and were for some time mainly sent
by the Mediterranean countries to the East.

(*h*) **The discovery of America** marked a new epoch in
territorial and mercantile expansion, and introduced
new problems among those handed down from an age
of political chaos.

(*i*) **Conclusion.** The middle period, with all its
inconsistencies in theory and practice, had nevertheless
taught men some lessons. The world-empire of Rome
showed a common political sovereignty by which the
acts of remote territories might be regulated; the

[1] Laws of Wisby contain early reference to marine insurance, § 66.
[2] Expanded in 1614.
[3] De Valroger, "Droit Maritime," I., § 1.

world-religion of the Church of the middle period added the idea of a common bond of humanity. Both of these conceptions imbued men's minds with the possibility of a unity, but a unity in which all other powers should be subordinate to a single power, and not a unity of several sovereign powers acting on established principles. The feudal system emphasized the territorial basis of sovereignty. The Crusades gave to the Christian peoples of Europe a knowledge and tolerance of each other which the honor of the code of chivalry made more beneficent, while the growth of the free cities opposed the dominance of classes feudal or religious. The fluctuations and uncertainties in theory and practice of international intercourse, both in peace and war, made men ready to hear the voice of Grotius (1583–1645), whose work marks the beginning of the modern period.

§ 12. Modern Period (1648–)

The modern period may be divided into three epochs for International Law: (a) from the Peace of Westphalia, 1648, to the Peace of Utrecht, 1713; (b) from the Peace of Utrecht, 1713, to the Congress of Vienna, 1815; (c) from the Congress of Vienna, 1815, to the present time.

(a) 1648–1713. It became evident at the termination of the Thirty Years' War in 1648 that the old doctrines of world-empire, whether of Pope or Emperor, could no longer be sustained. The provisions of the Peace of Westphalia, while not creating a code to govern international relations, did give legal recognition to the existence of such conditions as Grotius contemplated in

"De Jure Belli ac Pacis," viz.: sovereign states, equal
regardless of area and power. The decree of James I.,
in 1604, establishing a neutral zone by "a straight line
drawn from one point to another about the realm of
England," in which neither of the parties to the war
between the United Provinces and Spain should carry
on hostilities, formed a precedent in maritime jurisdiction, even though the decree was but imperfectly
enforced. This early part of the modern period was
especially fruitful in treatises and discussions upon the
nature of international law, and upon what it *ought to be*,
and also upon the law of the sea particularly Grotius's
"Mare Liberum," 1609, Selden's "Mare Clausum,"
1635, and Bynkershoek's "De Dominio Maris," 1702.[1]
During this period the public law was diligently studied,
the right of legation became generally recognized, French
gradually took the place of Latin in international intercourse,[2] with a corresponding modern spirit in the practice, though the discussions were usually ponderous and
abstract, the idea of the balance of power flourished and
formed a subject of frequent controversy, the principle
of intervention upon political grounds was propounded
and acknowledged, and the opinions of the great publicists, such as Grotius, gained great weight and were
widely studied. The general principles of neutral
trade, including "free ships, free goods," were laid
down, prize laws and provisions as to contraband were
adopted, numerous treaties of commerce gave witness

[1] The Marine Ordinance of Louis XIV, 1681, became the basis of
sea law.
[2] With the decline of the influence of the "Holy Roman Empire,"
the use of Latin in diplomacy became less general.

of the growth of international intercourse, and both men and states became somewhat more tolerant.

(b) 1713–1815. The Treaty of Utrecht (1713) contained recognition of many of the principles which had become fairly well accepted during the years since 1648. There are evidences of the growing influences of the New World upon the policy of the Old; the American fisheries question appears; the international regulations in regard to commerce are multiplied, and the central subject of the preamble is the subject of "the balance of power."[1] For many years the question of succession to the various seats of royal and princely power formed the chief subject of international discussion. During the eighteenth century the steady growth of England as a maritime power and the European complications over trans-Atlantic possessions brought new international issues. The basis of modern territorial acquisition was found in the Roman law of *occupatio*, and its laws of river boundaries were almost exactly followed.[2] From the Treaty of Aix-la-Chapelle (1748), in which former treaties were generally renewed, to 1815, the growth and observation of the principles of international law was spasmodic. By the Peace of Paris and by the Peace of Hubertsburg (1763), many questions of territorial jurisdiction were settled. England, now become the dominant power in North America, with greatly extended power in the East, impresses upon international practice adherence to actual precedent rather than to theoretically

---

[1] Abbé Saint-Pierre, in three volumes, 1729, "Abrégé du Projet de Paix perpétuelle," outlines a plan for peace by fixed system of balance of power. [2] "Institutes," II., 1, 21, 22.

correct principles. At the same time in Central Europe the conditions were ripe for that violation of international justice, the partition of Poland in 1772, followed by the further partition in 1793 and 1795. The rights which the concert of nations was thought to hold sacred were the ones most ruthlessly violated by the neighboring powers. The American Revolution of 1776 and the French Revolution of 1789 introduced new principles. The "armed neutrality" of 1780,[1] while maintaining the principle "free ships, free goods," made impossible the converse, "enemy's ships, enemy's goods," which had been held. Both the American and French Revolution made evident the necessity of the development of the laws of neutrality hitherto greatly confused and disregarded.[2] During the French Revolution it seemed that to Great Britain alone could the states of Europe look for the practice of the principles of international law. After the French Revolution it was necessary to define *just intervention* that Europe might not be again convulsed. It became clear that the state was an entity and distinct from the person of its king. No longer could the king of France or of any European state say "L'état c'est moi." Even though personal selfishness of monarchs might pervade the Congress of Vienna, the spirit of nationality could not long be restrained. The period from 1713 to 1815 had tested the general principles propounded during the seventeenth century, and it was found necessary to expand their interpretation, while

---

[1] Declaration of Russia, Feb. 28, 1780.

[2] The works of Moser (1701-1786) and his immediate followers attempt to make practical the principles of International Law.

the growth of commerce and intercourse made necessary new laws of neutrality and new principles of comity, such as were in part forthcoming in the early days of the nineteenth century, as seen in the resistance to the right of search, the declaration against African slave trade, establishment of freedom of river navigation, improved regulations in regard to trade in time of war, neutralization of Switzerland, placing of protectorate over Ionian Islands, and the determination of precedence and dignities of the various diplomatic agents and the states which they represented. By the year 1815 the theory of the seventeenth century had been severely tested by the practice of the eighteenth century, and it remained for the nineteenth century to profit by the two centuries of modern political experience.

(c) 1815 to date. The Peace of Westphalia (1648), the Peace of Utrecht (1713), and the Treaty of Vienna (1815) are the three celebrated cases of combined action of modern European powers. The " balance of power " idea had gradually been supplemented by " the concert of the powers " idea, which would not merely maintain the relative *status quo* of " the balance," but might enter upon a positive policy of concerted action. The " Holy Alliance " of 1815, to promote " Justice, Christian Charity, and Peace," [1] was first broken by its originators. There was a strong feeling that the principles of international law should be followed, however, and this, the " Declaration of the Five Cabinets," Nov. 15, 1818, distinctly avowed in " their invariable resolution, never to depart, either among themselves, or in their

[1] I. Hertslet, 317.

relations with other states, from the strictest observation of the principles of the Rights of Nations."[1]   The attempt to extend the principle of intervention in favor of maintaining the various sovereigns on their thrones, and in suppression of internal revolutionary disturbances by foreign force was made in the " Circular of the Three Powers," Dec. 8, 1820.[2]   Under many forms intervention has been one of the great questions of the nineteenth century, and the growing proximity and multiplication of relations of states during the century has added many complications.[3]   The Grecian War of Independence (1821–1829) brought the new principle of pacific blockade (1827), and at its conclusion the powers guaranteed the sovereignty of Greece.   The subjects of right of search, foreign enlistment, Monroe Doctrine, freedom of commerce and navigation, expatriation, extradition, neutralized territory, ship canals, consular rights, neutral rights and duties, arbitration, reciprocity, mixed courts, international postage, weights and measures, trade-marks and copyright, rules of war, submarine cables, and sphere of influence, which have come to the front during the nineteenth century, indicate in a measure the subject-matter of international negotiation.   Throughout the period since 1815 the tendency has been rather to regard what *is* the international practice.

§ 13. Writers.

Among the writers upon subjects connected with international law before the days of Grotius the most prominent are Victoria (–1550 ?), Ayala (1548–

---

[1] I. Hertslet, 573.   [2] *Ibid.*, 658.   [3] Hall, § 88, p. 297.

1584), Suarez (1548–1617), and Gentilis (1551–1611). While in many respects their contributions to the science were valuable, the work of Grotius stands out preëminent among all the early writers.

Hugo Grotius (b. Delft, Apr. 10, 1583; d. Rostock, Aug. 28, 1645). Scholar; jurist; statesman; good family; precocious; prodigious learning in many branches; at fifteen with special embassy to France; at twenty historiographer to the United Provinces; at twenty-five advocate-general of the fisc of Holland and Zealand; married next year Mary van Riegesberg, a worthy help-meet; at thirty pensionary of city of Rotterdam; same year one of deputation to England to settle maritime disputes. Grotius took active part in religious disputes, on which account in 1619 he was sentenced to imprisonment for life and confiscation of his property. Two years later, through cleverness of his wife, he escaped to Paris. Here days of adversity and study. In 1625 "De Jure Belli ac Pacis" published; brought no profit but immediate and lasting fame. Disappointed in his hope to return to permanent residence in Holland; is appointed Swedish ambassador at French Court, 1635–1645. Declines further service in 1645. Retires, honored in all lands; shipwrecked; died at Rostock, Aug. 28, 1645.[1]

Grotius's "De Jure Belli ac Pacis" (1625). An attempt to bring into a systematic treatment those principles which have since become known as international law. Touches upon many other subjects; rich in quotations; broad philosophical basis gives it permanent value. Conditions in Europe at time of appear-

[1] Walker, "Hist. Law of Nations," pp. 283, 326.

ance of work gave it immediate and powerful influence in determining course of modern political history.   Upon the foundation laid by Grotius the modern
science has been largely built.   Of course, many of the
principles expounded by Grotius are no longer applicable, and many new principles, as the doctrine of neutrality, have gained recognition.

Zouch (1590–1660), the successor of Gentilis, as professor of Roman Law at Oxford, while a follower of
Grotius in matter and method, deserves mention for his
distinction between *jus gentium* and that law to which
he gives the name *jus inter gentes*, in the French translation called *Droit entre les Gens*, later *Droit International*, and in the English, Law of Nations, and since
the latter part of the eighteenth century when Bentham
led the way, International Law.

Pufendorf (1632–1694) in his voluminous works in
general follows Grotius.

Toward the end of the seventeenth century a school
opposing the earlier writers arose.   This school, headed
by Rachel (1628–1691), assigned a stronger authority
to the principles of international law, and gave more
attention to usage, whether tacitly admitted or plainly
expressed, and to compacts.

Bynkershoek (1673–1743), limiting his work to particular subjects in international law, gave to the eighteenth century several authoritative treatises which are
justly regarded as of the highest worth.   He especially
defined the laws of maritime commerce between neutrals
and belligerents (*De Dominio Maris*, 1702), gave an outline of ambassadorial rights and privileges (*De Foro
Legatorum*, 1721), besides contributing to a much clearer

understanding of the general subject of international law.

Wolfe (1679–1754) published in 1749 his "Jus Gentium." This bases international law on a sort of state universal, *civitas maxima*, made up of the states of the world in their capacity as voluntarily recognizing a natural law.

Vattel (1714–1767), an ardent admirer of Wolf, published in 1758 his "Law of Nations," which he based upon the work of Wolf. This work of Vattel was clear and logical and gained an immediate and wide influence, far surpassing that of his master.

Moser (1701–1786) brings into the science the positive method which Rachel had hinted at in his work a hundred years before. He narrows his view to the principles underlying the cases of his own day, and would build the science on recent precedents. The method thus introduced has strongly influenced succeeding writers.

G. F. de Martens (1756–1801) combines in a measure the method of Vattel with the positive method of Moser in his "Précis du Droit des Gens Moderne de l'Europe," 1789. This treatise has been a recognized standard.

Many special and general works appeared in the latter years of the eighteenth and early years of the nineteenth century.

Wheaton (1785–1848), the foremost American writer on international law, published in 1836 his "Elements of International Law," which has long been recognized as a standard throughout the world.

Beside the great work of Wheaton justly stands Phillimore's "Commentaries upon International Law."

Many other works of highest merit have appeared during the latter half of the nineteenth century, such as those of Bluntschli, Travers Twiss, Calvo, Wharton, Pradier-Fodéré, and of the eminent authority, the late William Edward Hall. There are also many living writers whose contributions are of greatest worth.[1]

[1] See p. xix for list of authors and works.

CHAPTER IV

SOURCES

§ 14. Practice and Usage

If for a time international intercourse follows certain methods, these methods are regarded as binding in later intercourse, and departure from this procedure is held a violation of international right. That collection of customs known as "The Law Merchant" is an example of a source of this class. Of this it has been said, "Gradually, the usages of merchants hardened into a cosmopolitan law, often at positive variance with the principles of local law, but none the less acquiesced in for mercantile transactions, and enforced by tribunals of commanding eminence and world-wide reputation, such as the courts of the Hanseatic League and the *Parloir aux B*▮▮▮▮▮▮▮▮*ris.*"[1]

[1] Jenks, "Law ▮▮▮ ▮▮▮tics in the ▮ ▮ ▮ ▮

Sir W. Scott, in the case of the "Santa Cruz," 1798, said "Courts of Admiralty have a law and a usage on which they proceed, from habit and ancient practice."[1]

§ 15. Precedent and Decisions

The domestic courts of those states within the family of nations, may by their decisions furnish precedents which become the basis of international practice.

(a) Prize and Admiralty courts decisions form in themselves a large body of law. Jurisdiction in admiralty and maritime causes in the United States rests in the District Courts, the Circuit Courts, and the Supreme Court. The District Courts have original jurisdiction in civil causes of admiralty and concurrent jurisdiction with the Circuit and State Courts in suit of an alien, because of violation of international law or treaty of United States. The District Court also has full prize court powers. Appeals from prize courts decisions go directly to the Supreme Court for final judgment; appeals from admiralty decisions go to the Circuit Court for final judgment.[2] The prize courts of other powers vary in jurisdiction, nature, and procedure. British and American courts rely more particularly upon precedents, while the Continental courts follow more distinctly the general principles laid down in codes and text writers, and place less reliance upon previous interpretation of these principles as shown in court decisions.[3] Whatever the method of the prize

---

[1] The Santa Cruz, 1 C. Rob., 49, 61.
[2] Act of Congress, March 3, 1891. 26 U. S. Sts. at Large, 826.
[3] Lawrence, § 64.

court, its decision, if legally rendered, stands as valid in all states.[1]

(b) The decisions of **domestic courts** upon such matters as extradition,[2] diplomatic privileges, piracy, etc., tend to become a source of international law. In the United States the Supreme Court has original jurisdiction "in all cases affecting ambassadors, other public ministers, and consuls."[3]

(c) The decisions of **courts of arbitration** and other mixed courts are usually upon broad principles. Some of the principles involved may become established precedents, yet the tendency to render a decision, which by a compromise may be measurably acceptable to both parties, may lessen the value of the decision as a precedent. As arbitration is of necessity voluntary, there is generally a consensus upon certain points, even though the decision rendered may not become a precedent. The growth of the practice of arbitration of disputes is an indication of the general recognition of mutual confidence between states. The principles upon which the court of arbitration bases its decision, rather than the decision itself, furnish material valuable for international law.

§ 16. Treaties and State Papers

Treaties and state papers of whatever form[4] indicate the state of opinion, at a given time, in regard to the

---

[1] Bolton v. Gladstone. 5 East, 155, 160.

[2] United States v. Rauscher, 1886, 119 U. S., 407.

[3] United States Constitution, Art. III., § 2. For English view, see Walker, p. 46, who quotes 3 Burr, 1480.

[4] Declarations, protocols, conventions, proclamations, notes, etc.

matters of which they speak. Since they are binding
upon the parties to them, treaties may be regarded as
evidence of what the states, bound by their terms, accept
as law. When the same terms are generally accepted
among nations, treaties become a valuable evidence of
concrete facts of practice and proper sources of international law. The principles may be so well established
by successive treaties as to need no further treaty specifi-
cation. Treaties and state papers vary greatly in value
as sources of international law, however.

(a) Treaties and state papers may lay down new rules
or outline the operation of old rules. As instances of
those laying down new rules may be taken the several
Hague Conventions of 1898, the convention for the
protection of Submarine Cables, March 14, 1884, the
Geneva Convention of 1864; of those outlining and
determining the operation of old rules, there are many
instances, the most numerous in the treaties in regard
to maritime affairs and consuls.

(b) Treaties and state papers may enunciate established rules as understood by the parties to the treaty.
The Declaration of the Conference of London, Jan. 17,
1871, to which the major European states were parties,
announces that the signatory powers " recognize that it
is an essential principle of the Law of Nations that no
Power can liberate itself from the engagements of a
Treaty, nor modify the stipulations thereof, unless with
the consent of the Contracting Powers by means of an
amicable agreement." [1]

(c) Treaties and state papers may agree as to
rules which shall be held as binding upon the parties

[1] III. Hertslet, 1904.

to the treaty or paper. The Declaration of Paris, 1856, agreed as to certain principles and rules of maritime international law, which should be held as binding the signatory powers or those later agreeing to its provisions. This Declaration may be held as generally binding. The United States, by Proclamation of April 26, 1898, announced its adherence to the principles of the Declaration, and during the same year Spain acquiesced in its principles.

(*d*) Most treaties and state papers, however, deal with matters of interstate politics, and are not in any sense sources of international law. They are in most cases little more than interstate compacts.

§ 17. Text Writers

During the seventeenth and the first half of the eighteenth century, the writings of the great publicists were regarded as the highest source of authority upon matters now in the domain of international law. These writings not only laid down the principles which should govern cases similar to those which had arisen, but from the broad basis given the law of nations, deduced the principles for such cases as might arise. This latter method was especially common among the early writers, such as Victoria and Suarez in the sixteenth century. The philosophical school, from Grotius to the middle of the eighteenth century, continued to propound the principles which should govern in supposed cases, should they ever actually arise. Statesmen looked to these treatises as authoritative sources. The prolific Moser, in the middle of

D

the eighteenth century, made the historical method more prominent by giving less attention to the natural law, and by founding his system on usage and treaties. Bynkershoek (1673-1763) had anticipated him in this method in special lines, but Moser extended the system and made it most ample. Succeeding writers mingled the two systems, inclining to the one or the other. In the early days of the modern period, the writers upon the law of nations, outlined the course which states should pursue in their relations to one another. In the later days of the modern·period, the writers upon the law of nations, while sometimes discussing problems before they arise, in general attempt to expound the rules and principles which have entered already into interstate action. The works of the text writers, from Grotius to the present, must be regarded as sources of highest value.

§ 18. Diplomatic Papers

The diplomatic papers, as distinct from the state papers to which more than one state becomes a party, are simply papers issued by a state for the guidance of its own representatives in international intercourse. The papers are sometimes named state papers or included among the papers to which other states are parties, — in the United States, in the series known as "Diplomatic Correspondence, 1861-1868," and "Foreign Relations" since 1870; and in Great Britain in the "British and Foreign State Papers."

These papers, showing the opinions of various states from time to time upon certain subjects which may not come up for formal state action, afford a valuable source of information upon the attitude of states toward questions still formally unsettled. The simple expression to state agents in the way of instructions or information as to the position of the state on a given matter may, if continued and long accepted, give to the principle involved the force of international sanction. This was almost the case in the so-called Monroe Doctrine.[1] In these papers may often be found an indication of the line which the principles of international law will subsequently follow and a general concensus by several states in diplomatic instructions may be considered strong evidence of what the law is on a given point.

[1] In signing the Hague Convention for the Pacific Settlement of International Disputes, the representatives of the United States made the reservation that, "Nothing contained in this convention shall be so construed as to require the United States of America to depart from its traditional policy of not intruding upon, interfering with, or entangling itself in the political questions of policy or internal administration of any foreign state; nor shall anything contained in the said convention be construed to imply a relinquishment by the United States of America of its traditional attitude toward purely American questions."

PART II

PERSONS IN INTERNATIONAL LAW

CHAPTER V

STATES

19. DEFINITION.
    (*a*) Political.
    (*b*) Sovereign.
20. NATURE.
    (*a*) Moral.
    (*b*) Physical.
    (*c*) Communal.
    (*d*) External conditions.
21. RECOGNITION OF NEW STATES.
    (*a*) *De facto* existence.
    (*b*) Circumstances of recognition.
        (1) By division.
        (2) By union.
        (3) By admission of old states.
        (4) By admission of former barbarous communities.
        (5) Individual and collective recognition.
    (*c*) Act of recognition.
    (*d*) Premature recognition.
    (*e*) Conditions.
    (*f*) Recognition irrevocable.
    (*g*) Consequences.
        (1) The recognizing state.
        (2) The recognized state.
        (3) The parent state.
        (4) Other states.

§ 19. Definition

A State is a sovereign political unity. It is of the relations of states that public international law mainly treats. From the nature of its subject-matter it is a

39

juridical, historical, and philosophical science.[1] These sovereign political unities may vary greatly. The unity however

(*a*) Must be **political**, *i.e.* organized for public ends as understood in the family of nations and not for private ends as in the case of a commercial company, a band of pirates, or a religious organization.

(*b*) Must possess **sovereignty**, *i.e.* supreme political power beyond and above which there is no political power. It is not inconsistent with sovereignty, that a state should voluntarily take upon itself obligations to other states, even though the obligations be assumed under stress of war, or fear of evil.

§ 20. Nature

From the nature of the state as a sovereign political unity it must be self-sufficient, and certain conditions are therefore generally recognized as necessary for its existence from the standpoint of international law.[2]

(*a*) **Moral.** In order that a state may be regarded as within the "family of nations," and within the pale of international Law, it must recognize the rights of other states and acquiesce in its obligations toward them. This is considered a moral condition of state existence.

(*b*) **Physical.** A state must also possess those physical resources which enable it to exist as territory, etc.

(*c*) **Communal.** A state must possess a body of men so related as to warrant the belief in the continued

[1] Holtzendorff, "Introduction droit public," 44.
[2] Hall, § 1 p. 18; I., Rivier, § 3, 9, L

existence of the unity. Each state may be its own judge as to the time when these relations are established in a given body of men, and the recognition of a new state is fitting.

That such conditions are recognized as prerequisites of state existence from the point of view of international law is not due to the essential nature of the state, but rather to the course of development of international law; as Hall says, "The degree to which the doctrines of international law are based upon the possession of land must in the main be attributed to the association of rights of sovereignty or supreme control over human beings with that of territorial property in the minds of jurists at the period when the foundations of international law were being laid."[1]

(d) **External Conditions.** The external relationship of the state rather than the internal nature is the subject of consideration in international law. For local law a community may enter upon state existence long before this existence is recognized by other nations, as in the case of Switzerland before 1648. Until recognition by other states of its existence becomes general, a new state cannot acquire full status in international law; and this recognition is conditioned by the policy of the recognizing states.

§ 21. Recognition of New States

(a) **State existence de facto** is not a question of international law but depends upon the existence of a sovereign political unity with the attributes which

[1] Hall, § 1, p. 20.

necessarily appertain to it. This *de facto* existence is
not dependent upon the will of any other state or
states.[1] The entrance of the state into the international
statehood, however, depends entirely upon the recognition by those states already within this circle. Whatever advantages membership in this circle may confer,
and whatever duties it may impose, do not fall upon
the new state until its existence is generally recognized
by the states already within the international circle.
These advantages and duties, as between the recognizing
and recognized state, immediately follow recognition
but do not necessarily extend to other states than those
actually party to the recognition. The basis of this
family of nations or international circle which admits
other states to membership is historical, resting on the
polity of the older European states. These states,
through the relations into which they were brought

---

[1] The internal acts of a *de facto* state are valid, whatever the attitude of the international circle. As an example, in 1777, during the
Revolutionary War, the British governor of Florida made a grant of
land in what is now the southern part of the United States. Fifty
years later a descendant of the grantee laid claim to the land, but the
Supreme Court of the United States declared, "It has never been
admitted by the United States that they acquired anything by way
of cession from Great Britain by that treaty [of Peace, 1783]. It has
been viewed only as a recognition of preëxisting rights, and on that
principle the soil and the sovereignty, within their acknowledged
limits, were as much theirs at the Declaration of Independence as at
this hour. By reference to the treaty, it will be found that it amounts
to a simple recognition of the independence and limits of the United
States, without any language purporting a cession or relinquishment
of right, on the part of Great Britain . . . grants of soil made *fla-
grante bello* by the party that fails, can only derive validity from treaty
stipulations." Harcourt *v*. Gaillard, 12 Wheat., 523, 527. See also
M'Ilvaine *v*. Coxe's Lessee, 4 Cr., 209, 212.

by reason of proximity and intercourse, developed among themselves a system of action in their mutual dealings; and international law in its beginning proposed to set forth what this system was and should be.[1] This family of states could not permit new accessions to its membership unless these new states were properly constituted to assume the mutual relationships, and as to the proper qualifications for admission in each case, the states already within the family claim and exercise the right to judge.

(b) The circumstances of recognition vary.

(1) The most numerous instances are in consequence of *division* which involves the recognition of the existence of more than one state within the limits which had formerly been under a single jurisdiction. This may be preceded by recognition of the belligerency of a revolted community within the jurisdiction of an existing state, or may be preceded by division of an existing state into two or more states.[2] In the first case recognition is a question of national policy, in the second case recognition is usually readily accorded.

(2) In modern times a new state has frequently been formed by the *union* of two or more existing states.[3] The recognition in such a case usually follows immediately.

(3) A state *after existence for a period of years* may be formally admitted into the family of states. Japan, for centuries a *de facto* state, was only recently fully

[1] Suarez, "De Legibus," 6. [2] Wheat., D., 41 n.
[3] United States of Central America, Nov. 1, 1898, from Republics of Nicaragua, Salvador, and Honduras.

admitted to international statehood.[1]   Turkey, so long
the dread of Europe, was formally received by the
Treaty of Paris, 1856.

(4) New states may be formed in *territory hitherto
outside* any *de facto* state jurisdiction, or within regions
hitherto considered savage.   The examples of this class
are mainly African, as in the creation of the Congo
Free State under the International Association of the
Congo.   The United States recognized the Congo
Free State by acknowledging its flag, April 22, 1884.
Liberia, originally established by the American col-
onization Society in 1821, as a refuge for negroes from
America since 1847, has been recognized as an independent republic.

(5) From another point of view *recognition may
be individual or collective.*   Recognition is individual
when a state, independently of any other, acknowledges
the international statehood of a new state.   This was
the method of recognition of the United States.   Collective recognition is by the concerted action of several
states at the same time.   This has taken place most
often in the admission of minor states to the European
family of states, as in the cases of Greece by the powers
at the Conference of London, 1830 ; Belgium, 1831 ;
Montenegro, Servia, and Roumania, at the Congress
of Berlin, 1878.   The Congo Free State was acknowledged by the International Congo Conference at Berlin,
1885.

(*c*) **The act constituting recognition** of a new state
may be formal, as by a declaration, proclamation, treaty,

[1] Japan has been generally recognized since 1894, and her foreign
relations have been in course of readjustment.

sending and receiving ambassadors, salute of flag, etc.,
or informal, by implication through the grant of an *exequatur* to a consul from the new state, or other act
which indicates an acknowledgment of international
rights and obligations.[1] It should be observed, however, that the appointment by, or reception within, an
existing state of agents to carry on necessary intercourse between the existing state, and the aspirant for
recognition does not constitute recognition. It may be
essential to have relations with a community the statehood of which is not established, because of commercial
and other matters pertaining to the rights of the citizens of the existing state whose interests, or who in person may be within the jurisdiction of the unrecognized
community.[2] The definite act of recognition is, however,
in accord with the decision of the internal authority to
which this function is by state law ascribed. As foreign
states usually take cognizance of the acts of the executive
department only, it is the common custom to consider
recognition as an executive function, or as a function residing in the head of the state. In the United States,
the President is for foreign affairs the head of the state,
and has the authority to recognize new states in any manner other than by those acts, which by the Constitution
require the advice and consent of the Senate, as in the
conclusion of treaties, and appointment of ambassadors,
other public ministers, and consuls. President Grant,
in his second annual message, Dec. 5, 1870, said, " As
soon as I learned that a republic had been proclaimed
at Paris, and that the people of France had acquiesced
in the change, the minister of the United States was

[1] 1 Whart.,   [2] I. Rivier, §§ 44, 125.

directed by telegraph to recognize it, and to tender my congratulations and those of the people of the United States."[1] As President Jackson had in his message in December, 1831, and in the official correspondence with Buenos Ayres denied that country's jurisdiction over the Falkland Islands, Justice McLean said, in rendering his opinion in Williams v. Suffolk Insurance Company, "And can there be any doubt that when the executive branch of the government which is charged with our foreign relations, shall, in its correspondence with foreign nations, assume a fact in regard to sovereignty of any island or country, it is conclusive on the judicial department? And in this view it is not material to inquire, nor is it the province of the court to determine, whether the executive be right or wrong. It is enough to know that in the exercise of his constitutional functions he has decided the question."[2] "The President is the executive department."[3]

(d) Recognition may be **premature** and the recognized community may not be able to maintain its place in the international circle, or in case of a struggle with another state may be defeated. The recognizing state must assume in such case whatever consequences may come from its misjudgment, and the parent state may justly question the right of the recognizing state in its action, e.g. the recognition by France of the United

[1] See on this subject 1 Whart., § 70.
[2] 13 Pet., 415. See also Jones v. United States, 137 U. S. 202 ; Foster v. Neilson, 2 Pet., 253.
[3] State of Mississippi v. Johnson, President, 4 Wall., 475, 500. For late review of the question, see 32 Amer. Law Rev., 390, W. L. Penfield.

States in 1778 could justly be regarded by England as premature and as a hostile act.

(*e*) The recognition of a new state is the recognition of the existence of certain political conditions. This recognition of the state carries with it the acknowledgment of sovereignty, independence, equality, etc. It is an essential condition to just recognition that the new aspirant possess these qualifications absolutely or potentially to a reasonable extent.

(*f*) From its nature, recognition is irrevocable and absolute, unless distinctly conditional. Even when conditional, if the recognition is prior to the fulfillment of the condition by the recognized state, the recognition cannot be withdrawn because of non-fulfillment of the condition, but the recognizing state may resort to any other means which would be admitted in international law as justifiable against any other state failing to fulfill its obligations, *e.g.* suspension of diplomatic relations, retorsion, reprisals, or even war.[1] In the case of Belgium, the definition of its boundaries and establishing of permanent neutralization was an act subsequent to the recognition of its international statehood, and in case of violation of the treaty stipulations, Belgium would not lose its position as a state, but would be liable to such measures of reparation as the other parties to the treaty might employ.[2] If recognition could be withdrawn, it would work injustice to the recognized state, and to other states who, as third parties, will not permit their rights to be subject to the will of the recognizing state or states.

[1] I. Rivier, "Droit d......." §§ 8, 11.
[2] Hall, § 26*, note 1.

(*g*) The **consequences of recognition** immediately touch the relations of (1) the recognizing state, (2) the recognized, (3) the parent state if the new state is formed from an existing state, and (4) in a minor degree other states.

(1) The *recognizing state* is bound to treat the new state in all respects as entitled to the rights and as under duties accepted in international law.

(2) The *recognized state* is, as related to the recognizing state, entitled to the rights, and under the obligations prescribed in international law. As it is a new person in international law, it is entitled to full personal freedom in entering into relations with other states. So far, however, as the territory within the new state was under local obligations, these obligations are transferred to the new state. The general obligations resting on the parent state, by reason of treaties and responsibilities of all kinds which have been assumed by the parent state in the capacity of a legal unity, are not transferred, because the identity of the parent state remains intact.[1]

(3) The *parent state*, in cases where the new state is formed by separation from one already existing, is, as regards the recognizing state, on the same international footing as the new state. Both states are entitled to equal privileges, and under like obligations. The relations to other states are not necessarily much changed.

(4) The *relations* of the *states other than the recognizing, recognized*, and *parent states* are changed to the extent that they must respect the *de facto* relations set

[1] Hall, § 27, p. 100.

forth in (1), (2), and (3) above, *i.e.* while not recognizing the new state, they must accept the fact that the recognition exists for the states who are parties to it, and they are not entitled to pass judgment as to the justice of the recognition.

CHAPTER VI

LEGAL PERSONS HAVING QUALIFIED STATUS

§ 22. Members of Confederations and other Unions

A state in the sense of public law is not sovereign in the sense of international law, if there are any limitations upon its power to enter into relations with other states. Such a state may be a member of a confederation and exercise certain powers giving it a qualified international status. These loose unions may, as in the German Confederation from 1815 to 1866, leave to the local states a certain degree of autonomy in regulating international affairs while granting to the central government certain specified powers. This division of international competence is usually a temporary compromise ending in new states or in a close union. "Inasmuch as both the central and the separate states carry on diplomatic intercourse with foreign powers, they must each and all be regarded as Subjects of International Law ; and inasmuch as they carry on such intercourse only in a limited degree, they cannot be regarded as fully and absolutely sovereign." [1]

In the examples of personal and real unions and the like, the nature of the state is a matter of public law and little concerns international law. As related to international law, the question is how far are such states restricted in their dealings with other states. A union, such as that existing in the case of the ruler of the United Kingdom of Great Britain and Ireland and Empire of India, is of importance to international law only in its united capacity, while for public law the nature of the union is of much significance. The same might be said of the unions of Austria-Hungary, and Sweden-Norway.

§ 23. Neutralized States

Neutralized states are sovereign only in a qualified degree. While such states have a certain formal equal-

---

[1] Lawrence, § 51, p. 75.

ity, their actual competence is limited in regard to the exercise of sovereign powers. This limitation as to neutrality may be externally imposed or externally enforced, as in the case of Belgium, Switzerland, Luxemburg, Congo Free State, and till 1900, Samoa. This neutralization may take place for political or philanthropic reasons.[1] The degree of external sovereignty possessed by neutralized states varies. The fact that these states are not fully sovereign in the field of international law in no way affects their competence except in respect to matters covered by the conditions of neutralization. Such states are deprived of the right of offensive warfare, and have not therefore that final recourse possessed by fully sovereign states for enforcing their demands.

§ 24. Protectorates, Suzerainties

States under protectors — *protectorates* — usually possess all powers not specifically resigned. States fully sovereign may demand (1) that states under protectors afford reasonable protection to the subjects and to the property of subjects of fully sovereign states, and (2) that the protecting state use reasonable measures to give effect to the protection which it has assumed. Just how much responsibility the protecting state has depends upon the degree of protection exercised and assumed. The protectorate of Great Britain over the South African Republic by the agreement of 1884 was of a very moderate form. The right to veto within a certain time any treaty made with a foreign state, other than the Orange Free State and native princes,

[1] "Political Annuals," since 1887 rich in discussion of neutralization.

constituted practically the only restriction on the independence of the Republic.   Great Britain has several
other protectorates in Africa over which the degree
of authority varies.   In many instances protectorates
easily pass into colonies, as in the case of Madagascar,
which Great Britain recognized as under French protection in 1890, which protection the queen of Madagascar accepted in October, 1895, and in August, 1896,
Madagascar was declared a French colony.[1]

As distinct from a state under a protectorate which
possesses all competence in international affairs which
it has not specifically resigned, a state under *suzerainty*
possesses only such competence as has been specifically
conferred upon it by the suzerain.   The relations are
usually much closer than between protecting and protected states ; and in many cases only the suzerain has
international status, while the vassal is merely tributary,
though having a certain degree of internal independence which may be in some instances almost complete.
By the first article of the Treaty of Berlin, Bulgaria
is made a tributary and autonomous principality under
the suzerainty of the Sultan of Turkey.   Under Russian suzerainty are such vassal states as Bokhara and
Khiva.   Some of the states under the suzerainty of
European states have no status in international law, as
in the case of Bokhara and Khiva.   There exist such
anomalous cases as the co-suzerainty of the republic
of Andorra, the collective suzerainty of the Samoan
Islands till 1900,[2] and the absolute suzerainty of the
United States over the " domestic dependent nations "
of Indians.

[1] Statesman's Year Book 1901, p. 591.   [2] *Ibid.*, pp. 657, 1237.

§ 25. Corporations

From the point of view of international law, corporations are generally of two kinds : corporations organized for private purposes, and corporations organized for purposes involving the exercise of delegated sovereign powers.

(a) Corporations organized for private purposes come within the field of international law, when in time of war their property or other rights are impaired, when maritime law, whether of peace or war, may have been infringed, and when their rights are involved in the domain of private international law.

(b) Corporations organized for purposes involving the exercise of political powers have from time to time, for several centuries, been chartered and have often acquired a quasi-international status. While restricted to the performance of functions intrusted to them by their charters, the home governments have often sanctioned acts for which their charters gave no warrant. The companies that early entered America, India, Africa, and the later African companies, are of this kind. The development of the late doctrine of "the sphere of influence" has given an important position to these companies organized within those states desirous to share in "the partition of Africa."

Among the most notable of the earlier companies was the English East India Company,[1] which received its first charter in 1600. During more than two hundred and fifty years this company exercised practically sovereign powers, until by the act of Aug. 2, 1858,

[1] 6 American Cycl., 376.

the government heretofore exercised by the company was transferred to the crown, and was henceforth to be exercised in its name.

In recent years the African companies chartered by the European states seeking African dominions have had very elastic charters in which the home governments have generally reserved the right to regulate the exercise of authority as occasion might demand. These companies advance and confirm the spheres of influence of the various states, govern under slight restrictions great territories, and treat with native states with full authority. The British South Africa Company, chartered in 1889, was granted liberal powers of administration and full capacity, subject to the approval of the Secretary of State for the Colonies, to treat with the native states. The field of operations of this company was extended in 1891, so that it now includes over six hundred thousand square miles of territory. Of this company Lawrence says : " Clearly then it is no independent authority in the eye of British law, but a subordinate body controlled by the appropriate departments of the supreme government. Like Janus of old, it has two faces. On that which looks towards the native tribes all the lineaments and attributes of sovereignty are majestically outlined. On that which is turned towards the United Kingdom is written subordination and submission." [1] The acts of these companies become the basis of subsequent negotiations among the various European states, and the companies have a very important influence in molding the character of African development.

§ 26. Individuals

Without entering into discussion of "the doctrine of the separability of the individual from the state," it is safe to affirm that individuals have a certain degree of competence under exceptional circumstances, and may come under the cognizance of international law. By the well-established dictum of international law a pirate may be captured by any vessel, whatever its nationality. General admiralty and maritime procedure against a person admit the legal status of an individual from the point of view of international law. The extension of trade and commerce has made this necessary. This is particularly true in time of war, when individuals wholly without state authorization, or even in contravention of state regulations, commit acts putting them within the jurisdiction held to be covered by international law, as in the case of persons brought before Prize Courts. The principles of private international law cover a wide range of cases directly touching individuals.

§ 27. Insurgents

(a) **Definition.** Insurgents are organized bodies of men who, for public political purposes, are in a state of armed hostility to an established government.

(b) **Effect of Admission of Insurgency.** The practice of tacitly admitting **insurgent rights** has become common when the hostilities have assumed such proportions as to jeopardize the sovereignty of the parent state over the rebelling community, or seriously to interfere with customary foreign intercourse.[1]   The general effect of the admission is shown as follows : [2]

(1) Insurgent rights cannot be claimed by those bodies seeking other than political ends.[3]

(2) Insurgent acts are not piratical, as they imply the pursuit of " public as contrasted with private ends."[4]

(3) The admission of insurgent rights does not carry the rights of a belligerent, nor admit official recognition of insurgent body.[5]

(4) The admission of insurgent rights does not relieve the parent state of its responsibilities for acts committed within its jurisdiction.[6]

(5) When insurgents act in a hostile manner toward foreign states, they may be turned over to the parent state, or may be punished by the foreign state.[7] .

(6) A foreign state must in general refrain from interference in the hostilities between parent state and insurgents, *i.e.* cannot extend hospitality of its ports to insurgents, extradite insurgents, etc.[8]

(7) When insurgency exists, the armed forces of the insurgents must observe and are entitled to the advantages of the laws of war in their relations to the parent state.[9]

---

[1] Wheat., D., note 15, p. 37.

[2] For full discussion see Wilson, " Insurgency " lectures U. S. Naval War College, 1900.   [3] Hall, § 5, p. 31, ff.

[4] 3 Whart., § 381 ; United States *v.* " Ambrose Light," 25 Fed. Rep. 408.   Snow, 206, " Montezuma."

[5] President Cleveland's Message, Dec. 2, 1885.   U. S. For. Rel. 1885, pp. 254, 273.

[6] Parl. Papers, 1887, 1 Peru, 18.   [7] 3 Whart., § 381, " Huascar."

[8] 33 Albany Law Jour., 125.   [9] Lawrence, § 162.

NOTE. During the struggles between the parties in the United States of Colombia in 1885, the President of Colombia decreed: (1) That certain Carribean ports held by the opposing party should be regarded as closed to foreign commerce, and trade with these ports would be considered illicit and contraband, and that vessels, crews, etc., involved in such trade would be liable to the penalties of Colombian laws. (2) That as the vessels of the opposing party in the port of Cartagena were flying the Colombian flag, it was in violation of right, and placed that party beyond the pale of international law.[1]

The United States refused to recognize the validity of the first decree unless Colombia should support it by an effective blockading force.[2] (For similar position on part of Great Britain, see Parl. Deb. H. C., June 27, 1861.)

The United States also refused to recognize that the vessels of the insurgents were beyond the pale of international law or in any sense piratical.

The United States did not deny that closure might be a domestic measure similar to blockade in accord with municipal law, but emphatically maintained that effective blockade only could close a port in time of such insurrection.

It was further maintained that "The denial by this [U.S.] Government of the Colombian proposition did not, however, imply the admission of a belligerent status on the part of the insurgents." Message Pres. Cleveland, Dec. 8, 1885.[3]

The President's messages of Dec. 2, 1895, and Dec. 7, 1896, distinctly mention a status of insurgency as existing in Cuba.

During the rebellions in Chili in 1891 and in Brazil in 1894, the insurgents, while not recognized as belligerents by third powers, were nevertheless given freedom of action by these powers.

---

[1] 1885, For. Rel. U. S. 252, 264.   [2] 1885, For. Rel. U. S. 254, 273.
[3] See 3 Whart., § 381; Bluntschli, § 512; Hall, § 5, p. 34; U. S. For. Rel. (1885), 252, 254, 264, 273.

§ 28. Belligerents

(a) **Definition.** A community attempting by armed hostility to free itself from the jurisdiction of the parent state may, under certain conditions, be recognized as a belligerent.

(b) The general **conditions prior to recognition** are : (1) that the end which the community in revolt seeks shall be political, *i.e.* a mere mob or a party of marauders could have no belligerent rights, (2) the hostilities must be of the character of war and must be carried on in accord with the laws of war, (3) the proportions of the revolt must be such as to render the issue uncertain and to make its continuance for a considerable time possible, (4) the hostilities and general government of the revolting community must be in the hands of a responsible organization.

As each state, including the parent state, must judge as to the fact whether the conditions warranting recognition of belligerency exist, there may be great divergency of opinion in cases of recognition,[1] but the question of belligerency is a question of fact and never a question of theory.

(c) A community carrying on, in accord with the rules of war, an armed revolt of such proportions as to make the issue uncertain and acting under a responsible organization may not be recognized without offense to the parent state except upon certain **grounds.**   The generally admitted ground is, that the interests of the recognizing state be so far affected by the hostilities

[1] See numerous references in 51 Br. and Fr. St. Papers; also Hall, § 5, p. 39.

" as to make recognition a reasonable measure of self-protection."[1] "The reason which requires and can alone justify this step [recognition of belligerency] by the government of another country, is, that its own rights and interests are so far affected as to require a definition of its own relations to the parties. . . . A recognition by a foreign state of full belligerent rights, if not justified by necessity, is a gratuitous demonstration of moral support to the rebellion, and of censure upon the parent government."[2]

(*d*) **Recognition** of belligerency is naturally **an act of the executive authority.**[3]

The following is the proclamation of Queen Victoria of May 13, 1861 : —

" Whereas we are happily at peace with all sovereign powers and states :

"And whereas hostilities have unhappily commenced between the Government of the United States of America and certain states styling themselves the Confederate States of America :

"And whereas we, being at peace with the Government of the United States, have declared our royal determination to maintain a strict and impartial neutrality in the contest between the said contending parties :

"We, therefore, have thought fit, by [and with] the advice of our privy council, to issue this our royal proclamation :

"And we do hereby strictly charge and command all our loving subjects to observe a strict neutrality in and during the aforesaid hostilities, and to abstain from violating or contravening either the laws and statutes of the realm in

[1] Hall, § 5, p. 35.
[2] Wheat., D., note 15, p. 34.
[3] 1 Whart., §§ 69, 71.

this behalf or the law of nations in relations thereto, as they will answer to the contrary at their peril."

(*e*) **Certain consequences** follow the recognition of belligerency.

(1) *If recognition is by a foreign state.*

(a) From the date of recognition, the parent state is released from responsibility to the recognizing state for the acts of the belligerents.

(b) So far as the recognizing state is concerned, the parent state and the belligerent community would have the same war status, *i.e.* in the ports of the recognizing state, the vessels of both parties would have the same privileges, the merchant vessels of the recognizing state must submit to the right of search as justly belonging to both parties; in fine, so far as the prosecution of hostilities is concerned, the recognizing state must accord the belligerent community all the privileges of a full state.

(c) The recognizing state may hold the belligerent community, if it subsequently becomes a state, accountable for its acts during the period after the recognition of its belligerency. If, however, the parent state reduces the revolting community to submission, the recognizing state can hold no one responsible for the acts of the recognized community from the date of recognition.

(d) This recognition does not necessarily affect other than the three parties, the recognizing state, the belligerent community, and the parent state.

(2) *If recognition* of belligerency is by the *parent state.*

(a) From the date of recognition, the parent state is released from responsibility to all states for the acts of the belligerents.

(b) So far as the prosecution of hostilities is concerned, the community, recognized as belligerent by the parent state, is entitled to full war status.

(c) From the date of recognition by the parent state, the belligerent community only is responsible for acts within its jurisdiction, and if subdued by the parent state, no one can be held responsible, *i.e.* contracts made with a belligerent, or responsibilities assumed by a belligerent, do not fall upon the parent state, when victorious in the contest.

(d) Recognition of belligerency by the parent state gives the revolting community a war status as regards all states.

In a broad way, recognition by the parent state makes general those conditions which may exist only for the parties directly concerned, when recognition is by a single foreign state. In cases where several states recognize the belligerency of a hostile community, other states that have not recognized its belligerency may, without offense to the parent state, treat the hostile community as a lawful belligerent, which treatment would be constructive recognition. The general effect of recognition is to extend to the belligerent all the rights and obligations as to war that a state may possess, and to free the parent state from certain obligations while giving some new rights. The parent state may use the proper means for the enforcement of neutrality and demand reparation for any breach of the same, may maintain blockade, prize courts, and take other measures allowable in war.

The condition of insurgency is usually tacitly admitted for a period prior to the recognition of belligerency, and the vessels of the insurgents are not regarded as pirates either in practice or theory. They have not the *animus furandi*. The admission of insurgent status or the recognition of belligerency does not imply anything as to the political status of the community. In the first place there is conceded a qualified war status, and in the second full war status.

§ 29. Communities not fully Civilized

While there is no agreement as to what constitutes civilization, still international law is considered as binding only upon states claiming a high degree of enlightenment. Communities, whether or not politically organized and not within the circle of states recognized by international law, because they are not regarded as sufficiently civilized, are not treated as without rights. It is held that these communities not fully civilized should be treated as civilized states would be treated so far as the time and other circumstances permit. Unduly severe measures, whether in war or peace, should not be used by civilized states in dealing with those not civilized. It may be necessary that barbarians should be used as auxiliary forces in contests with barbarians, but it is now held that such forces should be officered and controlled by the civilized state. Extreme measures, in the way of devastation and destruction, have been used with the idea of impressing upon the minds of barbarians respect for the power of a state, but it is now questioned how far this is fitting for states claiming civilization. Many states not admitted to the circle of nations have now acquired such a status as entitles them to the general privileges of international law to the extent to which their action has not violated its provisions, and it is generally so accorded, as for many years to China, Persia, and other Asiatic states.

PART III

INTERNATIONAL LAW OF PEACE

CHAPTER VII

§ 30. Existence

The most comprehensive right of a state is the *right to exist* as a sovereign political unity. From this comprehensive right flow the general rights of *independence, equality, jurisdiction, property*, and *intercourse* and the obligations which the exercise of these rights imply. There are many classifications of the general rights of states. During the eighteenth century a classification into perfect and imperfect rights was common. A classification based on the essential nature of the state as a sovereign political unity, having (1) a right to existence and (2) from the point of view of international law, having relations to other states, has been widely followed. The rights based on the comprehensive right to existence were variously named as essential, fundamental, primitive, innate, absolute,

67

permanent, etc., while the rights derived from the practice of states in their mutual relations were called accidental, derived, secondary, acquired, relative, contingent, etc. The view now most generally recognized is that from the single comprehensive right of states *to exist*, all other rights flow, and all other rights are therefore related, if not directly, at least by virtue of their common source.

§ 31. Independence

Independence from the point of view of international law is freedom from external political control. While all states possessing freedom from external political control may not be admitted to the family of states, yet in order that a state may be admitted, it is regarded as essential that it be independent. The recognition of a state carries with it the recognition of independence. However, from the fact that there are states in the world having equal rights to independence, it follows that the field of action of each state is limited by the necessity of respect for the right of independence belonging to other states.

The recognition of a state presupposes autonomy as an essential for the existence of a sovereign political unity, and autonomy implies the right to determine and pursue such lines of action as may be in accord with its policy.

§ 32. Equality

All states, the existence of which has been recognized by the family of states, are regarded as possessed

of equal rights in political affairs, so far as legal competence is concerned.

This does not imply an equality of territorial area,
population, wealth, rank, and influence, etc., or that a
given state may not voluntarily limit the exercise of
its powers.

§ 33. Jurisdiction

The right of jurisdiction is the right to exercise
state authority. The right of jurisdiction is in general
coextensive with the dominion of the state. It may
be "laid down as a general proposition that all persons
and property within the territorial jurisdiction of a
sovereign are amenable to the jurisdiction of himself
or his courts ; and that the exceptions to this rule are
such only as by common usage and public policy have
been allowed, in order to preserve the peace and harmony of nations, and to regulate their intercourse in
a manner best suited to their dignity and rights."[1]

§ 34. Property

In international law, as against other states, a given
state has the right of property or domain in the territory and fixtures within its limits. This right of
property is not the right in the old feudal sense, for
in the public law of the state the title of ownership
may vest in the state only in a limited sense as over
territory to which none of its subjects have title, and
over such other forms it has ownership in corporate
capacity, as public buildings, forts, arsenals, vessels,

[1] Story, "Santissima Trinidad," 7 Wheat. 35'

lighthouses, libraries, museums, etc. The right of eminent domain as a domestic right may also vest in the state. While from the point of view of international law, a state has the right of property over all territorial and non-territorial possessions within its limits as against other states, yet the effect of this right is somewhat modified by the fact of public or private ownership, particularly as regards the laws of war, neutrality, and intercourse.

§ 35. Intercourse

In early periods of history intercourse among states was very limited and sometimes even prohibited. At the present time the necessities of state existence presuppose, in international law, the recognition of the right of intercourse in order that state business may be transacted. The principles upon which this intercourse is carried on are well established, and form the basis of diplomatic practice.

CHAPTER VIII

EXISTENCE

§ 36. Application of the Right

Besides the general rights of *independence, equality, jurisdiction, property, and intercourse,* the right of existence in its exercise may lead to certain acts for which the general principles of international law do not provide rules.[1]

(*a*) In face of actual dangers immediately threatening its existence, a state may take such measures as are necessary for self-preservation, even though not sanctioned by international law. Such measures, however, must be from "a necessity of self-defense, instant, overwhelming, and leaving no choice of means and no moment for deliberation," and further "must be limited by that necessity and kept clearly within it."[2] The wide discussion of the case of the *Virginius* involved the principle of the limits of the right of self-defense.[3]

[1] Hall, § 83, p. 281.
[2] "Caroline," 1 Whart., § 50 c; 2 *ibid.*, § 224. See Appendix, p. 434.
[3] 3 Whart., § 327, p. 147. Snow's Cases, § 179.

(*b*) The right to act in a manner which international law does not sanction or denies, even though it may be strictly to preserve the existence of the state so acting, cannot be upheld as freeing it from responsibility for such acts, and these acts may be regarded as hostile by states affected by them.

(*c*) As the domestic acts of a state are not within the province of international law, a state has the right to administer its internal affairs in such manner as it may determine fit to secure and further its existence. It may adopt any form of government; may plan for its growth by developing its resources, by encouraging immigration; may strengthen defenses and forces; may regulate trade, commerce, and travel. While acts of this character may work injury to other states, they are not in general just grounds for war, but may properly be met by like acts on the part of other states.

§ 37. Extension of the Right to Subjects of the State

As the subjects of a state are necessary for its existence, the right of self-preservation has been held to justify certain acts of states to secure to their subjects in their relations with foreign states such rights as the foreign states would accord to their own subjects under similar circumstances. That a local tribunal within a purely domestic division of a state cannot secure to foreigners rights to which they are entitled, in no way frees that state, whose sovereignty extends over such domestic division, from responsibility for violation of the foreigner's right. International law recognizes only the personality of the sovereign political unity, and cannot cognize the administrative and other subdivisions. Italy assumed a correct position in holding the United States government responsible for the murder of Italian subjects while in custody of officers of the State of Louisiana in 1891.[1] Hall says, "States possess a right of protecting their subjects abroad which is correlative to their responsibility in respect of injuries inflicted upon foreigners within their dominions."[2] "Fundamentally, however, there is no difference in principle between wrongs inflicted by breach of a monetary agreement and other wrongs for which the state, as itself the wrong-doer, is immediately responsible. The difference which is made in practice is in no sense obligatory; and it is open to governments to consider each case by itself, and to act as seems well to them on its merits."[3]

[1] U. S. For. Rel. 1891, pp. 628–658.   [2] § 87, p. 291.
[3] Hall, § 87, p. 294.

CHAPTER IX

§ 38. Manner of Exercise of the Right

Strictly, there can be no limitation or restriction of independence, for it is a recognized principle that independence must be absolute and inalienable. In fact, every state voluntarily accepts either formally by treaty or tacitly by practice, many conditions which restrain it in the exercise of its powers. The independence of ιe state is not thereby violated, since the restraint is

74

exercised by the state itself, and is not an act of external control. The number of these restraints which states voluntarily assume is continually increasing, owing to the closer relations of humanity.

The exercise of the right of independence involves the privilege of making treaties, alliances, contracts, and municipal laws, so far as these do not violate international law or the right of independence as possessed by other states. A state may go to war to maintain its independence. The international rights of a state are in general closely related to the right of independence, and derive force from this relationship.

§ 39. Balance of Power

Undoubtedly the idea of establishing a relationship among " neighboring states more or less connected with one another, by virtue of which no one among them can injure the independence or essential rights of another without meeting with effectual resistance on some side and consequently exposing itself to danger " [1] is not a modern idea. Ancient states united to prevent the growth of some neighboring power to such magnitude as would threaten their independence. [2] From the beginning of the modern period of international law, Peace of Westphalia (1648), the idea of maintaining an equilibrium among the powers of Europe has had great influence, and until the latter part of the nineteenth century was regarded as one of the fundamental principles of European international practice.

[1] Von Gentz, " Fragments upon the Balance of Power in Europe," 1806.

[2] Hume, " Essays," VII.

Many treaties aim to preserve this balance among the European powers, and the words "balance" and "equilibrium" often appear.[1] The Treaty of Utrecht in its provision between Spain and Great Britain, July 13, 1713, gives as its object *ad firmandam stabiliendamque pacem ac tranquillitatem christiani orbis justo potentiæ equilibro.* The idea that independence was to be preserved by some balance of power reappears in successive treaties. This idea of the balance of power has led to most diverse action. Unjust rulers have made it the cloak for action entirely outside the sanction of international law. Many times it has "served as the pretext for a quarrel, and repeatedly made hostilities general which would otherwise have been shut up within a comparatively small area."[2] The feeling that the balance of power was a necessary policy for the preservation of European states, led to the idea that states should be constrained to certain lines of action, which would prevent, in many cases, normal growth. Frequently the independence of a state was violated to anticipate an action which might disturb the European equilibrium. The partitions of Poland show a violation of the principles of international law for the sake of giving equal compensation to the parties to it.

The doctrine of the balance of power is not a principle of international law, but merely a maxim of European political practice pretending to state the means of maintaining the independence of European states.[3]

[1] Nys, "Origines," pp. 165 ff.
[2] Bernard Lectures on "Diplomacy," 98.
[3] Tucker, "Monroe Doctrine," 4.

§ 40. Monroe Doctrine

Another maxim of political action is that which has become known as the " Monroe Doctrine." While enunciated by a single state, it had in view the maintenance of the independence of the states of the American continent. For many years after the Revolutionary War the opinion prevailed that Europe viewed with disfavor the growth of the American republic. The Holy Alliance, formed on the downfall of Napoleon, was followed by several congresses of European powers, at one of which, held at Verona in 1822, the subject of helping Spain recover her revolting colonies in America was discussed. This led to the declaration of President Monroe in his message of Dec. 2, 1823, that there should be, (1) no more European colonies on these continents, (2) no extension of the European political system to any portion of this hemisphere, (3) no European interposition in the affairs of the Spanish-American republics. This doctrine has been repeatedly affirmed by the United States, and in some instances very liberally interpreted. It in no way embodies a principle of international law, though the European and other states may regard it as expressing the attitude of the United States upon the points covered, and if desirous of avoiding friction, govern themselves accordingly. If it were a principle of international law, the United States would not be justified in changing its attitude upon the doctrine, but probably it would not be seriously maintained that the United States might not enunciate another policy setting aside the Monroe Doctrine.[1] Reddaway well says, " that it produced its

[1] Hart, "Foundations of American For

desired effect as an act of policy, but in no way modified the Law of Nations." [1]

The doctrine has always failed of legislative indorsement, and at times has been strenuously opposed by European powers. That it has been recognized, however, to a certain extent, appears by the course of events.[2] It was in 1895 applied in the case of the intervention by the United States in the dispute over the boundary between Venezuela and British Guiana. Arbitration settled this difficulty.[3]

President Roosevelt in his message of December 3, 1901, said: "The Monroe Doctrine should be the cardinal feature of the foreign policy of all the nations of the two Americas, as it is of the United States. . . . The Monroe Doctrine is a declaration that there must be no territorial aggrandizement by any non-American power at the expense of any American power on American soil. . . . We do not guarantee any state against punishment if it misconducts itself, provided that punishment does not take the form of the acquisition of territory by any non-American power."

§ 41. Non-intervention

With the right of independence goes the correlative *obligation of non-intervention*, i.e. of refraining from all acts that would forcibly limit the freedom of another state. This obligation of non-intervention does not extend to the limitation of acts involving no display or threat of force, as in the case of mediation and arbitration. Nor can it be claimed that the *obligation of non-intervention* can be urged against measures undertaken by a state to preserve its fundamental right to existence. There is no *right* of intervention, as has been sometimes argued, though an act of intervention may be some-

[1] "The Monroe Doctrine," VI.   [2] See Tucker, "Monroe Doctrine."
[3] Ann. Cycl. (1895), p. 741; (1896), p. 804; (1899), p. 845, also U. S. For. Rel. 1896.

times justifiable in itself.[1] Intervention is the attempt of one or more states, by means of force, to coerce another state in its purely state action. The making of an alliance between two may influence a third state in its action, but it cannot be considered an intervention, nor is the tender of friendly offices in the settlement of a dispute to which a state is a party, intervention; but when a state directly interferes with the exercise of the authority in another state or by another state, it constitutes intervention. Intervention may vary greatly in degree and in character, whether it be armed or diplomatic. Each case must be considered separately on its merits, and if in any degree a justifiable measure, it must be on the highest grounds, and the motives of the intervening state must be pure. While it is still necessary to discuss the question of intervention in its various forms, yet, as Hall says: "It is unfortunate that publicists have not laid down broadly and unanimously that no intervention is legal, except for the purpose of self-preservation, unless a breach of the law as between states has taken place, or unless the whole body of civilized states have concurred in authorizing it."[2]

§ 42. Practice in Regard to Intervention

The nineteenth century might be called the century of interventions, for its whole political history has been closely related to the application of measures of intervention of the most varied sort. Naturally, all authorities do not agree as to the causes underlying the action of the several states, nor as to the nomenclature which

---

[1] Bonfils, No. 295; "Pradier-Fodéré," No. 355.
[2] § 92, p. 304.

should be used in describing these measures. A review
of some of the cases of intervention during the nineteenth
century shows that while the doctrine of non-intervention has been more and more widely professed, the
practice has been strongly influenced by political
expediency.

Intervention for any cause may always be regarded
by the state whose independence is impinged as a hostile act, and a ground for war, thus putting the matter
outside the international law of peace.[1]

(a) **Intervention for Self-preservation.** As the right
of existence is the first right of a state and universally
admitted, intervention may sometimes be used as a
means of maintaining this existence. In such a case
it is clearly a matter of policy as to the means which a
state shall use, and if it resorts to intervention rather
than other means, it must have ample grounds for its
action in the particular case. A case of intervention
on the grounds of self-preservation which has caused
much debate is that of England in the two attacks upon
Copenhagen in 1801 and 1807, on the ground that it
was necessary for English supremacy of the seas, which
formed her chief defense, to prevent the union of the
Danish forces with those of the other powers. Intervention cannot be justified by any appeal to general
principles which inhere in the act itself. " The facts
of intervention are acts of the political existence of
states. Good or bad, according as the intervention
is injurious or beneficial."[2] Of intervention as a
method of state action, Sir W. Harcourt says : " It is a
high and summary procedure which may sometimes

[1] Hall, § 88, p. 297.   [2] Bonfils, 295.

snatch a remedy beyond the reach of law. Nevertheless, it must be admitted that in case of Intervention, as in that of Revolution, its essence is illegality, and its justification is its success. Of all things, at once the most injustifiable and the most impolitic is an unsuccessful Intervention."[1] Non-intervention is the obligation which international law enjoins. It gives no sanction to a "right of intervention" which would be entirely inconsistent with the right of independence. The question of intervention is one of state policy only, and is outside the limits of the field of international law. Intervention is a method of state action which is justifiable only in rare cases, and less and less justifiable as the growing mutual dependence of states makes possible other methods less open to objection. International law at the present day undoubtedly regards intervention when *strictly* necessary to preserve the fundamental right of the intervening state to its existence as a permissible act though contravening the right of independence in another state.

(*b*) **Intervention to prevent Illegal Acts.** As international law must rest upon the observance of certain general principles, it may in extreme cases be necessary to intervene in order that these principles may be respected by certain states in their dealings with other states which, though weaker in physical force, have equal rights in international law. How far any state will act as champion of the law of nations is a question which it must decide for itself. Unquestionably international law would look with favor upon measures *necessary* for its own preservation.

[1] "Letters to Historicus," p. 41.

(c) **Intervention by General Sanction.** Some authorities have maintained that intervention when sanctioned by a group of states is justifiable. It is probable that a group of states would be less liable to pursue an unjust course than a single state, and that intervention under such sanction would be more liable to be morally justifiable. It is, however, no more legal than the same act by a single state; and if general consent is the only sanction, while the act may be expedient, advantageous, and morally just, it cannot be regarded as upheld by international law, nor can a single act of this kind establish a principle. The several cases of such intervention under general sanction can hardly be regarded as sufficiently similar to establish a principle even upon the Eastern Question in Europe.[1] It may be concluded that while general sanction of a considerable group of states may, for a given interference, free a state from moral blame and warrant the act as a matter of policy, yet it does not give any international law sanction for intervention by general consent.

(d) **Other Grounds of Intervention.** Many reasons have been advanced as justifying such measures as intervention.

(1) Intervention to carry out *provisions of treaties of guaranty* was formerly common, *e.g.* intervention by one state to preserve the same form of government in the other or to maintain the ruling family. It is now held that no treaty can justify interference in the internal affairs of a state not party to the treaty.

In general, intervention, because of treaty stipulations,

[1] See Rolin-Jaequemyns, R. D. I., XVIII., 378, 506, 591.

even when the state subject to the intervention is a party to the treaty, is a violation of independence unless the treaty provides for such measures, in which case the state has -become a protected state or entered into relations by which it has not full state powers. Such treaties must be clearly state acts and not acts of individuals " who from their position have the opportunity of giving to their personal agreements the form of a state act." [1] While there is still difference of opinion as to the question of intervention under treaty sanction, the weight of opinion seems to be decidedly to the effect that such intervention has no ground of justification in international law.

(2) Intervention to preserve the *balance of power*, which was regarded as a necessary means for the preservation of European peace, has been considered as justifiable till recent times. Since the middle of the nineteenth century the position has received less and less support, though advanced in behalf of the preservation of the Turkish Empire and the adjustment of the Balkan states. In 1854 Great Britain and France, on the appeal of the Sultan for assistance against the Russian aggressions, determined to aid him, " their said Majesties being fully persuaded that the existence of the Ottoman Empire in its present Limits is essential to the maintenance of the Balance of Power among the States of Europe." [2] The attitude at the present time is stated by Lawrence. " The independence of states is not to be violated on the ground of possible danger to some imaginary equilibrium of political forces." [3]

[1] Hall, § 91, p. 301. [2] Hertslet, 1181, 1193.
[3] § 85, p. 129. See also 1 Halleck, 507.

(3) Interventions upon the broad and indefinite
ground of *humanity* have been common and were generally upheld by the writers to the time of Vattel.
Since his day opposition to intervention of this kind
has gradually obtained favor. What the grounds of
humanity are, and which nation's ideas of humanity
shall be accepted as standard, have been questions
difficult to settle to the general satisfaction of states.
For a state to set itself up as judge of the actions
of another state and to assume that it has the right
to extend its powers to settling and regulating affairs
of morals, religion, and the relations of public authority to the subjects in another state, on the ground
of maintaining the rights of mankind as a whole, is to
take a ground which the conduct of any modern state,
even the most civilized, would hardly warrant. While
it is admitted that a state or states may sometimes interfere to prevent one state from unduly oppressing
another, as in the intervention of the powers in Greece
in 1827, yet it is generally held that to interfere because
the internal affairs of a given state are not conducted
in a manner pleasing to the foreign state is to give a
sanction to an act that would result in far more evil
than good. Such intervention has often taken place.
The "Holy Alliance," in attempting to guard Europe
from "the curse of Revolution," advocated in practice
a most dangerous form of intervention.[1] Indeed, much
of the European history of the nineteenth century is
but a history of successive interventions. In spite of
all this, as Walker says, "the rule regularly progresses
towards more general recognition, that non-interven-

[1] 1 Hertslet, 317. *Ibid.*, 658.

tion in the internal affairs of a state is a law which admits of no exception to foreign powers, so long as the operations of that state are confined in their effect to the limits of the national territory." [1]

Nevertheless, the United States interfered in the affairs of Cuba on the ground of humanity. The President, in his message of April 11, 1898, says, after a long statement of the facts : " I have exhausted every effort to relieve the intolerable condition of affairs which is at our doors. Prepared to execute every obligation imposed upon me by the Constitution and the law, I await your action." [2] By joint resolution of Congress of April 20, 1898, demand was made upon Spain to relinquish its authority in Cuba, and the President was authorized to use land and naval forces to carry the resolution into effect. [3]

(4) In time of *civil war*, on invitation of both parties, a foreign state may act as mediator, but unless the revolting party has been recognized, this is mediation in a domestic sense rather than intervention in the sense of international law.

Under other conditions there is a diversity of view as to the proper course of action. [4] Some deny with Vattel, G. F. de Martens, Heffter, Fiore, Bluntschli, Woolsey, and others maintain or permit intervention in civil war at the request of one of the parties, though some of the authorities do not permit intervention except on the invitation of the parent state and not on that of the rebelling party. Bluntschli (§ 476) and Wool-

[1] Walker, p. 151.
[2] Ann. Cycl. 1898, p. 159 ; U. S. For. Rel., 1898, p. 760.
[3] 30 U. S. Sts. at Large, 738.   [4] Bluntschli, § 477.

sey (§ 42) admit intervention only in behalf of the party
representing the state ; Vattel and some others permit
intervention in behalf of the party which the intervening state considers to have the right of the contest,
thus opening the arbitration of the contest to a foreign
state. Both of these positions are receiving less and
less of sanction. Intervention in behalf of the established state implies a doubt as to which power within
the state is the *de facto* power, and as Hall says : "the
fact that it has been necessary to call in foreign help
is enough to show that the issue of the conflict would
without it be uncertain, and consequently that there
is a doubt as to which side would ultimately establish
itself as the legal representative of the state."[1] It is
plain to see that intervention in behalf of the rebelling
party is a violation of the independence of the existing
state. It is equally clear that international law does
not give a foreign state a right to judge upon the justice or merits of domestic questions in another state.

The principle may now be regarded as established by
both theory and practice that the invitation of neither
party to a domestic strife gives a right to a foreign
state to intervene, and that no state has a right to
judge as to the merits of the contest and to interfere
in behalf of the party it thinks in the right. Indeed,
intervention because of civil war only is in no case
justifiable, though the consequences of such a disturbance may warrant intervention upon other grounds.[2]

(5) Intervention on the ground of *financial transactions* is not now sanctioned. A state may make any
injustice done its subjects by a foreign state a matter

[1] § 94, p. 307.   [2] 1 Hertslet, 664 ff.

of diplomatic negotiations. It has sometimes been held that contracts running between a state and the subject or subjects of another state may, if violated, become grounds of just intervention, and that the subjects had a right to demand action by their sovereign. This ground is manifestly insufficient, though each state is judge as to what measures it will take in a given case. International law does not guarantee the payment of loans which are merely personal transactions between the individual and the state in its corporate capacity, nor can the public law of one state be expected to hold in another. Interference on such grounds is a matter of expediency and not a matter of right.

(e) **Conclusion.** In general, the best authorities seem to agree that at the present time, owing to the ease with which other measures may be taken, intervention can be admitted only on the single ground of self-preservation. The numerous cases of intervention upon varied grounds amply show that any other ground would be open to wide abuse, as has often been the case. For general purposes of remedy for injury such measures as retorsion, reprisals, embargo, and pacific blockade may be taken when a state deems it expedient and is willing to assume the responsibility for such measures.[1] While intervention is, for the sake of preserving the existence of a state, a justifiable measure, it is not a *right*, but merely a means sometimes justifiable to preserve a right, — the right of a state to exist, which alone supersedes the obligation of non-intervention.

[1] See ch. XV.

CHAPTER X

EQUALITY

§ 43. Equality in General

The equality of states was an early premise of international law. This equality, however wide may have been its meaning, as interpreted by some of the earlier writers, can now be held to extend only to legal status. A state from its very being as a sovereign unity must be legally equal to any other state. Only those states members of the international circle are regarded as possessed of this equality from the point of view of international law. So far as legal attributes as *states* extend, the states members of the international circle are equal, yet that their weight in the world of affairs may vary by virtue of other circumstances must be admitted. The legal status of states is the same; regardless of the form of state organization, whether monarchy or republic; regardless of origin, whether by division or union of former states or even if created in a region hitherto outside the jurisdiction of any state; regard-

88

less of area, population, wealth, influence, etc. ; regardless of relations to other states provided sovereignty is not impaired ; regardless of any change in the form of state organization, as from a republic to a monarchy or even of a temporary lapse in the exercise of sovereignty.

§ 44. Inequalities among States

While all states, members of the family of states, are equal in international law so far as their legal attributes are concerned, they may be very unequal in other respects.

(*a*) One of the oldest marks of inequality is that of **court precedence**, which for many years was a fertile source of difficulty, and was at last settled to the extent of ranking by title of diplomatic representative by the Congress of Vienna in 1815.[1]

(*b*) **Inequalities in matters of ceremonial** of various kinds have not disappeared. These may be based upon tradition or conventional grounds, and frequently give rise to difficulties if disregarded. These ceremonials may be (1) political as between the sovereigns in their official personal capacity as emperors, kings, dukes, etc., (2) court and diplomatic in interstate negotiations, (3) treaty as in *alternat* or in the alphabetical signing of treaties, (4) maritime ceremonial in salutes, etc.

(*c*) **Inequalities in weight of influence in affairs.**

. (1) In Europe there is distinctly recognized in political practice an inequality of the states, and they are classed as "the great powers," "the minor powers,"

[1] See § 70 (*b*).

and sometimes such states as those of the Balkan penin-
sula are referred to as "the little powers" or "third-
rate states." These divisions are based merely upon
political grounds, and states may pass from one division
to another as their wealth, area, or influence increases
or decreases.

At the present time "the great powers," generally
mentioned *officially* upon the continent in the alphabetical order of their names in French, i.e. *Allemagne,
Angleterre, Autriche,* etc., are Germany, Great Britain,
Austria, France, Italy, and Russia. During the sixteenth
and seventeenth centuries Spain was numbered with "the
great powers." Sweden was so ranked in the seventeenth century. Italy was counted with "the great
powers" after 1870. The union of several powers upon
certain lines of policy, since early in the nineteenth century, has been called "the concert of Europe," "the
primacy of the great powers," etc. It was not the purpose
of these great powers to establish new rules of international law; but as enunciated by the five powers, Nov. 15,
1818, it was "their invariable resolution never to depart,
either among themselves, or in their relations with other
states, from the strictest observation of the principles
of the Rights of Nations."[1]

That the practice of the Great Powers has not been
strictly in accord with these expressed principles, a
glance will show. The immediate action of Austria,
Russia, and Prussia in the Congress of Troppau, 1820,
carried the principle of interference in the internal
affairs of states so far that Great Britain found itself
compelled to dissent. This continuance of the policy of

[1] 1 Hertslet, 574.

the Holy Alliance in putting down movements in favor of popular liberty, wherever arising, led to gross violations of international rights. Nor did Great Britain become a party to the acts of the Congress of Verona in 1822, which led to intervention to prevent changes in the internal organization of Spain in 1823. The struggles of the Greeks for independence at about this time were naturally regarded by those upholding the ideas of the Holy Alliance as dangerous to those states desiring to prevent revolutionary movements. But the narrow policy of the Alliance was gradually losing support. The opposition of Great Britain and the death of Alexander of Russia in 1825 hastened its speedy fall. Meantime the idea of a collective authority in the Great Powers had been maintained. This began to be exercised in behalf of the Greeks in 1826, and has throughout the nineteenth century been repeatedly exercised in the same behalf, sometimes unselfishly, often from motives of mixed character. During the latter half of the nineteenth century the Great Powers have continually kept a close surveillance over Grecian affairs, and enforced their judgments in regard to Greece by force (destruction of Turkish fleet at Navarino, 1827); by providing form of government and naming monarch (1829 and later); by fixing and changing boundaries (1829 and often); by pacific blockade (1827, 1850, 1886, 1897); by regulating financial affairs, and by other means of varying degree of force.[1]

The Eastern question has particularly occupied the Concert, and the disposition of the territory once within

[1] For detailed summary, 1826–1881, see Holland, " European Concert in the Eastern Question," Ch. II.

the Turkish jurisdiction has offered a fertile field for varying policy.

The establishment of Belgium as a neutral state by the treaty to which Belgium was itself a party afforded another example of the influence of the Great Powers.

Since 1839 Egypt has also been subject to frequent control by the Great Powers.

Since 1885 the unappropriated portion of Africa has been brought into the range of action of the Concert by the theory of the sphere of influence.

The Concert of the Great Powers shows then a policy which is liable to change with expediency. The two great treaties of the Concert are those of Paris, 1856, and Berlin, 1878. Of these Holland says, " The treaties of Paris and of Berlin thus resemble one another, in that both alike are a negation of the right of any one Power, and an assertion of the right of the Powers collectively, to regulate the solution of the Eastern question." [1] The fact that the action of the Great Powers has been regarded as binding and tacitly accepted in Europe in certain questions in the East, Egypt, Greece, and Belgium does not give the sanction of international law to the action. The most that can be said is that it is an alliance of a loose character, whose authority is in proportion to the force behind its decisions.[2]

(2) Another feature in European politics giving rise to further inequalities in practice was introduced by the alliance of Germany and Austria in 1879 and Italy in 1883, which is now commonly known as the Triple Alliance. This belt of powers separating Eastern from

[1] " European Concert in the Eastern Question," p. 221.
[2] Lawrence, " Disputed Questions," V.

Western Europe has materially affected the action of other powers.

The "friendly understanding" between France and Russia soon after the Triple Alliance affords a measure of counter-check upon the action of the other powers.

In spite of all these alliances and counter-alliances, the recognition of the weight of the decisions of the congresses and conferences of the Great Powers upon those subjects which are held to affect "the peace of Europe" have an influence comparable to that which might be assigned to a "Supreme Court of International Appeal." [1]

The United States upon the American continent in its enunciation of the Monroe Doctrine, and the subsequent interpretation of it, has assumed a position as arbiter among the American states in some respects similar to that of the European Concert among the European states. This attitude of the United States has weight in international practice, but cannot be regarded as a part of international law.

[1] Lawrence, "Disputed Questions," V., end.

CHAPTER XI

JURISDICTION

45. JURISDICTION IN GENERAL.

46. TERRITORIAL DOMAIN AND JURISDICTION.

47. METHOD OF ACQUISITION.
- (*a*) Discovery.
- (*b*) Occupation.
- (*c*) Conquest.
- (*d*) Cession.
    - (1) Transfer by gift.
    - (2) Transfer by exchange.
    - (3) Transfer by sale.
    - (4) Cession of jurisdiction.
- (*e*) Prescription.
- (*f*) Accretion.

48. QUALIFIED JURISDICTION.
- (*a*) Protectorates.
- (*b*) Sphere of influence.

49. MARITIME AND FLUVIAL JURISDICTION.

50. RIVERS.
- (*a*) Which traverse only one state.
- (*b*) Flowing through two or more states.
- (*c*) Under jurisdiction of two states.

51. THE NAVIGATION OF RIVERS.

52. ENCLOSED WATERS.
- (*a*) Wholly enclosed.
- (*b*) Gulfs, bays, estuaries.

(c) Straits: Danish Sounds, Dardanelles.
(d) Canals: Suez, Panama, Nicaraguan, Corinth, Kiel.

53. THE THREE-MILE LIMIT.

54. FISHERIES.
(a) Deep sea.
(b) Canadian.
(c) Bering Sea.

55. VESSELS.
(a) Classes.
   (1) Public.
   (2) Private.
(b) Nationality.
(c) Jurisdiction.
   (1) Public.
   (2) Private.
   (3) Semi-public.

56. PERSONAL, GENERAL — NATIONALITY.

57. NATURAL-BORN SUBJECTS.

58. FOREIGN-BORN SUBJECTS.

59. ACQUIRED NATIONALITY.
(a) By marriage.
(b) By naturalization.
(c) By annexation of territory.
(d) Effect of naturalization.
(e) Incomplete naturalization.

60. JURISDICTION OVER ALIENS.
(a) Over subjects abroad.
   (1) Emigration laws.
   (2) Recall of citizens.
   (3) Penal jurisdiction.
   (4) Protection of subjects.
(b) Over aliens within territory.
   (1) Exclusion.
   (2) Expulsion.
   (3) Conditional admission.

§ 45. Jurisdiction in General

Jurisdiction is the right to exercise state authority, and for the purposes of international law may be classified as, (a) territorial or land jurisdiction, (b) fluvial and maritime, and (c) jurisdiction over persons.

§ 46. Territorial Domain and Jurisdiction

The word " territory " is sometimes used as equivalent to domain or dominion or to an expression covering the sphere of state control. Territory is also used in the stricter sense of the land area over which a state exercises its powers. In this stricter sense, territorial jurisdiction refers to the exercise of state authority over the land within its boundaries and those things which appertain to the land. The growing international importance of railroads, telegraph, and other modern means of communication has introduced new topics not considered in early treatises, and these are still under discussion.

The fundamental law of territorial jurisdiction is that a state has within its boundaries absolute and exclusive jurisdiction over all the land and those things which appertain thereto. Certain exemptions are specially provided in international law to which all states are considered as giving express or tacit consent. In other respects than those mentioned under exemptions, the state may, as sovereign, exercise its authority at discretion within the sphere it has set for itself. The state has, as against all other states, an exclusive title to all property within its territorial jurisdiction. As regards its own subjects, it has the paramount title which is recognized in the right of eminent domain, or the right to appropriate private property when necessary for public use. A state may also in its corporate capacity hold absolute ownership in property, as in its forts, arsenals, ships, etc.

H

The state also has the right to enforce a lien on the land and what appertains to it in the form of taxes.

§ 47. Method of Acquisition

The method of acquisition of territorial jurisdiction is a subject which has received much attention in international law, particularly because of the remarkable expansion of the territorial area of states within the modern period of international law since 1648.

The methods commonly considered are : (1) discovery, (2) occupation, (3) conquest, (4) cession, (5) prescription, (6) accretion.

(a) In the early period of European expansion through **discovery**, the doctrine that title to land hitherto unknown vested in the state whose subject discovered the land was current. Gross abuse of this doctrine led to the modification that discovery without occupation did not constitute a valid title. As the field of discovery has grown less, the importance of a definition of occupation has decreased.

(b) **Occupation** is held to begin at the time of effective application of state authority, and strictly continues only during the exercise of such authority. In fact, however, the title by occupation is held to extend to the adjacent unoccupied territory to which the state might potentially extend the exercise of its authority, or where it may from time to time exercise its authority in an undisputed manner. Title by occupation extends as a rule to that area, not under the jurisdiction of another state, which is necessary for the safety of the occupied area or is naturally dependent upon it, as to the territory drained by a river of which a given state holds the mouth.

The "Hinterland Doctrine," brought forth during the latter years of the nineteenth century, advances the idea that no such limits as above shall bound the area which can be claimed on ground of occupation, but that coast settlements give a *prima facie* title to the unexplored interior.

While the uncivilized peoples living within an area to which a civilized state claimed jurisdiction by virtue of occupancy were often unjustly treated, they however "were admitted to be the rightful occupants of the soil, with a legal as well as just claim to retain possession of it, and to use it according to their own discretion, though not to dispose of the soil of their own will, except to the government claiming the right of preëmption. . . . The United States adopted the same principle, and their exclusive right to extinguish the Indian title by purchase or conquest, and to grant the soil, and exercise such a degree of sovereignty as circumstances required, has never been questioned."[1]

(*c*) **Conquest** in the technical sense of the status of a territory which has come permanently under the jurisdiction of the enemy is distinct from military occupation, which is a simple fact supported by force.

Military occupation may pass into conquest (1) by actual occupation for a long period, with intention on the part of the occupier to continue the possession for an indefinite period, provided there has not been a continued and material effort upon the part of the former holder to regain possession. If, after a reason-

[1] 3 Kent Com., 379, 380 ; 1 Gould and Tucker, 484.

able time, this effort to regain possession seems futile,
the conquest may be regarded as complete. Each state
must judge for itself as to the reasonableness of the
time and futility of the effort. (2) Conquest may be
said to be complete when by decree, to which the inhabitants acquiesce, a subjugated territory is incorporated under a new state. (3) A treaty of peace or act
of cession may confirm the title by conquest.[1]

(*d*) Transfer of territory by **cession** may be by gift,
exchange, sale, or other agreement.

(1) The *transfer by gift* is simple, and carries such
obligations as the parties interested may undertake.
In 1850, by a treaty with Great Britain, "Horse-shoe
Reef," in Lake Erie, was ceded to the United States for
the purpose of the erection of a lighthouse, " provided
the Government of the United States will engage
to erect such lighthouse, and to maintain a light
therein ; and provided no fortification be erected on
said Reef." [2]

(2) *Transfer of territory by exchange* is not common
in modern times. By the Treaty of Berlin, 1878, a portion of Bessarabia, given to Roumania by the Treaty of
Paris, 1856, was given back to Russia, and Roumania
received in exchange a portion of Turkey.[3]

(3) *Transfer of territory by sale* has been frequent.
From 1311, when the Markgraf of Brandenburg sold
three villages to the Teutonic knights, down to the
nineteenth century, instances of sale might be found,

[1] In case of the United States, while the President may after declaration of war conquer and hold foreign territory, the joint action of the
President and Senate is necessary to make the title complete by treaty.
   [2] Treaties of U. S., 444.
   [3] Woolsey, 496 ; Hertslet, 2745, 2791.

but the nineteenth century has numerous instances
which have established the principles. Napoleon sold
Louisiana to the United States in 1803, the Prince of
Monaco made a sale to France in 1851, Russia sold
Alaska to the United States in 1867, the Netherlands
sold African colonies to Great Britain in 1872, Sweden
sold the island of St. Bartholomy to France in 1877,
the United States bought the Philippines in 1898.
The fact of the sale is not a matter of international
law, but is purely within the range of the public law
of the countries concerned. The change of jurisdiction of the area gives rise to certain possible complications which may involve principles of international
law, though generally the conditions of sale settle such
questions.

(4) *Cession of jurisdiction* over a given portion of
territory as surety for the performance of a certain act,
by lease, by annexation agreements, as payment of an
indemnity or the like, are methods of acquiring temporary jurisdiction which frequently become permanent.

(e) **Prescription,** or the acquisition of territory by
virtue of long-continued possession, is similar to prescription in public law as applied to the acquisition of
property by persons. The recognition of this principle
prevents many disputes over jurisdiction of territory
which originally may have been acquired in a manner
open to question, *e.g.* the holding of the territory by
the states parties to the partition of Poland may through
long-continued possession be valid by prescription if
not by the original act.

In regard to prescription, it should be observed that
(1) it is a title valid only against other states. The

inhabitants do not necessarily lose rights originally possessed. (2) This method avoids perpetual conflicts on ground of defect of original title. (3) Prescription may be considered as effective when other states have for a considerable time made no objection, threatening the exercise of jurisdiction by the state in possession. While some authors deny this right, it is generally admitted in fact, and by most of the leading authorities acknowledged in theory.[1]

(f) When land areas in the neighborhood of the boundary of a state are changed, territory may be acquired by **accretion**. (1) Land formed by *alluvium* or other cause near the coast of a state is held to belong to that state. Lord Stowell, in 1805, held that mud islands formed by *alluvium* from the Mississippi River should for international law purposes be held as part of the United States territory.[2] In general, *alluvium* becomes the property of the state to which it attaches, following the Roman law.[3] (2) Where a river is the boundary, the rule is well-established that islands formed on either side of the deepest channel belong to the state upon that side of the channel ; an island formed mid-stream is divided by the old channel line. (3) When a river's channel is suddenly changed so as to be entirely within the territory of either state, the boundary line remains as before in the old channel. So also the boundary line of territory is not changed, even if the bed of a lake be changed.

[1] See discussion in Hall, § 36, note 1, p. 124.
[2] The "Anna," 5 C. Rob., 373.
[3] "Institutes," II., 1, 20.

§ 48. Qualified Jurisdiction

Two degrees of qualified territorial jurisdiction are exercised in the protectorate and the sphere of influence.

(*a*) **Protectorates.** The protecting state usually acquires the jurisdiction over all external affairs of the protected community, often including territorial waters, and assumes the direction of its international relations. A measure of jurisdiction of those internal affairs which may lead to international complications is also generally assumed by the protecting state, *e.g.* treatment of foreigners in the protected territory, relations of protected subjects in foreign countries, use of flag, etc. The conditions of protected states vary greatly, hardly the same description holding for any two. It may be safe to say that (1) the protecting state cannot be held responsible for the establishment of any particular form of government, (2) a reasonable degree of security and justice must be maintained. As to what constitutes a "reasonable degree," the circumstances of each case must determine; then the protecting state is bound to afford such justice and security and (3) must be able to exercise within the protected area such powers as are necessary to meet its responsibilities.

(*b*) The term "sphere of influence" has been used since the Berlin Conference, 1884–1885, to indicate a sort of attenuated protectorate in which the aim is to secure the rights without the obligations. First applied to Africa in the partition of the unexplored interior among the European powers, — Great Britain, Germany, France, Italy, Portugal, — it has since been extended to other regions. This •doctrine of mutual exclusion of each from the " spheres " of all the others cannot be held to bind any states not party to the agreement.

The method of exercise of " influence," while varying, usually consists in making with the native chiefs treaties which convey privileges other than the cession of sovereignty. These privileges are often commercial, and may be with the state direct or agreements with some company to whom the state has delegated a portion of its authority, as in the African trade companies.

The " spheres of influence," gradually with the growth of power of the influencing state and the necessity of protecting the "sphere," against other states, become less vague in their relations to the influencing state and merge into protectorates or some other more stable condition.

This " sphere of influence " idea, as well as the " Hinterland Doctrine," can be of only temporary importance, owing to the limited area still open to occupation. It is maintained that within the "sphere " the influencing state has jurisdiction to the exclusion of another state, and that it has a right to occupy the territory later, if advisable. The influencing state disclaims all obligations possible.[1]

§ 49. Maritime and Fluvial Jurisdiction

Wheaton states as a general principle of maritime and fluvial jurisdiction, "Things of which the use is in-

[1] See Lawrence, 153, 161, 164–167 ; Reinsch, " World Politics," pp. 60, 113, 184.

exhaustible, such as the sea and running water, cannot be so appropriated as to exclude others from using these elements in any manner which does not occasion a loss or inconvenience to the proprietor."[1] While the tendency of international policy is toward unrestricted freedom of river navigation, yet the principle as enunciated by Wheaton cannot be said to be established in practice. The American and Continental writers have generally favored the principle enunciated by Wheaton. English writers have contended against this position as a right, but admit that the principle is becoming established by numerous treaties and conventions. As to the sea, the principle may be said to be established.

§ 50. Rivers

The jurisdiction of rivers is a question which is not identical with the right of navigation of rivers, and may best be considered apart. The question of jurisdiction is one of general international principle, while the question of river navigation is one of particular provision, in many instances.

The rivers fall under three classes : —

1. Rivers which traverse only one state.
2. Rivers which traverse two or more states.
3. Rivers upon the opposite banks of which different states have jurisdiction.

(a) **Rivers which traverse only one state** are exclusively within the jurisdiction of that state. This jurisdiction may extend even to the forbidding of the use of

a river to other states, and justifies the state in pre-
scribing such regulations for its use as it may deem fit.

(b) **Rivers flowing through two or more states** are
for those parts within the boundaries of each state
under its jurisdiction for the purposes of police, tolls,
and general regulations. The right of absolute exclusion of the co-riparian states by any one of the states
through which a river flows has been the subject of
much discussion, and authorities of great weight can be
found upon either side.

(c) **When two states have jurisdiction** upon opposite banks of a river, the jurisdiction of each state
extends to the middle of the main channel or *thalweg*.
Before the Treaty of Luneville (Art. VI.), 1801, it had
been common to consider the limit of jurisdiction of
the two states the middle of the river, a line much more
difficult to determine, and more changeable than the
channel line. The *thalweg* has been frequently confirmed as the accepted boundary where no conventions
to the contrary existed.[1]

§ 51. The Navigation of Rivers

The laws of jurisdiction of rivers are generally
accepted. The early idea that there was a natural
right of navigation, and *innocent passage* has received
less support during the nineteenth century than formerly. The history of river navigation during the
nineteenth century, as shown in the discussions between the representatives of various nations, and in

[1] Ed. Engelhardt, "Du régime conventionnel des fleuves interna-
tionaux," Ch. II.

the treaties and conventions agreed upon, as well as in treaties and declarations voluntarily made in regard to navigation of rivers, seem to furnish general rules.

1. That international law gives to other states no right of navigation of rivers wholly *within* the jurisdiction of another state.

2. That when a river forms the *boundary* of two or more states it is open to the navigation of each of the states.

3. That when a river passes *through* two or more states, international law gives no right to one of the states to pass through the part of the river in the other state or states. There is a strong moral obligation resting upon the states below to allow freedom of navigation through the river to the states upon the upper course of the river. The right of *innocent use, innocent passage, freedom of river navigation,* has been maintained on various grounds and in various forms, by many authorities.[1] Those who take a position opposed to this claim, assert that the navigation of rivers is, and properly should be, to avoid more serious complications, a matter of convention.

In fact, since the French Revolution, the subject has so frequently been a matter of convention[2] as to establish the general principles, that in case of no special restrictions, river navigation is free, subject to such regulations as the state having jurisdiction may deem

[1] Grotius, II., ii., 12-14; Pufendorf, III., 3, 4; Vattel, §§ 104, 126-130, 132-134; Bluntschli, § 314; Calvo, §§ 259, 290-291; Fiore, §§ 758, 768; Carnazza-Amari, "Traite," § 2, Ch. VII., 17; Heffter, § 77; Wheat., D., § 193.

[2] Wheat., D., §§ 197-204; Whart., § 30; Pradier-Fodéré, "Traite," §§ 727-755.

necessary, and that the privilege of navigation carries with it the use of the river banks, so far as is necessary for purpose of navigation.[1]

§ 52. Enclosed Waters

(a) The rule in regard to **waters wholly within** the territory of a state such as lakes, etc., is that the jurisdiction is exclusively in that state.

(b) **Gulfs, bays, and estuaries** are regarded as within the jurisdiction of the state or states enclosing them, provided the mouth is not more than six miles in width. A line drawn from headland to headland on either side of the mouth is considered as the coast line of the state, and for purposes of maritime jurisdiction the marine league is measured from this line. Waters having wider openings into the sea have been claimed on special grounds, as the claim of the United States to territorial jurisdiction over the Chesapeake and Delaware bays. France and Germany claim jurisdiction over gulfs having outlets not over ten miles in width. Between states parties to treaties special claims have been made and allowed. These treaty stipulations do not necessarily bind states not parties to the treaty, e.g. treaty between Great Britain and France, 1839. "It is agreed that the distance of three miles, fixed as the general limit of the exclusive right of fishing upon the coasts of the two countries, shall, with respect to bays, the mouths of which do not exceed ten miles in width, be measured from a straight line drawn from headland to headland."[2]

---

[1] Justinian, "Inst.," 2, t. 1, §§ 1–5.
[2] 3 Whart., § 305 a.

The present tendency is toward a restricted jurisdiction and the acceptance of the six-mile limit of width of mouth, though there is a reasonable claim that some ratio should be fixed for very large interior water areas to which the entrance, though more than six miles, is yet relatively narrow.

(c) **Straits** less than six miles in width are within the jurisdiction of the shore state or states. In case two shores are territory of different states, each state has jurisdiction to the middle of the navigable channel.

Where a state owns both shores of a strait which does not exceed six miles in width, the strait is within its territorial jurisdiction, though other states have the right of navigation. This right of navigation is in general conferred upon both merchant and war vessels of states at peace with the territorial power. These vessels must, however, comply with proper regulations in regard to navigation. The claim to exclusive jurisdiction over such narrow straits has been abandoned.

The claim of the king of Denmark to jurisdiction over the Danish Sound and the Two Belts, which entitled him to levy tolls upon vessels passing through, was based on prescription and fortified by treaties as early as the one with the Hanse towns in 1368. Against these tolls, as an unjust burden upon commerce, the United States protested in 1848, at the same time maintaining that Denmark had not the right of exclusive jurisdiction. The European states in 1857 paid a lump sum in capitalization of the sound dues. The United States, refusing to recognize the right of Denmark to levy tolls, paid $393,011 in 1857 in consideration of Denmark's agreement to keep up lighthouses, etc.

The navigation of the Bosphorus and Dardanelles has been a subject of discussion and treaty since 1774, when Russia compelled Turkey to open these straits to the passage of merchant vessels. War vessels were excluded till 1856 when, by convention attached to the Treaty of Paris, such vessels were admitted for special purposes of service to the embassies at Constantinople and protection of improvements on the Danube waterway. By the Treaty of 1871 the Sultan may admit other war vessels, if necessary for carrying out terms of the Treaty of Paris. The United States has never acknowledged that the Sultan had the right to exclude its war vessels, though always asking permission of the Sultan to pass the Dardanelles.

As a generally accepted principle the law may be stated as follows : straits connecting free seas are open to the navigation of all states, subject of course to reasonable jurisdiction of the territorial power.

(d) **Canals** connecting large bodies of water have been regarded as in most respects subject to jurisdiction similar to that of straits. Yet as these canals are constructed at a cost, they must also be given exemptions from certain restrictions which properly apply to natural channels.

The position of the Suez Canal as an international waterway gives some indication of existing practice.

It is to be noted, (1) that the canal is an artificial waterway ; (2) that M. de Lesseps, a foreigner, in 1854, under authorization of the Viceroy, undertook its construction as a business venture ; (3) that it is wholly within the territory of Egypt.

The case is then one of an artificial waterway, constructed by private capital, wholly within the territory of a state.

The negotiations continued from 1869, when the canal was opened, to 1888, when a convention was signed by the Six Great Powers, and by the Netherlands, Spain, and Turkey, by which the status of the canal was defined. By Article I. of the Conventional Act, " The Suez Maritime Canal shall always be free and open, in the time of war as in the time of peace, to every vessel of commerce or of war, without distinction of flag.

"Consequently, the High Contracting Parties agree not in any way to interfere with the free use of the Canal, in time of war as in time of peace.

- " The Canal shall never be subjected to the exercise of the right of blockade."

By Article IV., the canal is not to become the base of hostile action. The marine league is to be respected in the action of foreign vessels. The twenty-four hour period was to elapse between the sailing of hostile vessels.

By Article VII., the powers might keep two war vessels in the "ports of access of Port Said and Suez," though "this right shall not be exercised by belligerents."

By Article X., the territorial jurisdiction for general administrative purposes is affirmed, and likewise for sanitary measures in Article XV.[1]

This Suez Canal of such great international importance is by this convention within the jurisdiction of Egypt, but the powers have assumed to provide that

[1] Parl. Papers, 1889, Commercial, No. 2; Holland, "Studies in International Law," p. 270.

this jurisdiction shall not be exercised in such a way as to prevent innocent passage.

The Hay-Pauncefote Treaty of 1901, setting aside the Clayton-Bulwer Treaty of 1850, leaves to the United States large jurisdiction over such canal as it may determine to construct across the Central American Isthmus.

The canal at Corinth, shortening somewhat the route to the Black Sea and Asia Minor, was opened in 1893. This canal does not, like the Suez, greatly change the current of the world's intercourse, and is entirely within the jurisdiction of Greece.

Similarly the canal at Kiel, opened in 1896, is wholly within the jurisdiction of Germany.

§ 53. The Three-mile Limit

One of the most generally recognized rules of international law is that the jurisdiction of a state extends upon the open sea to a distance of three miles from the low-water mark. In the words of the Act of Parliament passed in consequence of the case of the *Franconia*,[1] 1878 (41 and 42 Victoria, c. 73), " The territorial waters of Her Majesty's dominions, in reference to the sea, means such part of the sea adjacent to the coast of the United Kingdom, or the coast of some other part of Her Majesty's dominions, as is deemed by international law to be within the territorial sovereignty of Her Majesty ; and for the purpose of any offence declared by this Act to be within the jurisdiction of the Admiral,

---

[1] See Regina *v*. Keyn, 2 L. R. (Exch. Div.), 63.

any part of the open sea within one marine league of the coast measured from low-water mark shall be deemed to be open sea within the territorial waters of Her Majesty's dominions." The three-mile limit became more and more generally recognized after the publication of Bynkershoek's " De Dominio Maris," in which he enunciates the principle that the territorial jurisdiction ends where the effective force of arms ends, which being approximately three miles from shore at that time, has since been usually accepted.

For special purposes a wider limit of jurisdiction is maintained and sometimes accepted by courtesy, though it is doubtful whether any state would attempt to hold its position against a protest from another state. The claims are based on the jurisdiction over fisheries, the enforcement of revenue laws, and the maintenance of neutrality. Such claims as the former English claims to the " King's Chambers," announced in 1604 to be bounded by a " straight line drawn from one point to another about the realm of England," as from the Lizard to Land's End, would not now receive serious support; and since the rejection of the claims of the United States by the Bering Sea Tribunal, it can be safely stated that the expansion of territorial jurisdiction upon the open sea will only come through the consensus of states. The desirability of some new regulations upon marine jurisdiction was well shown in the discussions of the Institute of International Law at its meeting in Paris in 1894.[1]

Within the three-mile limit the jurisdiction extends to commercial regulations, rules for pilotage and anchor-

---

[1] Ann. Cycl. (1894), 292.

1

age, sanitary and quarantine regulations, control of fisheries, revenue, general police, and in time of war to the enforcement of neutrality.

§ 54. Fisheries

The existence of fisheries has given rise to some special claims to extension of maritime jurisdiction.

(a) As a general rule, the right of **fishing on the high sea** belongs to all states alike, but each must respect the rights of others. In order that these rights might be defined, it has in many cases been necessary to resort to conventions. One of the most recent examples of this kind is seen in the convention in regard to the North Sea Fisheries, May 6, 1882, to which Belgium, Denmark, France, Germany, Great Britain, and Holland are parties. The cruisers of any of these states may present the case of the fishing vessel violating the regulations of the convention in the country to which the vessel belongs, but the trial and penalty belong to the country of the vessel.[1]

(b) Special privileges granted by one state to another, or secured by custom, become servitudes, as in the case of the **Canadian** fisheries, and must depend upon the interpretation of the treaties by which they were granted.

By the Treaty of 1783 the United States have the right of fishing on certain parts of the coast of the British Dominion in North America.

Great Britain claimed that these rights were annulled by the Treaty of Ghent, 1814, which put an end to the

[1] Lawrence, pp. 138, 182.

War of 1812 as that treaty was silent upon the subject. The United States declared " they were not annulled by the war as they were enjoyed by the colonists before the separation from England in 1783, and so existed perpetually independent of treaty."

This claim was adjusted by the Treaty of 1818, which gave to the United States permission to take fish on certain parts of the coast of Newfoundland and Labrador, to dry and cure fish in certain inlets, and to enter other inlets for shelter, repairs, and supplies.

Disputes arising under this treaty were settled by the Treaty of 1854, which gave to Canadian fishermen certain rights of fishing along the eastern coast of the United States north of the thirty-sixth parallel of latitude.

The United States took action to terminate this treaty in accord with its terms in 1866. The conditions of the Treaty of 1818 revived.

The Treaty of Washington, 1871, practically reëstablishes the provisions of the Treaty of 1854, specifying that the difference in value between the rights granted by each state to the other should be determined by a commission. This commission awarded $5,500,000 to Great Britain in 1877.[1]

In accord with the provisions of the Treaty of 1871, it was terminated by the United States in 1886, the provisions of the Treaty of 1818 again coming in force.

A law of March 3, 1897,[2] provides that the President may in certain contingencies deny vessels of the British Dominions of North America entry into the waters of

---

[1] See Cushing's "Treaty of Washington."
[2] 24 U. S. Sts. at Large, 475.

the United States, and may also prohibit the importation of fish and other goods.[1]

(c) Another question which has given rise to much discussion is that of the seal-fishing in Bering Sea.

In 1821 Russia claimed that the Pacific north of latitude 51° was *mare clausum*. The United States and Great Britain denied this claim. By conventions, 1824 and 1825, Russia conceded to these nations rights of navigation, fishing, etc. After the United States in 1867 acquired Russian America, seal-fishing assumed importance. As the Canadian fishermen were not restrained by the laws binding the United States fishermen, it was feared that the seal would become extinct. In 1886 three Canadian schooners were by decree of the district court of Sitka confiscated for the violation of the laws of the United States in regard to seal-fishing, the judge charging the jury that the territorial waters of Alaska embraced the area bounded by the limits named in the treaty of cession to the United States of 1867 as those "within which the territories and dominion conveyed are contained."[2] This act with others of similar character led to a formal protest by Great Britain.

The questions in dispute were referred to a court of arbitration which decided against the claims of the United States, denying that the sea referred to as the Bering Sea was *mare clausum*, and denying that the United States acquired jurisdiction by prescriptive right from Russia in 1867. It was also decided that the United States had no right of property in the seals in the open sea, and that the destruction of these animals was contrary to the laws of nature. The

[1] See Whart., §§ 301–308.   [2] Treaties of U. S., 940.

United States and Grea⋯ ⋯ ⋯ ⋯
into an agreement in regar⋯ ⋯ ⋯ ⋯
ing of the seals by their su⋯⋯⋯⋯ ⋯ ⋯
also to be asked to become par⋯⋯ ⋯ ⋯ ⋯

It may be regarded as fina⋯⋯ ⋯⋯ ⋯ ⋯
the open sea is free to all, thou⋯⋯ ⋯ ⋯ ⋯
conventions establish regula⋯⋯⋯ ⋯⋯⋯ ⋯
upon their subjects.

§ 55. Vessels

At the present time every ⋯⋯⋯ ⋯⋯
jurisdiction of some state.

(a) **Classes.** — Vessels are divi⋯⋯
classes.

    (1) *Public vessels,* which ⋯
government vessels engage⋯ ⋯ ⋯
vessels employed in the ser⋯⋯
command of government o⋯⋯

    (2) *Private vessels,* ow⋯⋯
under regulations varying ⋯ ⋯

(b) The **nationality** of a pu⋯⋯ ⋯
by its flag. In an extreme ca⋯⋯ ⋯
mander is held to be sufficient p⋯⋯

In case of a private vessel ⋯⋯
evidence, but in case of doubt ⋯⋯
proper authorities its papers wh⋯⋯ ⋯

(c) The general exercise of j⋯⋯⋯
is as follows : —

    (1) Upon the high ⋯⋯
waters the jurisdiction o⋯ ⋯
and private vessels is ex⋯⋯

[1] Proceedings Fur Seal Arbitrati⋯⋯ ⋯⋯
Large, 947.

(2) Over *public vessels in foreign waters*, the jurisdiction of the state to which a public vessel belongs is exclusive for all matters of internal economy. The vessels are subject to port regulations in matters of anchorage, public safety, etc. As Dana says in his note to Wheaton, " It may be considered as established law, now, that the public vessels of a foreign state coming within the jurisdiction of a friendly state, are exempt from all forms of process in private suits."[1] In general practice the waters of all states are open to the vessels of war of all other states with which they are at peace. This is a matter of courtesy and not of right, and is in fact sometimes denied, as by the provision of the Treaty of Berlin, 1878, " The port of Antivari and all the waters of Montenegro shall remain closed to the ships of war of all nations."[2] Various regulations may require, without offence, notice of arrival, probable duration of stay, rank of commander, etc.

The boats, rafts, etc., attached to a vessel of war are regarded as a part of the ship while engaged in the public service.

While there is some difference of opinion as to the immunities of the persons belonging to a ship of war in a foreign harbor, a generally admitted rule seems to be that while the persons of a ship of war are engaged in any public service that is not prohibited by the local authorities, such persons are exempt from local jurisdiction. The ship's crew would not be arrested and detained by local authorities for minor breaches of local

[1] Note 63, § 105.   [2] IV. Hertslet, 2788.

regulations, though they might be sent on board their vessel with statement of reasons for such action. If the action of the crew constitutes a violation of the law of the country to which they belong, the commander of the ship may punish them, and report his action to the local authorities. In case of crimes of serious nature the commander may turn the offenders over to the local authorities, but must assure them a fair trial.

The commander of a vessel is, of course, always responsible to his home government, and his action may become the subject of diplomatic negotiations.

The question of *right of asylum* on board a ship of war has been much discussed. *First,* Most civilized states now afford asylum on board their ships of war to those who, in the less civilized regions, flee from slavery.[1] *Second,* In cases of revolution ships of war sometimes afford refuge to members of the defeated party, though the ship of war may not be used as a safe point from which further hostilities may be undertaken. *Third,* A commander may afford asylum to political refugees under circumstances which he thinks advisable. *Fourth,* In cases where asylum is granted to offenders whether political, or (in case of treaty right) criminal, if the request of the local authorities for the release of the criminal is refused by the commander of the ship, there is no recourse except to the diplomatic channels through extradition.

The immunities granted to vessels of war are also generally conceded to other vessels strictly upon public service, *e.g.* carrying an ambassador to his post. The largest possible exemption is given to a vessel con-

[1] Art. 28, Gen. Act Brussels Conference, July 2, 1890.

veying the sovereign of a state. Vessels transporting military forces in command of regularly commissioned government officers are usually granted immunities accorded to men-of-war.

(3) Over *private vessels in foreign waters* the amount of jurisdiction claimed by different states varies.

The principle which is meeting with growing favor, as shown by practice and by treaty stipulation, is stated by Chief Justice Waite in 1886 as follows, "Disorders which disturb only the peace of the ship, or those on board, are to be dealt with exclusively by the sovereignty of the home of the ship, but those which disturb the public peace may be suppressed, and, if need be, the offenders punished by the proper authorities of the local jurisdiction." [1]

The position of France is, briefly, to assume no jurisdiction over foreign merchantmen within her ports save in cases where the act affects some person other than those belonging to the ship, where the local authorities are expressly called upon to interfere, or, when the order of the port is disturbed.[2]

The British Territorial Waters Jurisdiction Act of Aug. 28, 1878, gives jurisdiction to the authorities over all acts committed within the marine league, even though the ships are not anchored but merely passing through territorial waters.[3] This is an extreme position, and not supported by the best authorities, even in Great Britain.

The position of France, as stated above, is open to little objection either in practice or theory, and is more and

---

[1] Wildenhus's Case, 120 U. S. 1, 18.

[2] Bonfils, "De la compétence des tribunaux français," § 326.

[3] Statutes, 41 and 42, Vict., p. 579.

more becoming a form of treaty agreement, and may be considered generally approved. Where these principles are adopted the jurisdiction of breaches of order within the ship may be referred to the home consul at the port, who has jurisdiction, and if necessary may call upon the local officers to assist him in enforcing his authority.

(4) In recent years special exemption from jurisdiction has been accorded to certain *semi-public* vessels engaged particularly in the postal and scientific service. Vessels in the postal service have by treaties been accorded special freedom from customs and port regulations; and by the Convention between Great Britain and France, Aug. 30, 1890 (Art. 9), it is agreed that in time of war such vessels shall be free from molestation till one of the states shall give formal notice that communication is at an end.

§ 56. Jurisdiction over Persons — Nationality

Under the discussion of jurisdiction of the state over persons comes the question of nationality. Nationality involves the reciprocal relations of allegiance and protection on the part of the person and state. It corresponds to citizenship in the broad sense of that term. In general a state may exercise jurisdiction over its own subjects or citizens as it will, and the relations of a state to its citizens are matters of municipal law only.

A state exercises jurisdiction over all persons within its limits except certain officers of other states by ex-territoriality entitled to exemption from local jurisdiction. In some of the Eastern states citizens of Western states are by treaty exempt from certain local laws.

This last exemption may properly be said to be by local
law, as a treaty becomes a part of the state law for the
subjects upon which it touches.

The jurisdiction also varies with the status of the
person as regards his relations to other states. The
conflict of laws in regard to nationality forms an important part of *private international law.*

§ 57. Jurisdiction over Natural-born Subjects

Children born within a state of which the parents are
citizens are natural-born subjects of that state. Such
persons are fully under the local jurisdiction.

Foundlings, because of the uncertainty of parentage,
are considered subjects of the state in which they are
found.

Illegitimate children take the nationality of the
mother, provided they are born in the state of which
the mother is subject.

The great bulk of the population of all states, except
those most recently founded, is natural-born, and therefore fully under local jurisdiction.

§ 58. Foreign-born Subjects

It is the general principle that each state determines
citizenship by its own laws. The status of persons born
abroad may become very uncertain by virtue of the conflict of laws of the state of which one or both the parents
are citizens and the state in which the child is born.

These laws in regard to children born to parents
while sojourning in foreign countries may be classified
as follows : —

(*a*) The child born in the foreign country is a sub-/ ject of the state of which his parents are citizens. That the child inherits the nationality of his father is a common maxim known as *jus sanguinis*. The United States law says, "All children heretofore born or here-after born out of the limits and jurisdiction of the United States, whose fathers were or may be at the time of their birth citizens thereof, are declared to be citizens of the United States ; but the rights of citizenship shall not descend to children whose fathers never resided in the United States." [1] The *jus sanguinis* is followed by Austria,[2] Germany,[3] Hungary,[4] Sweden,[5] Switzerland,[6] and by some of the smaller European states.

(*b*) Certain states follow the rule of *jus soli*, maintaining that the place of birth determines the nationality. Great Britain, by Article 4, of the Act of May 12, 1870, adopts this principle. By the Fourteenth Amendment of the Constitution of the United States, " All persons born or naturalized in the United States and subject to the jurisdiction thereof, are citizens of the United States and of the state wherein they reside." The laws of the United States have given rise to many questions.[7] Portugal and most of the South American states follow the *jus soli*.

(*c*) Other states follow sometimes the *jus sanguinis*, sometimes *jus soli*, and sometimes modifications of these laws. The laws of Belgium and Spain regard the child of an alien as an alien, though on attaining majority the child may choose the citizenship of the country of his birth.

---

[1] U. S. Rev. Sts., § 1993 ; 1 Gould and Tucker, 478 ; 2 *ibid.*, 178, 203.
[2] Civil Code, Art. 28.   [3] Law of June 1, 1870.   [4] Dec. 24, 1879.
[5] Feb. 27, 1858.   [6] July 3, 1876.   [7] Whart., § 183 ff.

The French laws of June 26–28, 1889, and July 22, 1893, consider as subjects the children born abroad to French citizens, also the children of foreigners born in France, unless these children within one year after attaining majority elect the nationality of their parents. Most states allow the descendants born to foreigners sojourning within their limits to elect their allegiance on attaining majority. Switzerland, however, strongly maintains the *jus sanguinis*, without according any choice to the descendants born to foreigners within her limits, or to her own subjects born abroad except by formal renunciation of citizenship. Thus the child of a citizen of Switzerland born in France would be by French law a citizen of France, and by Swiss law a citizen of Switzerland.

By the law of Germany, a citizen of Germany sojourning more than ten years abroad without registration at his consulate loses his German citizenship, without necessarily acquiring the citizenship of the country of his sojourn, thereby becoming *heimatlos*, or a "man without a country."

At the present time the laws in regard to descendants born to parents sojourning in a foreign state show the widest diversity and give rise to unfortunate complications.[1]

§ 59. Jurisdiction by Virtue of Acquired Nationality

The jurisdiction of a state extends to those who voluntarily acquire its citizenship.

(*a*) A woman in most states by marriage acquires the nationality of her husband. In some of the South American states the husband acquires the citizenship of

---

[1] 3 Pradier-Fodéré, 1648–1653.

his wife. By the law of Belgium, Aug. 6, 1881, and by the law of France, June 26, 1889, it was made easier for foreigners who had married women natives of those states to acquire Belgian or French nationality respectively. The United States law, while holding that a woman marrying a citizen of the United States acquires his nationality, does not hold that an American woman on marrying a foreigner thereby becomes expatriated, unless she takes up her residence in her husband's state.[1]

(b) A state may acquire jurisdiction over persons **by naturalization**, which is an act of sovereignty by which a foreigner is admitted to citizenship in another state. The method of naturalization is in accord with local law and varies greatly in different states.[2] The law of the United States prescribes that Congress has power " to establish an uniform rule of naturalization." [3] The foreigner desiring naturalization in the United States must declare on oath before a court " two years, at least, prior to his admission," his intent to become a citizen. After five years of residence he may obtain citizenship by taking an oath of allegiance to the United States and of renunciation of his former country. An alien who has resided in the United States the three years next preceding the attaining of his majority and who continues to reside in this country at the time of his application, may, after reaching twenty-one years of age, and after residing here five years including the three years of minority, become a citizen by making a declaration at the time of admission.[4]

---

[1] U. S. Rev. Sts., § 1994 ; 1 Gould and Tucker, 479 ; 2 *ibid.*, 178.
[2] 3 Pradier-Fodéré, 1656 ff.   [3] Constitution of U. S., Art. I., § 8.
[4] U. S. Rev. Sts., §§ 2165-2174 ; 1 Gould and Tucker, 513; 2 *ibid.*, 202.

(c) A state may acquire jurisdiction over persons by annexation of the territory upon which they reside. The territory may be acquired by cession, exchange, purchase, conquest, etc. The conditions of the transfer of allegiance from the state formerly possessing the territory is usually fixed by the treaty. This transfer is known as collective naturalization.

Ordinarily a right to choose the allegiance to either state is left to the inhabitants of an annexed territory. Removal from the new jurisdiction is usually required if the inhabitant does not choose to change his allegiance. If the inhabitant does not take any action, it is held that he thereby tacitly transfers his allegiance unless there are special treaty provisions.[1]

(d) The effect of naturalization, whatever the method, is to make the person a citizen of the state into which he is admitted, and over him that state has jurisdiction in all places outside the jurisdiction of the state whose allegiance he has forsworn.

There is conflict of the laws determining the relations to his native state of a person who has renounced his allegiance to one state by naturalization in another state. The general law is, that he becomes entitled to all the privileges of a subject of the state of his new allegiance, except that when he is within his first state he becomes liable for the performance of any obligation which he may have incurred prior to his naturalization.[2]

A state may determine what conditions must be fulfilled in order to constitute a valid severance of allegiance. Laws are diverse upon this subject. Many states

[1] 2 Pradier-Fodéré, 863; 3 ibid., 1671 ff.
[2] Treaties of U. S., 1262; 2 Whart., § 181.

have maintained, and some still maintain, that allegiance is inalienable.[1] England formally maintained this principle till 1870, and her attempts to enforce the principle brought on the War of 1812 with the United States.

In certain countries, as in the United States and Switzerland, minor children are held to follow the allegiance of their father in case of naturalization. The French law claims that the minor child's nationality is that of his birthplace. The subject has been determined in some instances by treaty stipulation, yet must be considered, like many questions of naturalization, as unsettled.

Many states distinguish in law and more in practice between that naturalization which carries with it protection of the state and allegiance of the subject (*naturalisation ordinaire*) and that naturalization which carries full political privileges (*grande naturalisation*).

(e) **Incomplete naturalization.** The fact that a person has taken the preliminary steps toward acquiring the nationality of a foreign state, by making a declaration of his intention or otherwise, may give the state to which the person has assumed an inchoate allegiance the right of protection of the declarant against third states,[2] though not necessarily against the native state of the declarant.[3] Of the privileges to be accorded to one who has declared his intention to become a citizen of the United States, Secretary Marcy said, " The declaration, indeed, is *prima facie* evidence that the person who made it was, at its date,

[1] Hall, § 71, p. 240 ff.
[2] 2 Whart., § 175, Frelinghuysen to Wallace, March 25, 1887.
[3] 2 Whart., § 175, Bayard to Williams, Oct. 29, 1885.

domiciled in the United States, and entitled thereby, though not to all, to certain rights of a citizen, and to much more consideration when abroad than is due to one who has never been in our country; but the declarant, not being a citizen under our laws, even while domiciled here, cannot enjoy all the rights of citizenship either here or abroad;"[1] and Mr. Marcy also says of the papers proving domicile, "And to this simple certificate . . . the European authorities are at liberty to pay such respect as they think proper."[2]

In 1853 a case arose in which the United States affirmed : " It is a maxim of international law that domicile confers national character; . . . international law looks only to the national character in determining what country has the right to protect. If a person goes from this country abroad, with the nationality of the United States, this law enjoins upon other nations to respect him, in regard to protection, as an American citizen."[3] This statement was made in support of the position assumed by the United States in the case of one Martin Koszta. Koszta, a Hungarian refugee of 1848–1849, went to Turkey, was imprisoned, later was released on condition of leaving the country, went to the United States, declared his intention to become a citizen, and in 1853 returned to Turkey. He went into business at Smyrna, obtained there a traveling pass certifying that he was under protection of the United States, was seized, thrown into the sea by persons employed by the Austrian consulate, and was picked up by an Austrian

[1] 2 Whart., § 193, Marcy to Seibels, May 27, 1854.
[2] 2 Whart., § 193, Marcy to Fay, May 27, 1854.
[3] 2 Whart., § 198, Marcy to Hülselmann, Sept. 26, 1853.

man-of-war, *Hussar*. The consul of the United States remonstrated, but the captain of the *Hussar* held Koszta. The chargé d'affaires requested the aid of a United States man-of-war, whose captain demanded Koszta's release. To avoid conflict in the port the mediation of the French consul was accepted, and Koszta was intrusted, pending settlement of claims, to the French consul. Finally Koszta was allowed to return to the United States, though Austria maintained her right to proceed against him if he returned to Turkey. The United States in this case undoubtedly took an extreme position in its claim of jurisdiction.

By an act of March 3, 1863, the United States declared that those who had taken the preliminary oath of intention to become citizens were liable to military service. Upon protest by foreign nations against this act of Congress, the President, by proclamation, announced that, as it had been claimed that " such persons, under treaties or the law of nations, retain a right to renounce that purpose, and to forego the privileges of citizenship and residence within the United States, under the obligations imposed by the aforesaid act of Congress," [1] to avoid all misapprehension, the plea of alienage would be accepted for sixty-five days, during which time such persons as had only declared their intention to become citizens might depart.

The position in the Koszta case, where the claim to the protection of the United States was made when the inchoate citizen was in trouble, and the claim of the inchoate citizens to renounce their allegiance when the state was in difficulties, show some of the problems to

[1] 6 Messages and Papers of President, 168.

x

which the diverse laws and practices in regard to naturalization have given rise.

The municipal laws of some of the local states of the United States admit to all political privileges of the local state those who have taken the first steps toward naturalization. It is generally conceded that such as have exercised the privileges of full citizens can properly be held to the obligations of full citizens, as was declared in the above proclamation.

The inconsistencies in regard to jurisdiction over those naturalized or incompletely naturalized are gradually yielding to treaty provisions which distinctly determine the position of such persons.

§ 60. Jurisdiction over Aliens

Citizens of one state, when sojourning in a foreign state, have a dual relationship by which they may claim certain privileges, both from their native state and from the foreign state.

(a) The native state naturally has **jurisdiction** of a qualified sort **over** its **subjects** even when they are **in a foreign state.**

(1) The right to make *emigration laws* may lead to restrictions binding in a foreign state. A state may banish its subjects. No other state is obliged to receive them, however.

(2) A state may *recall its citizens for special reasons*, as in the case of Greece in 1897, when Greek citizens were recalled for military service.

(3) There is much difference of opinion upon

the question of *penal jurisdiction* of the native state over its subjects who have committed crimes in a foreign state. In general American and English authorities agree that penal law is territorial. Some of the continental authorities take the view that a citizen on his return may be punished for crimes committed in a foreign state. The English law takes this position in certain crimes, as treason, bigamy, and premeditated murder. Usually a crime committed upon a vessel in a foreign harbor is held as within the jurisdiction of the state of the vessel's registry.

(4) A state may interfere to *protect its subjects* in a foreign state, thus extending its authority in their behalf. This has been frequently done to protect Western sojourners in Eastern states, *e.g.* the demands of Germany, in 1898, for concessions from China on account of injuries to missionaries. These demands, accompanied by a naval demonstration, resulted in the cession of Kaio-Chau.

(*b*) The jurisdiction of a state over aliens within its territory is very extensive.

(1) The absolute right of *exclusion* of all foreigners would hardly be maintained by any civilized state, though it could be deduced from the doctrine of sovereignty. Whether justly or not, Japan and China have been compelled by force to cede certain rights to states demanding admission for their citizens.

(2) The right of *expulsion* is, however, generally maintained. This right should, however, be

exercised most carefully, as the fact of admission carries with it some obligation on the part of the admitting state.

(3) The right to *conditional admission* is generally allowed, as seen in laws in regard to immigration.

(4) The foreign state may impose such restrictions upon *settlement* as it sees fit.

(5) A foreign state may *levy* such *taxes* upon the person and goods of aliens as are in accord with state law.

(6) Aliens are subject to the local *sanitary and police jurisdiction*.

(7) The foreign state has *penal jurisdiction* over aliens for crimes committed within territorial limits, and many states maintain, also, for such crimes as plotting against the state, counterfeiting state money, or crimes directly imperiling the state's well-being even when committed outside of state limits.

(8) The state may require aliens to render service such as is necessary to *maintain public order*, even military service, to ward off immediate and sudden danger, *e.g.* as an attack by savages, a mob, etc., but

(9) A state cannot compel aliens to enter its *military service for* the securing of *political ends*, or for the general ends of war.

(10) In nearly all states *freedom of commerce* is now conceded, the state giving to native and foreigner similar privileges. China still restricts trade to certain free ports.

(11) The *holding and bequeathing of property* of whatever sort is subject to local law.

(12) *Freedom of·speech and of worship* are also subject to local law.

All these laws are subject to the exemptions in favor of sovereigns, diplomatic agents, etc.

(c) Ordinarily the identity of an alien is established by a passport. This may also secure for him a measure of care in a foreign state. Below is the form of passport.

Good only for two years from date.

UNITED STATES OF AMERICA

DEPARTMENT OF STATE

To all to whom these presents shall come, Greeting :

I, the undersigned, Secretary of State of the United States of America, hereby request all whom it may concern to permit

DESCRIPTION

Age....Years................
Stature....Feet...Inches.., Eng.
Forehead......................
Eyes..........................
Nose ....
Mouth.........................
Chin..........................
Hair..........................
Complexion....................
Face ....

a Citizen of the United States
....
and freely to pass, and in case of
need to give him all lawful aid
and Protection:

Given under my hand and the
Seal of the Department of State
at the City of Washington, the
.......day of ....,
19.. and of the Independence of
the United States the one hundred
and ...

.....

(SEAL)

(Signature of the Bearer)
....
No......

§ 61. Exemptions from Jurisdiction — General

As a general principle, the sovereignty of a state within its boundaries is complete and exclusive. For various reasons there has grown up the custom of granting immunity from local jurisdiction to certain persons generally representing the public authority of a friendly state. This immunity may extend to those persons and things under their control.

This immunity has been called exterritoriality. The persons and things thus exempt from local jurisdiction are regarded as carrying with them the territorial status of their native state, or as being for purposes of jurisdiction within their own state territory, and beyond that of the state in which they are geographically. Wherever they may go they carry with them the territory and jurisdiction of their home state. Doubtless this doctrine of exterritoriality in the extreme form may be carried too far, as many late writers contend, and some have desired another term, as immunity from jurisdiction, as more exact and correct.[1] Such a term would have the merit of directing attention to the nature of the relation which the persons concerned sustained to the state. Hall sums up the case by saying, "If exterritoriality is taken, not merely as a rough way of describing the effect of certain immunities, but as a principle of law, it becomes, or at any rate is ready to become, an independent source of legal rule, displacing the principle of the exclusiveness of territorial sovereignty within the range of its possible operation in all

[1] Bonfils, 337.

cases in which practice is unsettled or contested."[1] Exterritoriality should be viewed as based on the immunities conceded to public persons, rather than as the source of these immunities.

§ 62. Exemption of Sovereigns

Sovereigns sojourning in their official capacity in foreign countries are exempt from local jurisdiction. This principle is based, not merely upon courtesy, but also upon convenience and necessity. The sovereign represents the state, and therefore cannot be subjected to the jurisdiction of another state without waiving the sovereignty, and in so far depriving the state of one of its essential qualities. Nor can the visiting sovereign exercise any authority which would infringe the sovereign powers of the state in which he is. The visiting sovereign can only claim immunity for such action as is in accord with the necessities of his convenient sojourn. He, his retinue, and effects, are exempt from civil and criminal jurisdiction. He is free from taxes, duties, police and administrative regulations. In the case of Vavasseur v. Krupp, 1878, it was decided that infringement of the patent law did not constitute a ground for suit against a sovereign. In this case Vavasseur brought action against Krupp for infringement of patent on shells in custody of the agents of the Mikado of Japan. The action resulted in an injunction preventing removal of the shells to the Mikado's ships, but on application of the Mikado to remove the shells as his property, the court held that,

[1] § 48, p. 173.

even if the property in question infringed a patent, the Mikado could not be sued and his property could not be held.[1] The principle that the sovereign is free from suit has frequently been decided by the courts of various countries. A sovereign sojourning in a foreign state cannot, however, set up his courts and execute judgment; such functions belong to his territorial courts. Criminals in his retinue must be sent home for trial. While the sovereign's *hôtel* or place of residence while abroad is exempt from local jurisdiction, the sovereign is not justified in allowing the *hôtel* to become an asylum for others than members of his retinue. On demand he must give up such refugees. In case the sovereign does not observe this principle or commits acts liable to endanger the peace of the foreign state, the authorities may invite him to depart, or if necessary expel him by force.

The sovereign may, in his private capacity, hold property and become party to a suit like any citizen.[2] A sovereign may travel *incognito*, and is then entitled only to the recognition accorded to the rank which he assumes. He can, however, assert his sovereign capacity and obtain its immunities at any time should he deem it proper.

§ 63. Exemptions of State Officers

(*a*) **Diplomatic agents,** or those commissioned to transact the political affairs of the state abroad, are conceded a wide immunity from local jurisdiction.

---

[1] Snow's "Cases," 72 ff., for this and other cases.
[2] Snow's "Cases," 82, Rothschild *v.* Queen of Portugal; Bynkershoek, "De Foro Legatorum," C. XVI.

As representing the political will of their state, diplomatic agents have immunities similar to those conceded to the sovereign, though by virtue of the fact that the sending of diplomatic agents has long been a common practice, their immunities are quite well defined. These immunities will be considered more in detail under the subject of International Intercourse, but in general a diplomatic agent is exempt from, (1) criminal jurisdiction, (2) civil jurisdiction, (3) local police and administrative regulations, (4) taxes and duties, (5) jury and witness duty, (6) regulations in regard to religious and social action, (7) all exercise of authority by the local state within his official residence or *hôtel*, (8) and from the exercise of similar authority over his household, official and unofficial.

(*b*) The exemptions granted to **consuls** vary in different states and under different circumstances. In general they are entitled to such exemptions as will enable them to perform their functions effectively.[1]

(*c*) Any foreign **army** within the territorial limits of a given state, by permission of the sovereign of said state, is free from the sovereign's jurisdiction. Chief Justice Marshall, in 1812, gave as his opinion : "In such case, without any express declaration waiving jurisdiction over the army to which this right of passage has been granted, the sovereign who should attempt to exercise it would certainly be considered as violating his faith. . . . The grant of a free passage, therefore, implies a waiver of all jurisdiction over the troops during their passage, and permits the foreign general to use that discipline, and to inflict those punishments,

---

[1] See § 80 (*f*) for full discussion.

which the government of his army may require."[1]
Permission, either general or special, must be obtained
in order that an army may enter a foreign state in
time of peace. The army must cause the least possible
inconvenience to the state during its sojourn.

The military attaché of an embassy is regarded as a
member of the official household of the diplomatic
agent.

(d) **Navy.** As a vessel of war can without inconvenience to a foreign state pass through or remain within
its maritime jurisdiction, it is customary to accord to
the vessel and crew immunity from local jurisdiction
and freedom of passage unless withheld for special
reason. "Their immunity from local jurisdiction has
come to be more absolute than that of the official residence of ambassadors, and probably for the reason that
they have the efficient means of resistance which an
ambassador has not."[2]

In general the exemption from local jurisdiction
which a vessel of war enjoys in a foreign state extends :
(1) to acts beginning and ending on board the vessel ;[3]
(2) to all boats, etc., of the vessel of war in charge of the
crew of the vessel and upon its service ; (3) to freedom
from customs and all such regulations as are not necessary for the safety of the port (it was held in case of
the United States frigate *Constitution*, in 1879, that
she was not liable to salvage charges ;[4] the vessel is
therefore liable to quarantine, anchorage, etc., rules

---

[1] Exchange *v.* M'Faddon, 7 Cr., 116, 139.
[2] "International Law," Naval War Col., 2d ed., p. 23.
[3] Hall, § 55.
[4] Snow's "Cases," p. 114.

which imply no derogatio...
all persons on board th...
the crew or others. In...
taken as warranting a gen...
of asylum on board vesse...
granted as an act of hospit...
who cannot use the vess...
trigue. Asylum to comm...
granted without offens...
criminals are usually surrende...
local authorities.

A commander cannot pu...
exercise external authori...

Hall sums up the gene...
immunities of a vessel...
plete instrument, ma...
intended to be used by...
the elements of which...
of separate use for...
are not exempted from...

In case of abuse...
waters the foreign...
depart; and if its requ...
force, though the...
diplomatic channels...

§ 64. ...

(a) In certain ...
ern states are by trea...
The extent of the exempt...

1 § 56, p. 2.

the treaty provisions.   The basis of this exemption is found in the "incompatibility of habits of thought on all legal and moral questions,"[1] and the consequent impossibility of obtaining what to the Western states seemed just treatment on the part of Oriental officials. Consular courts were established to meet the needs of foreigners within the jurisdiction of these Eastern states.[2]   The consuls in these states were invested with special judicial powers, though not considered by the laws of the United States judicial officers.   Each state determines the competence of its consular courts in foreign states.

The following rules are general, though not absolute, propositions in regard to the treatment of cases involving natives of Eastern countries and foreigners.

(1) *Penal Matters.*   If a native commits a crime against a foreigner, he is generally tried in the local court.

If a foreigner commits a crime against a native, he is generally tried in the consular court of his state.

If a foreigner commits a crime against a foreigner of another nationality, he is generally tried in the consular court of the injured foreigner.

If both parties to the crime are of the same nationality, the offenders are tried in the court of their own state.

If the crime is a grave one, such as murder,

---

[1] 1 Whart., § 125.

[2] By treaties with Japan, going into effect 1899, such courts were abolished in that empire.   29 U. S. Sts. at Large, 848.

sentence cannot be passed without the sanction of the home government, and in some cases the offender is sent home for trial.

(2) *Civil Matters.* In cases involving a foreigner and a native, the trial is generally by agents of the two countries.

In cases involving subjects of the same state, their consular court has jurisdiction.

In cases involving foreigners of different nationalities the consular court of the defendant has jurisdiction.

In cases involving large interests, there is an appeal from the consular to the higher courts of the state.

In the East registration of the head of the family at the consulate is necessary to obtain consular protection. Local statutes provide for the execution of treaty stipulations as to consular jurisdiction.[1]

(*b*) **In Egypt mixed courts** were instituted in 1875. This system, arranged by convention, has received the assent of nearly all the European states and of the United States.[2]

The majority of the judges in these courts are foreigners, and the courts have competence over cases against the Egyptian government, over civil and commercial matters between foreigners and natives, and between foreigners of different nationalities. Jurisdiction for other matters remains in the consuls.

[1] 1 U. S. Rev. Sts., §§ 4083-4130; 1 Gould and Tucker, 770-772; 2 *ibid.*, 503; Treaties of U. S., 1279, 1288; 1 Whart., § 125.

[2] Proclamation of March 27, 1876; 19 U. S. Sts. at Large, 662.

These courts have been the subject of much discussion and great difference of opinion.

§ 65. Extradition

Extradition is the act by which one state delivers a person accused of crime committed beyond its borders to another state for trial and punishment.

Many of the Continental states maintain that extradition is a duty binding upon all civilized states, on the ground that the prevention of crime which would result from certainty of punishment is an object to be sought by all for the general good. Grotius, Vattel, Kent, Fiore, and many other authorities maintain this position. Bluntschli, Foelix, Klüber, G. F. de Martens, Puffendorf, Phillimore, Wheaton and the majority of authorities make the basis of extradition the conventional agreement of treaties.[1] The large number of extradition treaties of the last half of the nineteenth century has made the practice general. Occasionally a state has, in the absence of treaties, voluntarily surrendered fugitives from justice as an act of courtesy. The extradition of Tweed by Spain in 1876 was an act of this kind.[2] Such cases are not common, however,[3] and it is safe to derive the principles from the general practice as seen in treaties.

(a) **Persons liable to extradition** vary according to treaties. It is the general practice to surrender on

---

[1] "The surrender of fugitives from justice is a matter of conventional arrangement between states, as no such obligation is imposed by the law of nations." In the Matter of Metzger, 5 How. 176, 188.

[2] 2 Whart., § 268.

[3] Snow's "Cases," 151 ff.; Treaties of U. S., 1289–1293.

demand of the state in which the crime is committed only those who are subjects of the state making the demand. This is the general rule of the Continental states. As Great Britain and the United States maintain the principle of territorial penal jurisdiction, it is customary for these states to uphold the idea of extradition even of their own subjects.[1] The practice is not uniform in the relations of these states to other states, as is shown in their treaties. The South American and Continental European states hold that their own citizens are not liable to extradition.

A large number of the modern writers are in favor of the extradition of subjects in the same manner as aliens, and it is evident that the drift of international practice, as shown by the treaties of the last quarter-century, is toward the refusal to grant protection to a subject who has sought refuge in his native state after committing a crime abroad.

In case the accused whose extradition is demanded is a citizen of a third state, the practice is not uniform, though the best authorities seem to favor the granting of the extradition only after communication with and assent of the third state, on the ground that the state to which the subject has fled is responsible to the third state for its treatment of him. This practice has been followed in many European treaties.

Ordinarily, not all criminals are liable to extradition, though treaty stipulations may cover cases usually excepted. Those accused of political crimes have, since the early part of the nineteenth century, been more and more generally exempt from extradition. Dur-

[1] J. Moore, "Extradition," 156.

ing the last quarter of the nineteenth century few
treaties have been made which do not make political
criminals specifically non-extraditable. Political crime
accompanied by attacks upon the person of the sovereign or of those holding political office or position are
not, however, in the above category, but are usually
extraditable.

(b) Even when an accused person is extradited there
are limitations as to the jurisdiction of the state to
which he goes. The trial must be for the offense or
offenses enumerated in the treaty. For example, a
treaty between two states enumerates among extraditable crimes murder, and does not enumerate larceny.
A fugitive from one of the countries is accused of both
murder and larceny. The country surrendering the
criminal would not permit the trial of the criminal for
any other crime than murder, until the criminal should
have had opportunity to return to the state from which
he was surrendered. For many years Great Britain
claimed that a person surrendered in accordance with
an extradition treaty should be tried only for the specific
offense for which he was surrendered. The United
States desired to include other offenses provided the
person had been once surrendered. This position of
Great Britain was accepted by the treaty of July 12,
1889.[1]

(c) The conditions necessary for a claim for extradition are : (1) that the crime shall have been committed
within the territorial or maritime jurisdiction of the

[1] 26 U. S. Sts. at Large, 1508 ; Snow's " Cases," 151 et seq. ; 2 Whart.,
§ 270 ; 1 Moore, " Extradition," 196 ff. ; Treaties of U. S., 1289 et seq. ;
1 Gould and Tucker, 987.

state making the demand, (2) that there be sufficient evidence of guilt to establish a case, and (3) that the application be from the proper authority and in the proper form.[1]

(*d*) The **procedure** in cases of extradition is based on definite principles. As it is an act of sovereignty, it must be performed by agents of the sovereign person, who for this purpose, although generally engaged in other functions, are executive officers.[2] The general rule is that the demand for extradition shall be made through the ordinary diplomatic channels. In colonies and under special circumstances an officer of first rank may be the medium of the demand.

The person demanded may be placed under provisional arrest pending the full proceedings of extradition.[3]

Reasonable evidence of the identity of the person and of the facts of the crime must be furnished by the state making the demand.

In case a person is demanded by two states, his native state and a third state in which he has committed a crime, it is customary to grant the request of the state in which he has committed the crime.

When a person is demanded on the ground of separate crimes committed in both states as above, if the crimes are equally grave, the request of his native state is granted. Sometimes, however, when the third state

---

[1] Treaties of U. S., 437 and 1289–1293 ; 26 U. S. Sts. at Large, 1510 ; U. S. Rev. Sts., §§ 5270–5280 ; 1 Gould and Tucker, 979–989 ; 2 Whart., §§ 274–280.

[2] In case of Chesapeake, 1863, the consul acted as agent. Wheat., D., § 428, note 207 ; 3 Pradier-Fodéré, 1876.

[3] 3 Pradier-Fodéré, 1877.

L

offers to surrender the fugitive to his native state after he has paid the penalty of his crime, the request of the third state is granted.

When the crime committed in one state is more grave than that committed in another, the request of the state maintaining the graver charge is granted.

When states other than the native state request the extradition of a fugitive, the state receiving the demand may take into consideration the gravity of the offense and the probability that a given state will, after securing justice, make it possible for other states to prosecute their claims. In cases of equal gravity priority of demand usually determines the course of action.[1]

If the person demanded is accused of a crime in the state of refuge, the demand for his extradition may be refused pending his trial in the state of refuge.

Many other questions arise which complicate the actual procedure in cases of extradition, but these belong mainly to the realm of *private international law*.

§ 66. Servitudes

Servitudes in international law constitute a restriction upon the exercise of the territorial jurisdiction of a state in favor of one or more states.

(*a*) **International servitudes** are : —

(1) *positive*, implying that a state is under obligation to permit within its territory another state to exercise certain powers, as by the Treaty of Berlin, 1878, Art. XXIX. " The administration

---

[1] " Annuaire de l'Institut de droit international," 1881–1882, p. 128.

of the maritime and sanitary police, both at Antivari and along the coast of Montenegro, shall be
carried out by Austria-Hungary by means of light
coastguard vessels ; "[1]

(2) *negative*, implying that a state is to refrain
from certain acts, otherwise customary, as " Montenegro shall neither have ships of war nor flag
of war."[2]

Among the *positive servitudes* are : those obligations of a state to allow within its own jurisdiction the
exercise of political or administrative authority by
another state, as in the execution of judicial or police
regulations ; those obligations to allow the exercise of
military authority, as in military occupation of a portion of the territory or the passage of troops. Among
the *negative servitudes* are : those obligations of a state
to refrain from exercising within its own jurisdiction certain political or administrative authority which
might be exercised, if the servitude did not exist, as in
the exemption of the citizens or corporate persons of
certain states from certain acts of jurisdiction or taxation ; those obligations to refrain from military acts,
such as the limitation of the army or navy to a certain
number, or the obligation not to fortify a certain place.

(*b*) There are also servitudes which may be called
general, because binding alike upon every state in favor
of all others, such as the innocent use of territorial seas.[3]

[1] IV. Hertslet, 2783.   [2] *Ibid.*
[3] For the general question, see 2 Pradier-Fodéré, 834, 845.

CHAPTER XII

§ 67. Property in General

The term "property" has been used in varying senses by writers upon international law. By virtue of the fact that a state has jurisdiction over all its public property there has sometimes been confusion between the two terms, but jurisdiction may, and does, extend to persons and things of which proprietorship cannot be affirmed by the state.

In the sense commonly used in international law the property of a state is held to be all the lands and water within its limits. Within this territory the state has rights to the exclusion of other states, and upon the land area may exercise the right of eminent domain.

The idea of property in this international sense is distinct from that of private ownership, which is merely relative and depends upon the regulations of the state; indeed, private property may be seized for the debts of the state.

A state may hold absolute possession of such objects as are capable of appropriation, as lands, buildings, and other material resources for public purposes. In some cases the state owns the railroads, telegraphs, mines, etc. In time of war such property receives treatment somewhat different from that of private property, and in time of peace it may receive special recognition, *e.g.* houses of ambassadors.

§ 68. State Property in International Law

Hall outlines this subject as follows: "A state may own property as a private individual within the jurisdiction of another state; it may possess the immediate as well as the ultimate property in movables, land, and buildings within its own territory; and it may hold property in its state capacity in places not belonging to its own territory, whether within or outside the jurisdiction of other states."[1] Property of the first class falls under the local law of the state in which it is. Property of the second class may come within the scope of international law in time of war. Property of the third class may come with the scope of international law both in time of peace and of war.

[1] § 43, p. 167.

CHAPTER XIII

DIPLOMACY AND INTERNATIONAL RELATIONS IN TIMES OF PEACE

69. GENERAL DEVELOPMENT.

70. DIPLOMATIC AGENTS.
    (a) Historical.
    (b) Rank.
        (1) Diplomatic agents of first class.
        (2) Envoys extraordinary.
        (3) Ministers resident.
        (4) Chargés d'affaires.

71. SUITE.
    (a) Official.
    (b) Non-official.

72. WHO MAY SEND DIPLOMATIC AGENTS.

73. WHO MAY BE SENT.

74. CREDENTIALS.

75. CEREMONIAL.
    (a) General.
    (b) Reception.
    (c) Precedence and places of honor.
    (d) Prerogatives.

76. FUNCTIONS.
    (a) Internal business.
    (b) Conduct of negotiations.
    (c) Relation to fellow-citizens.
    (d) Reports to home government.

77. TERMINATION OF MISSION.
    (a) Through death of agent.
    (b) In ordinary manner.
    (c) Under strained relations.
    (d) Ceremonial of departure.

78. IMMUNITIES AND PRIVILEGES.
    (a) Inviolability.
    (b) Exterritoriality and exemptions.
        (1) Criminal jurisdiction.
        (2) Civil jurisdiction.
        (3) Family and suite.
        (4) House of ambassador.
        (5) Asylum.
        (6) Taxation.
        (7) Religious worship.

79. DIPLOMATIC PRACTICE OF THE UNITED STATES.

80. CONSULS.
    (a) Historical.
    (b) Grades.
    (c) Nomination and reception.
    (d) Functions.
    (e) Special powers in Eastern states.
    (f) Privileges and immunities.
    (g) Termination of consular office.

§ 69. General Development

`Diplomacy may be broadly defined as the art and science of international negotiation. The conditions which make possible established relations among states are of comparatively recent origin. In the days when stranger and enemy were not distinguished, and when "strange air made a man unfree," there could be no extended relations among states. In very early times, however, states had some relations with each other, and general principles were observed in carrying on such business as might be necessary. These growing relations have given rise to what is known as the right of legation. Sometimes a right of intercourse between states has been claimed on the ground that the citizens of one state cannot be excluded from the natural advantages of another state, on the ground that all men have an equal right to innocent use of the earth's resources, ' or on more abstract grounds of moral duty variously interpreted. As the actual practice of states never has recognized such a right to contend for it would hardly be necessary. States put restrictions upon commerce, even to the exclusions of goods and persons. In some cases where the terms of the state enactment may not be prohibitive, the conditions of admission amount to practical prohibition.[1]

The influence of commerce in its many forms, the idea of unity of mankind in its various manifestations, the growth of neighborhood on the part of European states, and the necessity of respect for each other on the part of these states, made interstate relations imperative and convenient. While the right of intercourse might be questioned, the necessity and convenience of interstate relations admitted of no question.

§ 70. Diplomatic Agents

. (a) Historical. In very early times special privileges were extended to heralds, ambassadors, or other bearers of the state will. Laws[2] and history record as a fact

[1] U. S. Chinese Exclusion Act, 1882, 1 Gould and Tucker, 502 et seq.; 2 ibid., 193 et seq.

[2] Digest, LVII., 17.

this practice which had long been observed.   The ambassador was often one who in his own state held some
priestly office.   In the days of the Roman dominance,
the office of ambassador was commonly exercised by one
holding a religious office, and while the unity represented
by the church remained prominent, its officials were
often ambassadors.   Both from necessity and from the
sacred character of the person, the ambassador was
usually regarded as inviolable.   The person of the ambassador was respected long before there was any recognition of the rights and dignity of states as states.   In
order that there might be any such intercourse, it
was necessary that the agents should not be placed in
undue personal peril.[1]

With the preëminence of the Italian city states in
the Middle Ages there came the development of diplomacy as an art.   The most distinguished men of the
times were called to this state service.   Machiavelli's
name is inseparably linked to one school of diplomacy.
Dante, Petrarch, Boccaccio, and others whose names
have become famous, were sent on missions.[2]

During the thirteenth century, Venice outlined the
policy which her ambassadors should follow, and there
the system of foreign representation became well established.   This system included the granting of a commission, instructions, letter of credence, attachés, etc.
Italy may, indeed, be called the home of the diplomatic
system.

For many years, in fact till comparatively recent
times, ambassadors were looked upon with suspicion, as

[1] 3 Pradier-Fodéré, 1233.
[2] Nys, "Les Origines du Droit International," 297.

spies whom monarchs were more willing to give than to
receive.   Gradually, however, the practice of sending
and receiving ambassadors was seen to have much value.
During the fifteenth century, which marks the beginning of the modern period in the history of diplomacy,
the practice of sending permanent ambassadors seems
to have arisen.   There may have been isolated cases of
sending of permanent ambassadors before this time, but
from the fifteenth century the practice became more
and more common, though the different countries did
not observe any uniform regulations as to personnel,
procedure, or in other respects.   From this time diplomacy became more of a career, and one going on a
mission to a foreign country received careful preparation that he might outwit the representatives of the
state to which he was sent.   Sir Henry Wotton's oft-
quoted definition of an ambassador, " An ambassador is
an honest man, sent to *lie* abroad for the good of his
country," [1] describes the attitude taken in many countries toward the office, when early in the seventeenth
century he wrote the definition in Christopher Fleca-
more's album.   Gradually the rules of international
negotiation became established, and treatises upon the
subject appeared.

The Peace of Westphalia in 1648, which marks the
beginning of modern international relations, showed
that modern diplomacy had already obtained a recognition, and served to give it a more definite form.
This date serves as a boundary to the first division of
the modern period in the history of diplomacy.   The
years from the early part of the fifteenth century to

[1] Walton, " Life of Wotton," 155.

the Peace of Westphalia are the years of beginnings. From this time the system of permanent ministers, which so greatly changed the character of international negotiations, became almost a necessity through the development of the equilibrium of the states of Europe.[1]

During the years 1648 to 1815 the relations of states became more complex, and the business of international negotiation more delicate. Diplomatic practice, always tending to look to precedent, suffered severe strains under the ambitious monarchs occupying the thrones of Europe after the Peace of Westphalia. Principles and precedent were often disregarded to obtain political ends. So great was the friction that at length some of the more commonly disputed questions were settled at the Congress of Vienna, 1815.

(b) The question of relative **rank** of state agents gave rise, in the days before the Congress of Vienna, to many difficulties. The protocol of that Congress of March 9, 1815, together with the eighth article adopted at the Congress of Aix-la-Chapelle, Nov. 21, 1818, give the basis of present practice as follows : —

" In order to prevent in future the inconveniences which have frequently occurred, and which may still occur, from the claims of Precedence among the different Diplomatic characters, the Plenipotentiaries of the Powers who signed the Treaty of Paris have agreed on the following Articles, and think it their duty to invite those of other Crowned Heads to adopt the same regulations : —

[1] Calvo, § 1311 ff.

DIVISION OF DIPLOMATIC CHARACTERS

ART. I. Diplomatic characters are divided into **Three** classes: That of Ambassadors, Legates, or Nuncios.

That of Envoys, Ministers, or other persons accredited to Sovereigns.

That of Chargés d'Affaires accredited to Ministers for foreign affairs.

REPRESENTATIVE CHARACTER

ART. II. Ambassadors, Legates, or Nuncios only shall have the Representative character.

SPECIAL MISSIONS

ART. III. Diplomatic characters charged with any special Mission shall not, on that account, assume any superiority of Rank.

DIPLOMATIC PRECEDENCE

ART. IV. Diplomatic characters shall rank in their respective classes according to the date of the official notification of their arrival.

REPRESENTATIVES OF THE POPE

The present Regulation shall not occasion any change respecting the Representative of the Pope.

FORM FOR RECEPTION OF DIPLOMATIC AGENTS

ART. V. There shall be a regular form adopted by each State for the reception of Diplomatic Characters of every Class.

DIPLOMATIC AGENTS OF COURTS ALLIED BY FAMILY OR OTHER TIES

ART. VI. Ties of consanguinity or family alliance between Courts confer no Rank on their Diplomatic Agents. The same rule also applies to political alliances.

ALTERATION OF SIGNATURES IN ACTS OR TREATIES

ART. VII. In Acts or Treaties between several Powers that admit alternity, the order which is to be observed in the signatures of Ministers shall be decided by ballot.[1]

ART. VIII. It is agreed between the Five Courts that Ministers Resident accredited to them shall form, with respect to their Precedence, an intermediate class between Ministers of the Second Class and Chargés d'Affaires."[2]

To the articles, except the last, Austria, Spain, France, Great Britain, Portugal, Prussia, Russia, and Sweden were parties. Spain, Portugal, and Sweden were not parties to the eighth article. Theoretically these rules are binding only upon those states parties to the treaties, but practically they are accepted by all civilized states.

The four grades are as follows : —

1. Ambassadors, legates, and nuncios.

2. Envoys, ministers, or other persons accredited to sovereigns.

3. Ministers resident.

4. Chargés d'affaires.

The first three grades are accredited to the sovereign. The fourth grade, chargés d'affaires, is accredited to the minister of foreign affairs.

The rank of the agent does not necessarily have any relation to the importance of the business which may be intrusted to him. The titles given to the different

[1] I. Hertslet, 62, 63.

[2] I. Hertslet, 575. These rules have been adopted by the U. S. Department of State.

diplomatic agents, at the present time, are in a general way descriptive, as follows : —

(1) *Diplomatic agents of the first class* are held to represent the person of the sovereign. Ambassador ordinary usually designates one holding a permament mission. Ambassador extraordinary designates one on a special mission, or having power to act in exceptional circumstances. This, however, is most often a title of somewhat superior honor giving no other advantage. Papal legates rank, and for practical purposes, are, ambassadors extraordinary, though representing particularly ecclesiastical affairs and the Pope as head of the Church. Legates are chosen from the cardinals and sent to countries recognizing the papal supremacy. Nuncios of the Pope rank as ambassadors ordinary on a permanent mission, and are usually intrusted with power to transact general affairs.[1]

(2) *Envoys extraordinary, envoys ordinary, and ministers plenipotentiary* have in general the same functions and rank. With these rank the papal internuncio. The general idea is that the agents of the second class do not stand for the person of the sovereign, but for the state.

(3) *Ministers resident* are regarded as upon a less important mission than the agents of the first or second class. They are frequently sent by the greater powers to the lesser powers.

(4) *Chargés d'affaires* ceremonially rank below the ministers resident. They are accredited to the minister of foreign affairs, while members of the first three classes are accredited to the sovereign. A chargé d'affaires may perform the functions of the higher grades

[1] Calvo, § 1328 ff.

of agents and has the same general privileges. When a consul is charged with a diplomatic mission he ranks with the chargés d'affaires. Commissioners on various missions are sometimes accorded the same rank ; but, as they do not bear the title, commissioners cannot claim the rank of the chargé d'affaires, though in their functions there may be no difference.

There is no rule as to the grade of diplomatic agent which one state shall send to another, though it was formerly held that only states entitled to royal honors could send ambassadors. It is now customary for states to agree among themselves as to the relative rank of their diplomatic agent. Thus the United States by a recent act provided that " whenever the President shall be advised that any foreign government is represented or is about to be represented in the United States by an ambassador, envoy extraordinary, minister plenipotentiary, minister resident, or special, envoy or chargé d'affaires, he is authorized in his discretion to direct that the representative of United States to such government shall bear the same designation. This provision shall in no wise affect the duties, powers, or salary of such representative." [1]

The rank of a diplomatic agent is a mark of dignity and honor particularly of consequence in matters of etiquette and ceremonial. Reciprocity between states is the general rule in the grade of agents. The old theory that agents of the first rank had access to the ear of the sovereign is no longer held, and all grades alike represent both the sovereign and the state from which they come.

[1] March 1, 1893, 27 U. S. Sts. at Large, c. 182.

§ 71. Suite

The personnel of a mission may be distinguished as the official and the non-official.

(a) The **official suite** consists of the functionaries, and varies in number according to the dignity and importance of the mission. Formerly the number was scrutinized with great care, owing to the fear that a numerous suite might endanger the safety of the receiving state. The official suite may include, (1) the counsel to the mission, (2) the secretaries, (3) the attachés, military, naval, and others, (4) the interpreters and dragomans, (5) the clerks and accountants, (6) the couriers, (7) the chaplain, (8) the doctor, and in some instances other officers necessary for the performance of the official functions.

(b) The **non-official suite** includes the family of the diplomatic agent and those in his household employ. This may include, beside his immediate family, (1) the private chaplain, (2) the private doctor, (3) the private secretaries, (4) the domestic servants of various grades.

§ 72. Who may send Diplomatic Agents

It is the general rule that sovereign states only may send ambassadors or other diplomatic agents. Sometimes diplomatic relations are maintained between states when both are not fully sovereign, as in the relations between Bavaria, a member of the German Empire, and France. In general, where the sovereignty of a state is not complete, its right of legation is fixed by the treaty which impairs its sovereignty. A state which has not full sovereign powers may have a partial right of legation, either active or passive, or a right to send diplomatic agents with limited functions.

The sending of a diplomatic agent is essentially an act of the sovereign person, whether he be a monarch, president, council, or have other title.   The domestic law determines who this person shall be.   International law makes no distinction.

In each state a department, usually called the department of foreign affairs, has the business of international intercourse in charge.   The organization of this department and the general methods are matters of domestic law.   All foreign states need to know is to what extent this department is competent to carry on negotiations.

§ 73. Who may be Sent

Before actually sending a diplomatic agent, a state usually obtains assurance from the receiving state that the proposed agent will be an acceptable person.   If the proposed agent is a *persona non grata*, it is held that the foreign state is not obliged to give its reasons for refusing to receive him.   To refuse a given person does not imply any lack of courtesy to the sending state on the part of the refusing state.   A state may refuse to receive one of its own citizens as the minister of a foreign state.   Sometimes states have refused to receive those who have in the sending state taken positions manifesting hostile disposition toward the receiving state.

In 1885 the Italian government refused to receive Mr. Keily as United States representative on the

ground that he had denounced the overthrow of the
temporal power of the Pope. It was considered probable that one who had taken so decided an attitude
toward an action of the government to which he was
sent would hardly be acceptable. Mr. Keily had just
before been refused by Austria-Hungary on the ground
that his wife was a Jewess and his marriage only a
civil one. President Cleveland showed his attitude
toward this action in his first annual message, 1885.
"The Austro-Hungarian government finally decided
not to receive Mr. Keily as the envoy of the United
States, and that gentleman has since resigned his commission, leaving the post vacant. I have made no new
nomination, and the interests of this government at
Vienna are now in the care of the secretary of legation,
acting as chargé d'affaires *ad interim*."[1]

§ 74. Credentials, Instructions, Passport

Before starting upon his mission, a diplomatic representative receives, if of one of the first three classes,
from the head of the state, if of the fourth class (chargé
d'affaires) from the minister of foreign affairs, a letter of
credence. In the United States the President signs the
letters of credence of diplomatic agents above the rank
of chargé d'affaires. In these instances the letter is
addressed to the head of the foreign state. In the case
of chargé d'affaires the letter is addressed to the minister of foreign affairs and signed by the Secretary of
State. A letter of credence gives the name, the character and general object of the mission, and requests

[1] 1 Whart., §§ 82, 82 *a*, 83.

for the agent full faith and credence as the state's representative. In case of representatives to Turkey, besides the letter to the Sultan, formerly letters were also taken to the grand vizier and to the minister of foreign affairs. Representatives of the Pope carry in place of letters of credence papal bulls. Sometimes a diplomatic agent receives also letters of recommendation to persons of importance in the foreign country. These letters have a semi-official character in many cases. While a letter of credence may give power to open treaty negotiations, it is usual to give a special letter conferring *full powers* or *general full powers* to close and sign a treaty, or to act in behalf of the state in some manner not covered by his instructions. These letters are commonly letters patent.

The diplomatic agent also customarily receives instructions which may be either for his own guidance or to be communicated to the foreign state. If to be communicated to the foreign state, the instructions make more fully known his special functions. In all cases the agent is bound by his instructions, and if there is doubt as to method of action it is easy, in these days of rapid communication, to entertain a memorandum.

The diplomatic agent also receives for himself and suite a special passport. The special passport differs from the ordinary passport in that it describes the official rank or occupation of the bearer, often also the purpose of the travel, and while generally omitting the description of the person. This may serve not only the purpose of

1 "The American Passport," U. S. Dept. State

passport, but may also give an official introduction to the bearer.

The papers furnished to diplomatic representatives of the United States include : —

1. A sealed letter of credence to the head of the state or minister of foreign affairs according to rank of the representative.

2. " An open office copy of the letter of credence."

3. The special passport above mentioned.

4. "A copy of the Register of the Department of State."

5. A letter of credit upon the bankers of the United States.

6. A copy of Instructions to the Diplomatic Officers of the United States.

7. A copy of the Consular Regulations of the United States.

(FORM OF)

LETTER OF CREDENCE

A............... B..............,
President of the United States of America.

To...............................
....
....

GREAT AND GOOD FRIEND:

I have made choice of.................................
one of our distinguished citizens, to reside near the Government of Your............in the quality of.................................
He is well informed of the relative interests of the two countries an of our sincere desire to cultivate to the fullest extent the friendshi which has so long subsisted between the two Governments. M knowledge of his high character and ability gives me entire confiden

vised a ceremonial commensurate with this estimate, for what was once done out of respect for and in response to the demand of a personal sovereign, is now done out of respect for the dignity of the state itself. Thus in the days of more democratic sovereignties international representatives are clothed with a dignity which both elevates the attitude of participants in international negotiations and gives greater weight to their conclusions. The ceremonial also fixes a definite course of procedure which any state may follow without giving offense to another, whether it be weak or powerful.

(b) While the minor details of the ceremonial of reception of a diplomatic agent are not invariable, certain customs are well established. A diplomat officially notifies the receiving state of his arrival by sending, (1) if he be of the first rank, a secretary of the embassy to the minister of foreign affairs, with a copy of his letter of credence and a request for a day and hour when he may have an audience with the head of the state in order to present his credentials, (2) if of the second rank, while sometimes the above procedure is allowed, he usually makes the announcement and request in writing, (3) if of the third rank he always observes the last-mentioned procedure, (4) if of the fourth rank, chargé d'affaires, he notifies the minister of foreign affairs of his arrival and requests an audience.

The audience may be for any grade more or less formal, public or private. Usually diplomats of the first rank are received in public audience. At the audience the diplomat presents his letter of credence, and usually makes a brief address, of which he has earlier furnished a copy to the minister of foreign affairs in order that a suitable reply may be prepared. Diplomats of the second rank customarily receive a similar solemn audience. This may or may not be granted to ministers of the third rank. Official ... varying somewhat in ceremonial in different states follow.

(c) From the time when permanent missions began to be common, conflict between the representatives of different states made necessary fixed rules of precedence. As Wicquefort said in the latter part of the seventeenth century, "One of the things that most ... Embassadors from paying one another civilities ... Contest they have concerning Honours and ... only on Account of the Competition of ... but sometimes also by Reason of some ... have amongst themselves."[1] Wicquefort ... cases give ample evidence of the confusion ... in his day. Bynkershoek, in "De For... Ch. I. and XII., shows that the confusion ... less in 1721, though the rank by ... to be more fully recognized. Vattel ... that there had arisen a more definite ... a fairly clear gradation, yet as the ... agreed to by any considerable number ... was not in accordance with any general principle, there were contests still ... of Vienna (1815) and Aix-la-Chapelle ... the disputed points in regard ...

[1] Wicquefort, "The Embassador and ... translation, Ch. XXII., p. 201.

[2] "Droit des gens," Liv. IV., Ch. VI.

adjusted.   Certain general propositions are now ad-
.mitted, such as, that no diplomat can pretend to
special honors or immunities above other diplomats of
the same rank.[1] The rule of the Congress of Vienna
is followed, by which diplomats of the same class rank
according to the precedence in the date of the official
notification of their arrival.

Places of honor are now quite definitely fixed.   On
ceremonial occasions, where the representatives are
seated at a table, as in an international congress, it
may be somewhat varied as fronting the main window,
opposite the main entrance to the room, in the place
receiving the light over the left shoulder.   When the
place is determined by the relation to the head of the
table or the presiding officer, the first honor, except in
Turkey, is at his right, the second at his left, the third
in the second place on the right, the fourth in the
second place on the left, and so on.   In processions the
place of honor is sometimes first, sometimes last.   For
relatively short processions, certain more definite rules
are usually observed.   When only two participate, the
first place is the place of honor ; when three participate,
the middle place, the place in advance being the second
honor and the place in the rear the third ; when four
participate, the second place is the place of honor, the
place in advance the second, the third and fourth being
in honor in order ; when five participate, the middle is
the place of honor, the second place being the second in
honor, the first the fourth in honor, the fourth the third
in honor, and the fifth the fifth in honor.[2]

[1] Calvo, § 1328 ff.
[2] Lehr, "Manuel des Agents Diplomatiques," § 367 ff.

To avoid friction as to place of honor in signing treaties, etc., the principle of the alternat is usually followed, by which the copy going to a given nation has the name of its own representative first in order.[1] Sometimes the order is determined by lot, and sometimes is alphabetical in the order of the names of the states parties to the treaty.

(*d*) Certain **prerogatives** are held to appertain to the office of ambassador and to diplomats of the first rank. Among these are : (1) the title of Excellency, (2) the right to remain covered in the presence of the sovereign, unless the sovereign himself is uncovered, (3) the privilege of a dais in his own home, (4) the right to use a "coach and six" with outriders, (5) military and naval honors, (6) the use of the coat of arms over the door, (7) invitations to all court ceremonies. This last is usually extended to all diplomats. Those of lower rank than the ambassador sometimes claim modified forms of the above prerogatives.

Many of the interesting phases of diplomatic ceremonial are survivals of forms which in earlier days were most jealously and strenuously guarded. The closer relations of states and better understanding of mutual relations have made unnecessary the observance of many forms once vital to harmony.

Many courtesies are regarded as due diplomatic representatives by virtue of their rank. These are not uniform at the various courts, but general notification of accession to the throne, notification of births and deaths in the royal family, congratulations

---

[1] The Department of State instructs the representatives of the United States to follow this practice.

and condolences as public events warrant, and many others.

Diplomats are also entitled to receive salutes, which are usually arranged for in advance.   The ambassador receives a salute of nineteen guns; envoy extraordinary and minister plenipotentiary, fifteen; the minister resident, thirteen; and the chargé d'affaires, eleven.

§ 76. Functions

The functions of a diplomatic representative in a broad sense are, to direct the internal business of the legation, to conduct the negotiations with the state to which he is accredited, to protect citizens of his state [1] and to issue passports under proper restrictions,[2] and to make reports to his home government.

(a) The **internal business** of the mission may in general be classified as concerned with (1) the custody of archives, (2) diplomatic correspondence [3] involving at times the use of cipher, (3) record of the work of the legation, (4) the exercise of a measure of jurisdiction over the household.   In grave cases the diplomat must send the offender home for trial, or under certain circumstances, if a native of the state, hand the offender over to the local authorities.   Otherwise his jurisdiction is mainly of a minor disciplinary sort.   The assumption of such authority as claimed by Sully, in 1603, when he tried and condemned to death one of the French suite,

---

[1] U. S. Rev. Sts., § 2000.

[2] U. S. Rev. Sts., § 4075.

[3] Till the reign of Louis XIV., Latin was the language of diplomacy; from that time, French became more and more used.   Since the Congress of Vienna, 1815, any language may be used without offense, Art. 120.

is now absolutely denied. Indeed, James I. pardoned the offender whom Sully had delivered to him for execution. In 1896 Great Britain denied the right of the Chinese ambassador to detain a Chinaman who was held in the legation under charge of political conspiracy, and compelled his release.

(*b*) The **conduct of negotiations** with the state to which he is accredited may involve, (1) verbal communications with the sovereign or ministers. The purport of such communications may be preserved in writing known as *briefs of the conversation*, or *aids to the memory*. In cases of somewhat formal conversations the written reports may be called *notes* or *memoranda*. To the *procès-verbaux*, or reports of international conferences for the discussion of treaty. stipulations, the name *protocol* is usually given. (2) Formal communications with the sovereign or ministers, (3) the maintenance of diplomatic privileges and immunities, (4) such action as may be necessary to protect his state's interests so far as possible, and particularly its treaty rights.

(*c*) The diplomat's **relations to the citizens of his own country** are largely determined by the domestic law of his own state, and usually involve, (1) a measure of protection to his fellow-citizens; (2) issue and *visé* of passports, and in some countries the issue of certificates of nationality and travel certificates; (3) in cases of extradition of citizens of his own state from the foreign state, the presentation of the requisition for extradition; and in cases of extradition of citizens of the state to which he is accredited from his own state, usually the certification that the papers submitted as evidence

are "properly and legally authenticated."[1] In some
states diplomats are authorized to perform notarial
acts.[2] (4) The exercise of a reasonable courtesy in
the treatment of his fellow-citizens.

All these functions vary with local law. The practice is not uniform, as is evidenced in the inconsistencies in regard to regulations as to the marriage by the
diplomatic agent.[3]

(d) In making reports the diplomat is supposed to
keep his own government informed upon, (1) the views
and policy of the state to which he is accredited, and
(2) such facts as to events, commerce, discoveries, etc.,
as may seem desirable. These reports may be regular
at specified periods, or special.

§ 77. Termination of Mission

The mission of a diplomatic representative may terminate in various ways.

(a) A mission may terminate through the death of
the diplomat. In such a case there may properly be
a funeral befitting the rank of the diplomat. The
property and papers of the mission are inventoried and
sealed by the secretary, or in case of absence of secretaries and other proper persons, by the diplomats of
one or more friendly powers. The inheritance and
private property of the diplomat, of course, follow the
law of his country, and the property of the deceased
is exempt from local jurisdiction.

[1] 22 U. S. Sts. at Large, 216, § 5.
[2] U. S. Rev. Sts., § 1750; 1 Gould and Tucker, 446; 2 ibid., 158.
[3] Hall, § 53, n. 1., p. 192.

(*b*) The mission may terminate in **ordinary course** of events, by (1) expiration of the period for which the letter of credence or full power is granted, (2) fulfillment of the purpose of the mission if on a special mission, (3) change of grade of diplomat, (4) the death or dethronement of the sovereign to whom the diplomatic agent is accredited, except in cases of republican forms of government. In the above case new letters of credence are usually regarded as essential to the continuance of the mission. The weight of opinion seems to indicate that the mission of a diplomat is terminated by a change in the government of his home country through revolution, and that new letters of credence are necessary for the continuance of his mission.

(*c*) A mission may be interrupted or broken off through **strained relations** between the two states or between the diplomatic agent and the receiving state. (1) A declaration of war immediately terminates diplomatic relations. (2) Diplomatic relations may be broken off by the personal departure of the agent, which departure is for a stated cause, such as the existence of conditions making the fulfillment of his mission impossible, or the violation of the principles of international law. (3) Diplomatic relations may be temporarily suspended, owing to friction between the states, as in the case of the suspension of diplomatic relations between Great Britain and Venezuela from 1887 to 1897, owing to dispute upon questions of boundary. In 1891 Italy recalled her minister from the United States on account of alleged tardiness of the United States authorities in making reparation for the lynching of Italians in New

Orleans on March 14, 1891.[1]   (4) A diplomatic agent
is sometimes dismissed either on grounds personal to
the diplomat, or on grounds involving the relations of
the two states.   When, in 1888, the demand for the
recall of Lord Sackville, the British minister at Washington, was not promptly complied with, Lord Sackville
was dismissed and his passport sent to him.   Lord
Sackville had, in response to a letter purporting to be
from an ex-British subject, sent a reply which related
to the impending presidential election.   His recall was
demanded by telegraph Oct. 27.   The British government declined to grant it without time for investigation, and his passport was sent him on Oct. 30.   In
1871, " The conduct of Mr. Catacazy, the Russian minister at Washington, having been for some time past
such as materially to impair his usefulness to his own
Government, and to render intercourse with him for
either business or social purposes highly disagreeable,"
it was the expressed opinion of the President that "the
interests of both countries would be promoted . . . if
the head of the Russian legation here was to be changed."
The President, however, agreed to tolerate the minister
till after the contemplated visit of the grand duke.   The
communication also stated, " That minister will then be
dismissed if not recalled." [2]

(d)- The ceremonial of departure is similar to that of
reception.   (1) The diplomat seeks an interview according to the method outlined in the ceremonial of
reception, in order to present his letter of recall.   (2) In
case of remoteness from the seat of government the
agent may, if necessary, take leave of the sovereign by

[1] 16 Ann. Cycl., 833.   [2] 1 Whart., § 84.

letter, forwarding to the sovereign his letter of recall.
(3) It very often happens that a diplomatic agent presents his successor at the time of his own departure.
(4) In case of change of title the diplomat follows the
ceremonial of departure in one capacity with that of
arrival in his new capacity.   (5) It is understood that
the agent, after the formal close of his mission, will depart with convenient speed, and until the expiration of
such period he enjoys diplomatic immunities.

§ 78. Immunities and Privileges

Few subjects involved in international relations have
been more extensively discussed than the privileges
and immunities of diplomatic agents.   Many of the
earliest treatises on international affairs were devoted
to such questions.   In order that any business between states might be carried on, some principles upon
which the diplomatic agent could base his action were
necessary.   The treatment of the agent could not be
left to chance or to the feeling of the authorities
of the receiving state.   Gradually fixed usages were
recognized.   These immunities and privileges may be
considered under two divisions : personal inviolability,
and exemption from local jurisdiction, otherwise known
as exterritoriality.

Inviolability.   The person of the agent was by
ancient law inviolable.   According to the dictum of the
Roman Law, *sancti habentur legati*.   In accord with this
principle the physical and moral person is inviolable.
Any offense toward the person of the ambassador is in
effect an offense to the state which he represents, and to

the law of nations.   The receiving state is bound to
extend to the diplomatic agent such protection as will
preserve his inviolability.   This may make necessary
the use of force to preserve to the diplomatic agent his
privileges.   The idea of inviolability, as Calvo says, is
absolute and unlimited, and based, not on simple convenience, but upon necessity.   Without it diplomatic
agents could not perform their functions, for they would
be dependent upon the sovereign to whom they might
be accredited.[1]   In many states laws have been enacted
during the last half of the nineteenth century fixing
severe penalties for acts which affect the diplomatic
agent unfavorably in the performance of his functions,
or reflect upon his dignity.[2]

The privilege of inviolability extends, (1) alike to
agents of all classes, (2) to the suite, official and non-
official, (3) to such things as are convenient for the
performance of his functions, (4) during the entire
time of his official sojourn, i.e. from the time of the
making known of his official character to the expiration
of a reasonable time for departure after the completion
of his mission.   This also holds even when the mission
is terminated by the outbreak of war between the state
from which the agent comes and the state to which he
is accredited.   (5) By courtesy the diplomatic agent
is usually accorded similar privileges when passing
through a third state in going to or returning from his
post.

A diplomatic agent may place himself under the
law, says Despagnet, so far as attacks upon him are
concerned : (1) when he voluntarily exposes himself

[1] "Droit Int.," § 1481, ff.   [2] Lehr, "Manuel," §§ 988–998.

to danger, in a riot, duel, civil war; (2) when in his private capacity he does that which is liable to criticism, *e.g.* as a writer or artist, provided the criticism should not degenerate into an attack upon his public character; (3) when the attacks upon him are in legitimate personal self-defense; (4) when, by his actions, he provokes on the part of the local government precautionary measures against himself, *e.g.* if he should plot against the surety of the state to which he is accredited.[1] Only in the case of extreme necessity, however, should any force be used. It is better to ask for the recall of the agent. In case of refusal or in case of urgent necessity the agent may be expelled.

(*b*) **Exemption from local jurisdiction** of the state to which a diplomatic agent is sent, or exterritoriality in a limited sense, flows naturally from the admitted right of inviolability. The term "exterritoriality" is a convenient one for describing the condition of immunity which diplomatic agents enjoy in a foreign state, but it should be observed that the custom of conceding these immunities has given rise to the "legal fiction of exterritoriality," rather than that these immunities are based on a right of exterritoriality. The practice of granting immunities was common long before the idea of exterritoriality arose.[2] The exemptions give to diplomatic agents large privileges.

(1) The diplomatic agent is exempt from the *criminal jurisdiction* of the state to which he is accredited.

---

[1] Despagnet, "Droit international public," 2d ed., § 235; Heffter, § 204.

[2] Grotius, "De Jure Belli," II., 18.

N

In case of violation of law the receiving state has to decide whether the offense is serious enough to warrant a demand for the recall of the agent, or whether it should be passed without notice. In extreme cases a state might order the agent to leave the country, or in case of immediate danger might place the agent under reasonable restraint. Hall considers these "as acts done in pursuance of a right of exercising jurisdiction upon sufficient emergency, which has not been abandoned in conceding immunities to diplomatic agents." [1]

(2) The diplomatic agent is exempt from *civil jurisdiction* of the state to which he is sent, and cannot be sued, arrested, or punished by the law of that state.[2] This rule is sometimes held to apply only to such proceedings as would affect the diplomat in his official character; but unless the diplomat voluntarily assume another character, he cannot be so proceeded against. If he become a partner in a firm, engage in business, buy stocks, or assume financial responsibilities, it is held in theory by some authorities that the diplomatic agent may be proceeded against in that capacity. The diplomatic agent of the United States is distinctly instructed that "real or personal property, aside from that which pertains to him as a minister, . . . is subject to the local laws." [3] The practice is, however, to extend to the diplomat in his personal capacity the fullest possible immunity, and in case of need to resort to his home courts, or to diplomatic methods by appeal

[1] § 50.

[2] U. S. Rev. Sts., §§ 4063, 4064 ; Wheat., D., 308–310.

[3] Instructions to Diplomatic Officers, 1897, § 47.

to the home government, for the adjustment of any difficulties that may involve its representative in foreign court proceedings. The real property of the diplomatic agent is, of course, liable to local police and sanitary regulations. In cases where a diplomatic agent consents to submit himself to foreign jurisdiction, the procedure and the judgment, if against him, cannot involve him in such manner as to seriously interfere with the performance of his functions. He cannot be compelled to appear as witness in a case of which he has knowledge ; however, it is customary in the interests of justice for the diplomatic agent to make a deposition before the secretary of the legation or some proper officer. By the Constitution of the United States, in criminal prosecutions the accused has a right to have the evidence taken orally in his presence. The refusal to give oral testimony of M. Dubois, the Dutch minister to the United States in 1856, resulted in his recall.[1] The Venezuelan minister, however, testified in open court as a courtesy to the United States government in the trial of the assassin of President Garfield.[2] The United States at the present time maintains that "a diplomatic representative cannot be compelled to testify, in the country of his sojourn, before any tribunal whatsoever." This may be considered the generally accepted principle, though the interests of general justice and international courtesy frequently lead to voluntary waiving of the rule with the consent of the accrediting state.

(3) *The official and non-official family* enjoy the immunities of their chief as necessary for the conven-

[1] 1 Whart., § 98.   [2] *Ibid.*

ient performance of his mission. Questions in regard
to the immunities of the non-official suite have sometimes arisen. To avoid this it is customary for the
diplomat to furnish the receiving state with a list
of his family. Great Britain does not admit the full
immunity of domestic servants. When Mr. Gallatin
was United States minister to Great Britain, his coachman, who had committed an assault beyond the *hôtel*
of the minister, was held liable to the local jurisdiction. As a diplomatic agent can voluntarily turn
over an offender to the local authorities, and as he
would naturally desire the observance of local law,
there would be little danger of friction with local
authorities anywhere, provided a just cause could
be shown.

Couriers and bearers of dispatches are entitled to
immunities so far as is necessary for the free performance of the specific function.

(4) *The house and all grounds and buildings* within
the limits of the diplomatic residence are regarded as
exempt from local jurisdiction. Great Britain claimed
the right of entry to arrest Mr. Gallatin's coachman
above mentioned, though admitting that such entrance
should be made at a time to suit the convenience of the
minister if he did not care to hand him over directly.
This immunity extends also to carriages and other
necessary appurtenances of the mission.

Children born to the official family in the house of
the diplomatic agent are considered as born in the state
by which the agent is accredited.

(5) *The right of asylum* in the house of the ambassador is now generally denied. In 1726 the celebrated

case of the Duke of Ripperda, charged with treason, gave rise to the decision by the Council of Castile that the duke could be taken from the English legation by force if necessary, because the legation, which had been established to promote good relations between the states, would otherwise be used for overthrowing the state in which it had been established.[1] It may be regarded as a rule that, in Europe and in the United States, the house of a diplomatic agent affords only temporary protection for a criminal, whether political or otherwise, and that on demand of the proper authority the criminal must be surrendered. Refusal is a just ground for demand for recall of the diplomatic agent. The United States instructs its agents that "The privilege of immunity from local jurisdiction does not embrace the right of asylum for persons outside of a representative's diplomatic or personal household."[2] This right is, however, recognized in practice, both by the United States and European nations, so far as pertains to the houses of the diplomats in South American states. The United States, in 1870, tried without avail to induce the European nations to agree to the discontinuance of the practice. In 1891, in Chile, Minister Egan, of the United States, afforded refuge in the legation to a large number of the political followers of Balmaceda. Chile demanded his recall, but the United States maintained that there must be sufficient grounds for such action. In Eastern countries it has been the practice to afford asylum in legations in times of political disturbance and to politic[1]

---

[1] De Martens, "Causes Cél.," I., 174.
[2] Instructions to Diplomatic Officers, 1897, § 50.

offenders.   In 1895 the British ambassador at Constantinople gave asylum to the deposed grand vizier
at Constantinople.   It can be said, however, that the
tendency is to limit the granting of asylum to the fullest possible extent,[1] and finally to abolish the practice
altogether, as has been the case with the ancient extension of this privilege to the neighborhood of the
legation under the name of *jus quarteriorum*.[2]

(6) In general, the diplomatic agent is *exempt from
personal taxes* and from taxes upon his personal goods.
The property owned by and devoted to the use of the mission is usually exempt from taxation.   In this respect the
principle of reciprocity is followed among some states.
The taxes for betterments, such as paving, sewerage,
etc., are regarded as proper charges upon the mission.
A state has a right to make such regulations as it
deems necessary to prevent the abuse of this immunity
from taxation.   It is also customary for a third state
to grant to a diplomat passing through its territory
immunity from duties.   Diplomatic agents are also exempt from income, military, window, and similar taxes.

(7) It is hardly necessary now to mention the fact
that the diplomatic agent is entitled to *freedom of religious worship* within the mission, provided there be no
attempt by bell, symbol, or otherwise to attract the
attention of the passer-by to the observance.   This
privilege was formerly of importance, but now is never
questioned.

---

[1] Hall, § 52, p. 189.

[2] See the "Right of Asylum in the Legations of the United States
in Central and South America," by Barry Gilbert, in *Harvard Law
Review* for June, 1901, p. 118.

§ 79. Diplomatic Practice of the United States[1]

Some of the minor points of procedure and functions may be seen by the study of the customs and rules of any large state, as in the United States.

(a) Official communications involving international relations and general international negotiations are within the exclusive province of the Department of State, at the head of which stands the Secretary of State.   In other states this department is commonly called the Department of Foreign Affairs, and its chief is the Minister or Secretary for Foreign Affairs, and was so designated in the United States from 1781 to 1789.   The Department of State of the United States, however, performs many functions not strictly within a Department of Foreign Affairs, as an enumeration of the Bureaus will show.

(1) Bureau of Appointments.

(2) Diplomatic Bureau.

(3) Consular Bureau.

(4) Bureau of Indexes and Archives.

(5) Bureau of Accounts.

(6) Bureau of Rolls and Library, which, besides other duties, has charge of the publication of the laws, treaties, proclamations, and executive orders.

(7) Bureau of Foreign Commerce (before July 1, 1897, called Bureau of Statistics).

(b) The Constitution provides that, " In all cases affecting ambassadors, other public ministers, and consuls," the Supreme Court has original jurisdiction.[2]

---

[1] Concise bibliography, Hart, "Foundations of American Foreign Policy," pp. 241-293.   [2] U. S. Constitution, Art. III., § 2, 2.

(c) A diplomatic agent cannot, without consent of Congress, " accept of any present, emolument, office, or title of any kind whatever from any king, prince, or foreign state." [1]   This provision does not, however, prevent the rendering of a friendly service to a foreign power, and it may be proper for him, having first obtained permission from the Department of State, to accede to the request to discharge temporarily the duties of a diplomatic agent of any other state.[2]

(d) In case of revolution a diplomatic agent may extend protection to the subjects of other friendly powers left for the time without a representative.[3]   In neither this nor in the preceding case does the United States become responsible for the acts of its diplomatic representative in so far as he is acting as agent of the other state or states.

(e) " It is forbidden to diplomatic officers to participate in any manner in the political concerns of the country of their residence ; and they are directed especially to refrain from public expressions of opinion upon local political or other questions arising within their jurisdiction.   It is deemed advisable to extend similar prohibition against public addresses, unless upon exceptional festal occasions, in the country of official residence.   Even upon such occasions any reference to political issues, pending in the United States or elsewhere, should be carefully avoided." [4]   A diplomatic agent is forbidden to recommend any person for office

---

[1] U. S. Constitution, Art. I., § 9, 8.   [2] 1 Whart., § 100.
[3] 1 Whart., § 105.
[4] Instructions to Diplomatic Officers, U. S., 1897, §§ 68, 69.

under the government to which he is accredited.[1] The diplomatic agent should not become the agent to prosecute private claims of citizens.[2] The diplomatic agent should not retain any copy of the archives, nor allow the publication of any official document, without authorization of the Department of State. The Department in general disapproves of residence of the agent elsewhere than at the capital of the receiving state.

(*f*) Joint action with the diplomatic agents of other powers at a foreign court is deprecated, although conferences resulting in a common understanding in cases of emergency are considered desirable.[3]

(*g*) It is permitted that the diplomatic agent of the United States wear the uniform and bear the title of the rank attained in the volunteer service of the Army of the United States during the rebellion.[4] It is prohibited by a later statute to wear "any uniform or official costume not previously authorized by Congress."[5] This has been interpreted as applying to dress denoting rank, but not to the prescribed court dress of certain capitals ;[6] and "diplomatic officers are permitted to wear upon occasions of ceremony the dress which local usage prescribes as appropriate to the hour and place."[7]

(*h*) The United States has never been liberal in compensating diplomatic agents for their services. In 1784 the salary of the highest grade was fixed at nine

---

[1] U. S. Rev. Sts., § 1751. [2] 1 Whart., § 99.
[3] 1 Whart., § 102. [4] U. S. Rev. Sts., § 1226.
[5] *Ibid.*, § 1688. [6] Schuyler, "Amer. Dip.," 144.
[7] Instructions to Diplomatic Officers, U. S., § 67.

thousand dollars, and it had only been doubled at the end of the nineteenth century. Other states of equal dignity provide far more liberally for their representatives.

The whole matter of diplomatic agents has been the subject of numerous statutes.[1]

§ 80. Consuls

(a) **Historically** the office of consul preceded that of ambassador. The merchants of different states had dealings with each other long before the states, as such, entered into negotiations. The Egyptians, apparently as early as the fourteenth century B.C., intrusted the trial of certain maritime cases to a designated priest. The Mediterranean merchants appealed to the *judicium mercatorium et maritimum* in the sixth century B.C. The Greek *proxenos* performed some consular functions. Rome later had similar public servants. The consular system, however, did not develop during the long period of decay of the Roman Empire. In the days of the Crusades, the merchants settled in the coast cities of the Mediterranean. Quarters of the cities practically came under the jurisdiction of the foreign occupants. The consuls, probably at first chosen by the merchants, exercised this jurisdiction, under which the law of the state of the origin of the merchants was regarded as binding. Their functions were somewhat similar to those exercised in some Eastern states at the present time. As soon as condi-

[1] U. S. Rev. Sts., §§ 1674–1752; 1 Gould and Tucker, 439–447; 2 *ibid.* 155–158.

tions became more settled, the states gradually assumed control of these consular offices. The laws of Oleron, Amalfi, Wisby, the Consolato del Mare, and the early Lex Rhodia show that many of the consular functions were recognized in the Middle Ages, and the institution of consuls seems to have been quite well established by the year 1200. The Hanseatic League in the fourteenth century had magistrates in many cities entitled *aldermen*, who were performing functions similar to those of the consuls of the Mediterranean.[1] England began to send consuls in the fifteenth century; the system rapidly spread, and the powers and functions of consuls were wide. From this time, with the growth of the practice of sending resident ambassadors, the extent of the consular duties was gradually lessened. The diplomatic functions formerly in the charge of the consuls were intrusted to the ambassadors, and other functions of the consuls were reduced by making them the representatives of the business interests of the subjects of the state in whose service they were, rather than of the interests of the state as such.[2] From the middle of the seventeenth century, when the responsibility of states to each other became more fully recognized, and government became more settled, the exterritorial jurisdiction of consuls was no longer necessary. The growth of commerce among the nations has increased the duties of the consul. The improved means of communication, telegraphic and other, has relieved both consuls and ambassadors of the responsibility of deciding, without

[1] Nys, "Les origines du droit international," "Le Commerce," p. 286.
[2] Lawrence, "Commentaire sur Wheaton," IV., p. 6.

advice from the home government, many questions of serious nature.

(b) **The rank of consuls** is a matter of domestic law, and each state may determine for its own officers the grade and honors attaching thereto in the way of salutes, precedence among its domestic officials, etc. There is no international agreement in regard to consuls similar to that of 1815–1818 in regard to diplomatic agents.

The United States differentiates the consular service more fully than most states, having the following: consuls-general, vice-consuls-general, deputy consuls-general, consuls, vice-consuls, deputy consuls, commercial agents, vice-commercial agents, consular agents, consular clerks, interpreters, marshals, and clerks.[1] The term "consular officer," however, includes only consuls-general, consuls, commercial agents, deputy consuls, vice-consuls, vice-commercial agents, and consular agents.[2] The full officers are consuls-general, consuls, and commercial agents. The vice consular officers are "substitute consular officers" and the deputy consuls-general, deputy consuls, and consular agents are "subordinate consular officers."[3]

Consuls-general ordinarily have a supervisory jurisdiction of the consuls within the neighborhood of their consulate, though sometimes they have no supervisory jurisdiction. This is often exercised by the diplomatic agent accredited to the same state.

Most states have consuls-general, consuls, vice-consuls, consular agents, sometimes also consular students.

---

[1] Consular Regulations, 1896, 1.   [2] U. S. Rev. Sts., § 1674.
[3] U. S. Rev. Sts., § 1674.

(c) **The nomination of consuls** is an attribute of a sovereign state. They may be chosen either from among its own citizens or from those of the foreign state. Consuls chosen from the citizens of the state to which they are accredited exercise only in part the full consular functions, the limit of the functions being determined by the laws of the accrediting state and by the laws of the receiving state. Some states refuse to receive their own citizens as consuls ; others do not accredit foreigners as consuls.

The commission or patent by which a consul-general or consul is always appointed is transmitted to the diplomatic representative of the appointing state in the state to which the consul is sent, with the request that he apply to the proper authority for an *exequatur*, by which the consul is officially recognized and guaranteed such prerogatives and immunities as are attached to his office. The vice-consul is usually appointed by patent, though he may be nominated by his superior, and is recognized by granting of an *exequatur*. The *exequatur* may be revoked for serious cause, though the more usual way is to ask the recall of a consul who is not satisfactory to a state. The *exequatur* may be refused for cause. It is usually issued by the head of the state. If the form of government in the receiving state or in the accrediting state changes, it is customary to request a new *exequatur*.

NOTE. The consular agents, while appointed and confirmed as are the higher consular officers, do not in the practice of the United States receive an *exequatur*.

(FORM OF)

FULL PRESIDENTIAL EXEQUATUR

....

President of the United States of America.

To all to whom it may concern :
                       Satisfactory evidence having been exhibited to me
that ....
has been appointed...
I do hereby recognize him as such, and declare him free to exercise
and enjoy such functions, powers, and privileges as are allowed to
....
                    In Testimony whereof, I have caused these Letters
                to be made Patent, and the Seal of the United States
[SEAL   to be hereunto affixed.
OF THE   Given under my hand at the City of Washington
UNITED   the..............day of.............., A.D. 19....,
STATES]   and of the Independence of the United States of
               America, the............

By the President, ...

....
                 Secretary of State.

(*d*) **Functions.** The consul, as the officer representing particularly the commercial and business interests
of the state from which he comes, and in a minor degree
the other individual interests, has a great variety of
functions. His functions are in general such as affect
only indirectly the state in which he resides. He is
not, like the diplomatic agent, directly concerned with
affairs of state; he has no representative character,
though in effect he is often the local representative of
the diplomatic agent accredited to the state.

The functions of a consul are largely matters determined by custom, treaty stipulation, and by special

provisions of his *exequatur*. Within these limits
domestic law of the accrediting state determines the
consul's functions. (1) In general the consul has many
duties in connection with the *commercial interests* of
the subjects of the state which he serves. These duties
extend both to maritime and land commerce. The consul is to care that the provisions of commercial treaties
are observed, that proper invoices of goods are submitted, and that shipment is in accord with the regulations of the state which he serves. He is to furnish
such reports in regard to commercial and economic
conditions as are required. These reports often involve many subjects only indirectly related to trade
and commerce. (2) The consul has many duties relating to the *maritime service* of the state which
accredits him. This usually includes such supervision
of merchant vessels as the domestic law of his state may
grant to him, together with that accorded by custom.
His office is a place of deposit of a ship's papers while the
ship remains in port. When necessary he may super-
vise the shipment, wages, relief, transportation, and
discharge of seamen, the reclaiming of deserters, the
care of the effects of deceased seamen, in some states
the adjudication of disputes between masters, officers,
and crews, and if necessary he may intervene in cases of
mutiny or insubordination. In case of wrecked vessels
the consul is usually left considerable latitude in his
action. The consul may also authenticate the bill of
sale of a foreign vessel to the subject of the state which
accredits him. This authentication entitles the vessel
to the protection of the consul's state. The consul
may also be intrusted with other duties by treaties and

custom of given states. (3) The consul *represents*
the *interests of the citizens* of the state in whose service
he is, in matters of authentication of acts under seal, in
administration of the property of citizens within his
district, in taking charge of effects of deceased citizens,
in arbitration of disputes voluntarily submitted to him,
visé of passports, and minor services. (4) The consul
furnishes to the state which he represents *information*
upon a great variety of subjects particularly relating to
commercial, economic, and political affairs, the condi-   .
tions of navigation, and general hydrographic information.   Besides this he is expected to keep his state
informed of the events of interest transpiring within
his district.

As Hall says: " In the performance of these and similar duties the action of a consul is evidently not international.   He is an officer of his state to whom are
entrusted special functions which can be carried out in
a foreign country without interfering with its jurisdiction.   His international action does not extend beyond
the unofficial employment of such influence as he may
possess, through the fact of his being an official and
through his personal character, to assist compatriots
who may be in need of his help with the authorities of
the country.   If he considers it necessary that formal
representations shall be made to its government as to
treatment experienced by them or other matters concerning them, the step ought in strictness to be taken
through the resident diplomatic agent of his state, — he
not having himself a recognized right to make such
communications." [1]   In late years there has been in the

[1] § 105, p. 331.

consular conventions between different states a tendency
to extend to consuls the right of complaint to the local
authorities in case " of any infraction of the treaties or
conventions existing between the states," and " if the
complaint should not be satisfactorily redressed, the
consular officer, in the absence of the diplomatic agent
of his country, may apply directly to the government
of the country where he resides." [1]

(e) In some of the **Eastern and non-Christian states**
consuls have special powers and functions in addition
to the ordinary powers and functions.   The extent of
the powers varies, and is usually determined by treaty.
With the advance of civilization these special functions
are withdrawn, as by the Treaty of the United States
with Japan, Nov. 22, 1894,[2] the jurisdiction of the consular courts of the United States in Japan came to an
end July 17, 1899.

In general, in Mohammedan and non-Christian states,
treaty stipulations secure to the consuls of Western
states the right of exercising extensive criminal and
civil jurisdiction in cases involving citizens of their own
and the Eastern states, or in cases involving citizens of
their own and other Western states.[3]   In some of the
Eastern states the consuls have exclusive jurisdiction
over all cases to which citizens of their states are

[1] See Treaties : United States and Colombia (New Granada), 1850;
United States and France, 1853 ; United States and Austria, 1870;
United States and Germany, 1871 ; Austria and Portugal, 1873 ; Ger-
many and Russia, 1874 ; France and Russia, 1874 ; United States and
Italy, 1878 ; Portugal and Belgium, 1880 ; United States and Rou-
mania, 1881 ; United States and Congo Free State, 1891, and others.

[2] 29 U. S. Sts. at Large, 848.

[3] See § 64 for extent of jurisdiction.

o

parties ;[1] in others the cases involving citizens of the Eastern and Western states are tried in the court of the defendant in the presence of the "authorized official of the plaintiff's nationality," who may enter protest if the proceedings are not in accord with justice,[2] while in certain states or for certain cases mixed courts are constituted. Certain Western states in their domestic laws make provisions for appeal from the decision of the consular court to specified authorities as to the diplomatic agent or to some domestic tribunal.

This jurisdiction is exceptional, furnishes no precedents for international law, tends to become more restricted, and will doubtless gradually disappear.[3]

(f) The **privileges and immunities** vary according to the states and from the fact that a consul may be, (1) a citizen of the state in which he exercises his consular functions, (2) a domiciled alien, (3) an alien engaged in business or some other occupation in the state where 'he exercises his functions, or (4) a citizen of the accrediting state engaged exclusively upon consular business.[4] It is, however, necessary that the state which grants an *exequatur* to, or receives as consul a person from one of the first three classes, grant to such person a measure of privilege and immunity consistent with the free performance of his consular duties.

Each consul has the privilege of placing above the door of his house the arms of the state which he serves,

[1] U. S. Treaty with Borneo, June 23, 1850, Art. IX., Treaties of U. S., 102.

[2] U. S. Treaty with China, Nov. 17, 1880, Art. IV., Treaties in Force, 120.

[3] Hall, § 105 note, p. 338.

[4] Lehr, § 1236 ff.

generally also of flying its flag.   The archives and official property are inviolable.

In the case of a consul not a citizen of the receiving state and engaged exclusively in consular business, exemption from arrest except on a criminal charge, when he may be punished by local laws or sent home for trial; exemption from witness duty, though testimony may be taken in writing; exemption from taxation; exemption from military charges and service, — is usually conceded by custom and often by treaty.   It is not, however, conceded that the consular residence may be used as an asylum.

The consul of the third class, who, though an alien to the receiving state, engages in business other than consular duties, is subject to all local laws governing similarly circumstanced foreigners, except when in the performance of his functions.   His consular effects must be kept distinct from those appertaining to his business capacity, which last are under local law.

The domiciled alien exercising consular functions is subject to local law as others similarly circumstanced, which, in some states, may involve considerable obligations.   The freedom from local restrictions sufficient for the convenient performance of his consular duties is implied in the grant of the *exequatur.*

The reception of a citizen as a consular representative of a foreign state does not confer upon him the personal privileges and immunities of any of the other classes, but only the immunities attaching to the office itself, and absolutely necessary for the performance of its duties, as the right to use the arms above the office door, the inviolability of archives, and respect for his authority while in the performance of his functions.

In some of the Eastern states and in some of the non-Christian and semicivilized states consuls are entirely exempt from local jurisdiction, enjoying exemptions similar to those of diplomatic agents.

In time of war the house of the consul is, when flying the flag of the state which he serves, specially protected, and liable to injury only in case of urgent military necessity. Consuls do not necessarily withdraw because of hostilities with the accrediting state.[1]

In general, the consul, by virtue of his public office, is entitled to more respect than a simple citizen, or, as Heffter puts it, " consuls are entitled to that measure of inviolability which will enable them to exercise their consular functions without personal inconvenience." [2]

(g) The consular office may be vacated by a given occupant, (1) by death, (2) by recall, (3) by expiration of his term of service, (4) by revocation of his exequatur. This last cause is the only one needing attention. The exequatur may be revoked by the state issuing it, if the conduct of the holder be displeasing to the state. The state issuing the exequatur is sole judge. This does not necessarily imply any discourtesy to the accrediting state, as the consul does not represent the sovereignty of the state. It is customary, however, to give the accrediting state an opportunity to recall its consul. Exequaturs have, on several occa-

---

[1] " De Clercq et de Vallat," I., pp. 106, 107.
[2] § 244.

sions, been withdrawn from consuls who have directly or indirectly aided the enemies of the receiving state, or have given offense by their participation in the public affairs of the receiving state.   Consequently consuls are usually officially advised to refrain so far as possible from expressions of their opinions upon public affairs, either of the receiving or sending state.

CHAPTER XIV

TREATIES

§ 81. Definition

A treaty is an agreement, generally in writing, and always in conformity with law, between two or more states. A treaty may establish, modify, or terminate obligations. These obligations must be such as are legally within the capacity of the states concerned to negotiate. A treaty runs between states only. As distinguished from other forms of international agreement, a treaty is usually concerned with matters of high state importance, with a considerable number of questions, or with matters involving several states.

Separate articles are clauses attached to a treaty after ratification, and to be interpreted with reference to the whole.

§ 82. Other Forms of International Agreements

Besides the treaty, which is the most formal international agreement, there may be various other methods of expressing the terms of international agreements. The importance of the matter contained in the various documents is not necessarily in proportion to their formality.

The terms " convention " and " treaty " are very generally used interchangeably, though strictly the scope of a convention is less broad, and usually applies to some specific subject, as to the regulation of commerce, navigation, consular service, postal service, naturalization, extradition, boundaries, etc. The terms below are often used loosely in practice.

(a) A protocol, or procès verbal, is usually in the form of official minutes, giving the conclusions of an international conference and signed at the end of each session by the negotiators. This does not require ratification by the sovereign as in the case of treaties and conventions, though it is equally binding upon the good faith

of the states concerned.   Ordinarily the persons signing the protocol have been duly authorized by their
respective states in advance.   The term "protocol" is
sometimes applied to the preliminary draft of an agreement between two or more states as to the agreements
entered into by negotiators in preparation of a more
formal document, such as a treaty or convention.[1]

(b) **Declarations** are usually documents containing reciprocal agreements of states, as in granting equal privileges in matters of trade-marks, copyrights, etc., to the
citizens of each state.   The term is used for the documents, (1) which outline the policy or course of conduct
which one or more states propose to pursue under certain circumstances, (2) which enunciate the principles
adopted, or (3) which set forth the reasons justifying a
given act.

(c) The terms "**memoranda**" and "**memoires**" are
used to indicate the documents in which the principles
entering an international discussion are set forth, together with the probable conclusions.   These documents
may be considered by the proper authorities, e.g. may be
sent to the foreign secretaries of the states concerned,
and contre-memoires may be submitted.   These documents are generally unsigned.

(d) Besides the above, there may be in diplomatic
negotiations **letters** between the agents, in which the use
of the first or second person is common, and **notes**, which
are more formal and usually in the third person.   These

[1] For various protocols, see Treaties of U. S., 824, 1148 ; 30 U. S.
Sts. at Large, 1593 ; ibid., 1596.   For the recent protocol between the
United States and Spain as to terms of peace, see 30 U. S. Sts. at Large,
1742.

letters, if made public, may have much force, as in the case of the collective note of the powers commonly called the "Andrassy note," by which the Powers of Europe in 1875 held that in Turkey "reform must be adopted to put a stop to a disastrous and bloody contest."

(e) When representatives of states not properly commissioned for the purpose, or exceeding the limits of their authority, enter into agreements, their acts are called treaties **sub spe rati** or **sponsions**. Such agreements require ratification by the state. This ratification may be explicit in the usual form, or tacit, when the state governs its action by the agreements.

(f) Of the nature of treaties are **cartels**, which are agreements made between belligerents, usually mutual, regulating intercourse during war. These may apply to exchange of prisoners, postal and telegraphic communications, customs, and similar subjects. These documents are less formal than conventions, usually negotiated by agents specially authorized, and do not require ratification, though fully obligatory upon the states parties to the agreement.[1] Here also may be named the suspension of arms, which the chief of an army or navy may enter into as an agreement for the regulation or cessation of hostilities within a limited area for a short time and for military ends. When such agreements are for the cessation of hostilities in general, or for a considerable time, they receive the name of armistices or truces. These are sometimes called conventions with the enemy. These last do not imply international negotiation.

[1] Wheat., D., §§ 254, 344.

The following is the beginning and end of the **Treaty of Washington** relative to the Alabama Claims, etc., including the President's proclamation thereof : [1] —

"BY THE PRESIDENT OF THE UNITED STATES OF AMERICA

"A PROCLAMATION

"Whereas a treaty, between the United States of America and her Majesty the Queen of the United Kingdom of Great Britain and Ireland, concerning the settlement of all causes of difference between the two countries, was concluded and signed at Washington by the high commissioners and plenipotentiaries of the respective governments on the eighth day of May last; which treaty is word for word, as follows : —

" ' The United States of America and her Britannic Majesty, being desirous to provide for an amicable settlement of all causes of difference between the two countries, have for that purpose appointed their respective plenipotentiaries, that is to say: The President of the United States has appointed, on the part of the United States, as Commissioners in a Joint High Commission and Plenipotentiaries [here, follow the names]; and her Britannic Majesty, on her part, has appointed as her High Commissioners and Plenipotentiaries [here follow the names].

" ' And the said plenipotentiaries, after having exchanged their full powers, which were found to be in due and proper form, have agreed to and concluded the following articles : —

[Here follow 42 articles.]

" ' ARTICLE XLIII

" ' The present treaty shall be duly ratified by the President of the United States of America, by and with the advice

[1] 17 U. S. Sts. at Large, 863 ; Treaties of U. S., 478.

and consent of the Senate thereof, and by her Britannic Majesty; and the ratifications shall be exchanged either at Washington or at London within six months from the date hereof, or earlier if possible.

"'In faith whereof, we, the respective plenipotentiaries, have signed this treaty and have hereunto affixed our seals.

"'Done in duplicate at Washington the eighth day of May, in the year of our Lord one thousand eight hundred and seventy-one.'

[Here follow the seals and signatures.]

"And whereas the said treaty has been duly ratified on both parts, and the respective ratifications of the same were exchanged in the city of London, on the seventeenth day of June, 1871, by Robert C. Schenck, Envoy Extraordinary and Minister Plenipotentiary of the United States, and Earl Granville, her Majesty's Principal Secretary of State for Foreign Affairs, on the part of their respective governments:

"Now, therefore, be it known that I, Ulysses S. Grant, President of the United States of America, have caused the said treaty to be made public, to the end that the same, and every clause and article thereof, may be observed and fulfilled with good faith by the United States and the citizens thereof.

"In witness whereof, I have hereunto set my hand and caused the seal of the United States to be affixed.

"Done at the City of Washington this fourth day of July, in the year of our Lord one thousand eight hundred and seventy-one, and of the Independence of the United States the ninety-sixth.

"U. S. GRANT.

"By the President:

"HAMILTON FISH, *Secretary of State.*"

There is no diplomatic language, though various languages have from time to time been more commonly

used. In early treaties and diplomatic works Latin
was very common, and it was used so late as the Treaty
of Utrecht in 1713. Spanish prevailed for some years
toward the end of the fifteenth century. From the days
of Louis XIV., when the French particularly became the
court language, it has been widely used in congresses and
treaties. Frequently, when used, there have been inserted in the treaties provisions that the use of French
should not be taken as a precedent. The French language is, however, commonly employed in congresses in
which a considerable number of different languages are
represented, and the original forms of the treaties are
drawn in French. During the nineteenth century this
has been very common, as in the acts of the Congress
of Vienna, 1815 ; Aix-la-Chapelle, 1818 ; Paris, 1856 ;
Berlin, 1878 and 1885 ; Brussels, 1890. Even other
states of Europe, in making treaties with Asiatic and
African states, have agreed upon French as the authoritative text for both states. In some of the treaties of
the United States and the Ottoman Porte, the French
language is used.

It is customary, when the treaty is between states
having different official languages, to arrange for ver-
sions in both languages in parallel columns, placing at
the left the version in the language of the state to
which the treaty is to be transmitted.

(c) In signing the treaty each representative **signs
and seals** in the first place the copy to be sent to his
own state. The order of the other signatures may be
by lot or in the alphabetical order of the states represented. The signing of the treaty indicates the completion of the agreement between those commissioned

in behalf of the states concerned. This does not irrevocably bind the states which the signers represent, though the fact that its representative has signed a treaty is a reason for ratification which cannot be set aside except for most weighty cause.

(*d*) **Ratification** is the acceptance by the state of the terms of the treaty which has been agreed upon by its legally qualified agent. The exchange of ratifications is usually provided for in a special clause, *e.g.* " The present treaty shall be ratified, and the ratifications exchanged at . . . as speedily as possible." By this clause the state reserves to itself the right to examine the conditions before entering into the agreement. At the present time it is held that even when not expressed, the "reserve clause " is understood.

The ratification conforms to the domestic laws of each state. Ordinarily it is in the form of an act duly signed and sealed by the head of the state. In the act of ratification the text of the treaty may be reproduced entire, or merely the title, preamble, the first and last articles of the body of the treaty, the concluding clauses following the last article, the date, and the names of the plenipotentiaries.

In many states prior approval of the treaty by some legislative body is necessary. In the United States the Constitution provides that the President "shall have power by and with the advice and consent of the Senate, to make treaties, provided two-thirds of the Senators present concur." [1] In the United States it has frequently happened that the Senate has not approved of treaties, and they have therefore failed of

[1] Art. II., § 2, 2.

ratification. This was the fate of the Fishery Treaty with Great Britain in 1888.

The ratification may be refused for sufficient reason. Each state must decide for itself what is sufficient reason. The following have been offered at various times as valid reasons for refusal of ratification : (1) error in points essential to the agreement, (2) the introduction of matters of which the instructions of the plenipotentiaries do not give them power to treat, (3) clauses contrary to the public law of either of the states, (4) a change in the circumstances making the fulfillment of the stipulations unreasonable, (5) the introduction of conditions impossible of fulfillment, (6) the failure to meet the approval of the political authority whose approval is necessary to give the treaty effect, (7) the lack of proper credentials on the part of the negotiators or the lack of freedom in negotiating.

The exchange of ratifications is usually a solemn, *i.e.* highly formal, ceremony by which parties to the treaty or convention guarantee to each other the execution of its terms. As many copies of the act of ratification are prepared by each state as there are state parties to the treaty. When the representatives of the states assemble for the exchange of ratifications, they submit them to each other. These are carefully compared, and if found in correct form, they make the exchange and draw up a *procès verbal* of the fact, making as many copies of the *procès verbal* as there are parties to the treaty. At this time also a date for putting into operation the provisions of the treaty may be fixed. Sometimes clauses explanatory of words, phrases, etc., in the body of the treaty are agreed upon.

Such action usually takes the form of a special *procès verbal* or protocol.

Unless there is a stipulation as to the time when a treaty becomes effective, it·is binding upon the signatory states from the date of signing, provided it is subsequently ratified.

A state may assume a more or less close relation to the agreements contained in treaties made by other states, by measures less formal than ratification. These measures are commonly classed as acts of, (1) *approbation*, by which a state without becoming in any way a party to the treaty assumes a favorable attitude toward its provisions, (2) *adhesion*, by which a state announces its intention to abide by the principles of a given treaty without becoming party to it, and (3) *accession*, by which a state becomes a party to a treaty which has already been agreed upon by other states.

NOTE. After the completion of the negotiation it is customary to promulgate and publish the treaty or convention. Both these acts are matters of local rather than international law. The *promulgation* is the announcement by the chief of the state that the treaty or convention has been made, and the *publication* is the official announcement of the contents of the treaty or convention. See p. 204.

§ 84. Validity of Treaties

Four conditions are very generally recognized as essential to the validity of a treaty.

(*a*) The parties to the treaty must have the **international capacity** to contract, *i.e.* **ordinarily** they must be independent states.

P

(*b*) The agents acting for the state must be **duly authorized**, *i.e.* the plenipotentiaries must act within their powers.

(*c*) There must be **freedom of consent** in the agreements between the states. This does not imply that force, as by war, reprisals, or otherwise, may not be used in bringing about a condition of affairs which may lead a state, without parting with its independence, to make such sacrifices as may be necessary to put an end thereto. No constraint can be put upon the negotiators of the treaty by threats of personal violence, or in any way to prohibit their free action, without invalidating their acts. There is no freedom of consent when the agreement is reached through fraud of either party, and treaties so obtained are not valid.

(*d*) The treaties must be in **conformity to law**, as embodied in the generally recognized principles of international law and the established usage of states. States could not by treaty appropriate the open sea, protect the slave trade, partition other states unless as a measure of self-protection, deprive subjects of essential rights of humanity, or enter into other agreements that could not be internationally obligatory.

§ 85. Classification of Treaties

Treaties have been variously classified, but the classifications serve no great purpose. The most common classification is clearly set forth by Calvo. As regards form, treaties may be, (1) transitory, or (2) permanent or perpetual; as regards nature, (1) personal, relating to the sovereign, or (2) real, relating to things and not dependent on the sovereign person; as regards effects, (1) equal or (2) unequal, or according to other effects, simple or conditional, definitive or preliminary, principal or accessory, etc.; as regards objects, (1) general or (2) special.[1] In a narrower sense treaties may be divided into many classes, as political, economic, guarantee, surety, neutrality, alliance, friendship, boundary, cession, exchange, jurisdiction, extradition, commerce, navigation, peace, etc., and conventions relating to property of various kinds, including literary and artistic, to post and telegraph, etc. Most of these classes are sufficiently described by their titles. The nature of some of the classes is not fully indicated in the title.

A treaty of guarantee is an engagement by which a state agrees to secure another in the possession of certain specified rights, as in the exercise of a certain form of government, in the free exercise of authority within its dominions, in freedom from attack, in the free navigation of specified rivers, in the exercise of neutrality, etc. In 1831 and 1839, by the Treaties of London, the independence and neutrality of Belgium were guaranteed, and in the Treaty of 1832 the affairs in Greece were adjusted under guarantee. The Treaty of Paris, 1856, guarantees " the independence and the integrity of the Ottoman Empire." When the guaranteeing state is not only bound to use its best efforts to secure the fulfillment of the treaty stipulations, but to make good the conditions agreed upon in the treaty provided one of the principals fails to meet its obligations, the treaty is not merely one of guarantee, but also a treaty

[1] Calvo, §§ 643-668.

of surety.   This happens in case of loans more particularly.

Agreements of states to act together for specific or general objects constitute treaties of alliance.   The nature of these treaties of alliance varies with the terms.   They may be defensive, offensive, equal, unequal, general, special, permanent, temporary, etc., or may combine several of these characteristics.

§ 86.   Interpretation of Treaties

Sometimes clauses interpreting treaties are discussed and adopted by the states signing a treaty.   These acts may take the form of notes, protocols, declarations, etc. The dispatch of the French ambassador at London, Aug. 9, 1870, to the foreign secretary interprets certain clauses of the treaty guaranteeing the neutrality of Belgium.   In cases where no preliminary agreement in regard to interpretation is made. there are certain general principles of interpretation which are ordinarily accepted.   Many treatises follow closely the chapters of Grotius and Vattel upon this subject.[1]

The *rules usually accepted* are : (1) Words of the treaty are to be taken in the ordinary and reasonable sense as when elsewhere used under similar conditions. (2) If the words have different meanings in the different states, the treaty should so far as possible be construed so as to accord with. the meaning of the words

[1] Grotius, II., 16 ; Vattel, II., 17.   The rules of Vattel are briefly and well stated by Baker, ''First Steps in International Law,'' 1899. p. 105.

in the states which accepted the conditions. (3) In default of a plain meaning, the spirit of the treaty or a reasonable meaning should prevail. (4) Unless the fundamental rights of states are expressly the subject of the agreement, these rights are not involved. (5) That which is clearly granted by the treaty carries with it what is necessary for its realization.

In the *cases of conflicting clauses* in a single treaty or conflicting treaties, the general rules are : (1) Special clauses prevail against general clauses; prohibitory against permissive, unless the prohibitory is general and the permissive special; of two prohibitory clauses, the one more distinctly mandatory prevails; of two similar obligatory clauses the state in whose favor the obligation runs may choose which shall be observed. (2) In case of conflict in treaties between the same states the later prevails ; in case a later treaty with a third state conflicts with an earlier treaty with other states, the earlier treaty prevails.[1]

" The most favored nation " clause is now common in treaties of commercial nature. This clause ordinarily binds the state to grant to its co-signer all the privileges similarly granted to all other states, and such as shall be granted under subsequent treaties. When privileges are granted by one state in exchange for privileges granted by another, as in a reciprocal reduction in tariff duties, a third state can lay claim to like reduction only upon fulfillment of like conditions. Under " the most favored nation " clause, Art. VIII., of the

---

[1] For the subject of interpretation, see Hall, §§ 111, 112, p. 350 ff. ; 2 Phillimore, Pt. V., Ch. VIII. ; Calvo, §§ 1649–1650 ; Pradier-Fodéré, §§ 1171–1188.

Treaty of 1803, between France and the United States, France claimed that its ships were entitled to all the privileges granted to any other nation whether so granted in return for special concessions or not. This position the United States refused to accept, and by Article VII. of the Treaty of 1831 France renounced the claims.[1]

§ 87. Termination of Treaties

Treaties in general come to an end under the following conditions : —

(*a*) The complete fulfillment of all the treaty stipulations terminates a treaty.

(*b*) The expiration of the limit of time for which the treaty agreement was made puts an end to the treaty.

(*c*) A treaty may be terminated by express agreement of the parties to it.

(*d*) When a treaty depends upon the execution of conditions contrary to the principles of international law or morality or impossible of performance, it is not effective.

(*e*) A state may renounce the advantages and rights secured under a treaty, *e.g.* England renounced the protectorate of the Ionian Islands in 1864, which she had held since 1815.

(*f*) A declaration of war may put an end to those treaties which have regard only to conditions of peaceful relations, as treaties of alliance, commerce, navigation, etc., and may suspend treaties which have regard

[1] For discussion of the "most favored nation" clause, see 2 Whart., § 134, also Appendix to Vol. III., p. 888, and J. R. Harod, "Favored Nation Treatment."

to permanent conditions, as treaties of cession, boundaries, etc. The treaty of peace between China and Japan, May 8, 1895, Article 6, asserts that, " All treaties between Japan and China having come to an end in consequence of the war, China engages, immediately upon the exchange of ratifications of this act, to appoint plenipotentiaries to conclude, with the Japanese plenipotentiaries, a treaty of commerce and navigation, and a convention to regulate frontier intercourse and trade." In the war between the United States and Spain the royal decree issued by Spain, April 23, 1898, Article I., asserts that " The state of war existing between Spain and the United States terminates the treaty of peace and friendship of the 27th October, 1795, the protocol of the 12th January, 1877, and all other agreements, compacts, and conventions that have been in force up to the present between the two countries." The declaration of war also gives special effect to certain treaties and conventions, as to those in regard to care of wounded, neutral commerce, etc.

(g) A treaty is voidable when, (1) it is concluded in excess of powers of contracting parties, (2) when it is concluded because of stress of force upon negotiators or because of fraud, (3) when the conditions threaten the self-preservation of the state or its necessary attributes. Hall gives as the test of voidability the following : " Neither party to a contract can make its binding effect dependent at his will upon conditions other than those contemplated at the moment when the contract was entered into, and on the other hand a contract ceases to be binding so soon as anything which formed an implied condition of its obligatory force at the time

of its conclusion is essentially altered." [1] The condition
rebus sic stantibus is always implied.

(*h*) A treaty may be terminated by the simple act
of denunciation when this right of denunciation is
specified in the treaty itself, or when the treaty is of
such a nature as to be voidable by an act of one·of the
parties. "There can be no question that the breach of
a stipulation which is material to the main object, or if
there are several, to one of the main objects, liberates
the party other than that committing the breach from
the obligations of the contract; but it would be seldom
that the infraction of an article which is either discon-
nected from the main object or is unimportant whether
originally or by change of circumstances, with respect
to it, could in fairness absolve the other party from
performance of his share of the rest of the agreement,
though if he had suffered any appreciable harm through
the breach he would have a right to exact reparation,
and end might be put to the treaty as respects the subject-matter of the broken stipulation." [2]

[1] Hall, § 116, p. 367.   [2] *Ibid.*, p. 369.

CHAPTER XV

AMICABLE SETTLEMENT OF DISPUTES AND NON-HOSTILE REDRESS

§ 88. The Amicable Settlement of Disputes

It is now generally admitted that in the settlement of international disputes war should be regarded as a last resort. Other means of amicable settlement should be exhausted before any measures of force are tried. Among these amicable means the most common are diplomatic negotiations, the good offices or friendly mediation of a third state, conferences and congresses, and arbitration.[1]

---

[1] See Holls's " Hague Peace Conference," 1

(*a*) The settlement of disputes **by diplomatic nego-tiation** follows the ordinary course of diplomatic busi-ness, whether committed to regular or special agents. The larger number of disputed questions are settled by diplomatic negotiation.

(*b*) In the case of disputes not easily settled by diplomatic negotiations, a third state sometimes offers its **good offices** as mediator. Its part is not to pass on a disputed question, but to devise a means of settle-ment. The tender involves the least possible interfer-ence in the dispute, and is regarded as a friendly act. Either disputant may decline the tender without offense. One of the disputants may request the tender of good offices or of mediation. The distinction between these is not always made in practice. Ordinarily good offices extend only to the establishing of bases of, and the com-mencement of, the negotiations. The more direct work of carrying on the negotiations is of the nature of mediation. Either party may at any time refuse the mediator's offices.

(*c*) The Hague Convention provides for an **Inter-national Commission of Inquiry** to facilitate the solution of differences which diplomacy has not settled "by elucidating the facts by means of an impartial and con-scientious investigation." "It leaves the conflicting Powers entire freedom as to the effect to be given to its statement."[1]

(*d*) The settlement of questions liable to give rise to disputes by **conferences and congresses** is common, and implies a meeting of representatives of the inter-ested parties for consideration of the terms of agree-ment upon which a question may be adjudicated. In

[1] Appendix, p. 448.

general, the conclusions of a congress are more formal
and are regarded as having more binding force than
those of a conference, though this distinction is not
always made. States not directly interested may participate in conferences or congresses, and sometimes as
mediators play a leading part.

(e) **Arbitration** involves an agreement between the
disputants to submit their differences to some person or
persons by whose decision they will abide. Arbitration
has been common from early times. The Hague Convention for the Pacific Settlement of International Disputes [1] proclaimed for the United States, November 1,
1901, provides that " The Signatory Powers undertake
to organize a permanent Court of Arbitration, accessible
at all times . . . competent for all arbitration cases,
unless the parties agree to institute a special Tribunal,"
for the general organization of the Court at the Hague,
for the procedure, and for an award without appeal,
unless the right to revision be reserved in the " Compromis." Other powers may adhere, and any contracting power may withdraw its adherence one year after
notification. The United States gave its adherence
under reservation in regard to the Monroe Doctrine.

Of about thirty cases of arbitration during the nineteenth century, the decision in one case was rejected by
both parties to the dispute, and in one case rejected by
one of the parties. In several other instances one party
has refused to submit to arbitration questions readily
lending themselves to such settlement, even though
requested by the other party.[2]

[1] Appendix X., pp. 445 et seq.
[2] See, on this entire subject, Moore's "International Arbitration ";
Holls's " Hague Peace Conference," 176–305.

§ 89. Non-hostile Redress

Good offices, mediation, and arbitration can only extend to international differences of certain kinds. Such measures are not applicable to all cases of disagreement, nor are such measures always acceptable to both parties. Consequently certain other practices have arisen with the view of obtaining satisfaction by measures short of war. Formerly an individual might be commissioned by a letter of marque and reprisal to obtain satisfaction from a state for injuries which he had suffered. This practice is, however, discontinued,[1] and satisfaction must be obtained through the proper state channels. The means by which satisfaction may be claimed vary, and are usually classed as retorsions, reprisals, of which embargo is an important variety, and pacific blockades.

§ 90. Retorsion

Retorsion is a species of retaliation in kind.[2] Retorsion may not consist in acts precisely identical with those which have given offense, though it is held that the acts should be analogous. The offense in consequence of which measures of retorsion are taken may be an act entirely legitimate and desirable from the point of view of the offending state. Another state may, however, consider the act as discourteous, injurious, discriminating, or unduly severe. In recent years commercial retorsion has become a very important means of retaliation which, bearing heavily upon mod-

[1] 3 Phillimore, 21, 22.　[2] Pradier-Fodéré, 2634-2636.

ern communities, may lead to a speedy settlement of difficulties. The tariff wars of recent years show the effectiveness of commercial retorsion, *e.g.* the measures in consequence of the tariff disagreements between France and Switzerland in 1892. These measures of retorsion should always be within the bounds of municipal and international law.

§ 91. Reprisals

Reprisals are acts of a state performed with a view to obtaining redress for injuries. The injuries leading to reprisals may be either to the state or to a citizen, and the acts of reprisal may fall upon the offending state or upon its citizens either in goods or person. The general range of acts of reprisal may be by (1) the seizure and confiscation of public property or private property, and (2) the restraint of intercourse, political, commercial, or general. In extreme cases, acts of violence upon persons belonging to one state, when in a foreign state, have led to similar acts upon the part of the state whose subjects are injured against the subjects of the foreign state. This practice is looked upon with disfavor, though it might be sanctioned by extremest necessity. Acts of retaliation for the sake of revenge are generally discountenanced.

§ 92. Embargo

Embargo consists in the detention of ships and goods which are within the ports of the state resorting to this means of reprisal. It may be (1) civil or pacific embargo, the detention of its own ships, as by the act of the United States Congress in 1807, to avoid risk on account of the Berlin Decree of Napoleon, 1806, and the British Orders in Council, 1807; or (2) hostile, the detention of the goods and ships of another state. It was formerly the custom to detain within the ports of a given state the ships of the state upon which it desired to make reprisals, and if the relations between the states led to war to confiscate such ships. Hostile embargo may now be said to be looked upon with disfavor, and a contrary policy is generally adopted, by which merchant vessels may be allowed a certain time in which to load and depart even after the outbreak of hostilities. The Naval War Code of the United States provides that "Merchant vessels of the enemy, in ports within the jurisdiction of the United States at the outbreak of war, shall be allowed thirty days after war has begun to load their cargoes and depart."[1] By the proclamation of the President of the United States declaring that war with Spain had existed since April 21, 1898, it was also declared that "Spanish merchant vessels, in any ports or places within the United States, shall be allowed till May 21, 1898, inclusive, for loading their cargoes and departing from such ports or places."[2] Spain, by the royal decree of April 23, 1898, declared "A term of five days from the date of the publication of the present royal decree in the *Madrid Gazette* is allowed to all United States ships anchored in Spanish ports, during which they are at liberty to depart."[8]

---

[1] Art. 15, U. S. Naval War Code; Proclamations and Decrees, p. 77. See Appendix, p. 405.

[2] 30 U. S. Sts. at Large, 1770.   [8] Proclamations and Decrees, p. 93.

§ 93. Pacific Blockade

Pacific blockade is a form of reprisal which consists in the blockading by one state of certain ports of another state without making war upon that state. In the conduct of blockades practice has varied greatly. In general, however, the vessels of states not parties to the dispute are not subject to seizure. Such vessels are liable to arrest by a ship of the blockading squadron under ordinary proof of identity. Whether vessels under the flag of the blockading party are liable to other inconveniences or to any penalty is not defined by practice or opinion of jurists.

"The Institute of International Law in 1886 provided that pacific blockade should be allowed provided that the vessels of the blockaded party only were detained; that pacific blockade should be one which could in general not bind the vessels of third powers. From the nature of pacific blockade as an act short of war, its consequences should be limited to the parties concerned. The pacific blockade of 1886 extended only to vessels flying the Greek flag, but the admirals of the Great Powers in the blockade of Crete in 1897 endeavoured to control other than Greek troops and merchandise for the Greek troops within the island. As no case arose, the question cannot be regarded as settled.

The provisions of the pacific blockade of 1897 were as follows : —

"The blockade will be general under the Greek flag.

¹ Parl. Papers, Greece.

"Ships of the six powers or neutral may enter into the ports occupied by the powers and land their merchandise, but only if it is not for the Greek troops or the interior of the island. These ships may be visited by the ships of the international fleets.

"The limits of the blockade are comprised between 23° 24' and 26° 30' longitude east of Greenwich, and 35° 48' and 34° 45' north latitude."[1]

The Secretary of State of the United States, in acknowledging the receipt of the notification of the action of the powers, said, "I confine myself to taking note of the communication, not conceding the right to make such a blockade as that referred to in your communication, and reserving the consideration of all international rights and of any question which may in any way affect the commerce or interests of the United States."[2] The weight of authority supports the position of the United States.

The first attempt to establish a blockade without resorting to war was in 1827, when Great Britain, France, and Russia blockaded the coasts of Greece with a view to putting pressure upon the Sultan, its nominal ruler. Since that time there have been pacific blockades varying in nature: blockade of Tagus by France, 1831; New Granada by England, 1836; Mexico by France, 1838; La Plata by France, 1838 to 1840; La Plata by France and England, 1845 to 1848; Greece by England, 1850; Formosa by France, 1884; Greece by Great Britain, Germany, Austria, Italy, and Russia, 1886; Zanzibar by Portugal, 1888; and Crete by Great Britain, Germany,

---

[1] The *London Gazette*, March 19, 1897.
[2] U. S. For. Rel., 1897, p. 255.

Austria, France, Italy, and those ...
instances it may be deduced ...
a legitimate means of constrai ...
those states parties to the ...
consequences, (3) that it ma...
advisable to resort to pacific ...
the more serious resort to war a...
parties to the pacific ...
to observe it, though their ...
they are required to establish ...
nary manner.   To determine ...
the so-called " right of appeal ...

PART IV

INTERNATIONAL LAW O

CHAPTER XVI

WAR

§ 94. Definition

Gentilis, one of the earliest writers on the laws of war, defined war in 1588 as "a properly conducted contest of armed public forces."[1] The nature of such contests varied with circumstances, and wars were, accordingly, classified by early writers as public, private, mixed, etc., distinctions that now have little more than historical value.[2] Wars are now sometimes classified as international and civil.

§ 95. Commencement

It is now assumed that peace is the normal relation of states. When these relations become strained it is customary for one or both of the states to indicate this

---

[1] "De Jure Belli," I., II., "Bellum est publicorum armorum justa contentio;" Instr. U. S. Armies, § 20.

[2] Halleck, Ch. XIV.; Calvo, § 1866 ff.

229

condition by discontinuing some of the means of peaceful intercommunication, or by some act short of war. The withdrawal of a diplomatic representative, an embargo, or any similar action does not mark the commencement of war. War commences with the first act of hostilities, unless a declaration fixes an earlier date, and in case of a declaration subsequent to the first act of hostilities, war dates from the first act. A proclamation of the blockade of Cuban ports preceded the declaration of war between Spain and the United States in 1898.[1] Similarly, hostilities were begun before the declaration of war between China and Japan in 1894.[2] Indeed, few of the wars of the last two centuries have been declared before the outbreak of hostilities, and many have not been declared formally at all. Declaration at the present time is usually but a formal acknowledgment of a well-known fact. In the case of the war in South Africa, early in October, 1899, the government of the Transvaal requested the government of Great Britain to give "an immediate and affirmative answer" not later than 5 P.M. on October 11th to certain questions in the accompanying ultimatum as to settling differences by arbitration, the withdrawal of British troops, etc., stating that if the answer was not satisfactory, it would be regarded as "a formal declaration of war." The government of Great Britian replied that the conditions demanded were such that the government deemed it impossible to discuss them. Hostilities immediately followed.

Civil war naturally is not preceded by a declaration, but exists from the time of the recognition of the

[1] 30 U. S. Sts. at Large, 1769, 1776.   [2] Takahashi, 42 et seq.

belligerency by an outside state, or from the date
when the parent state engaged in some act of war
against the insurgent party.[1] In the case of the Civil
War in the United States, the proclamation of blockade
of the Southern ports by President Lincoln was held
to be sufficient acknowledgment of a state of war.[2]

§ 96. Declaration

In ancient times wars between states were entered
upon with great formality. A herald whose person
was inviolate brought the challenge, or formal declaration, which received reply with due formality. At
the beginning of the eighteenth century this practice had
become unusual, and in the days of Vattel (1714–1767)
the theory of the necessity of a formal declaration was
set aside. It was, however, maintained that a proclamation or manifesto should be issued for the information of the subjects of the states parties to the war, and
for the information of neutrals. The practice is now generally followed, and may be regarded as obligatory.[3]
Such action is reasonable in view of the changes which
a state of war brings about in the relations of the
parties concerned, and of neutrals. The proclamations
usually specify the date from which the war begins, and
hence have weight in determining the nature of acts
prior to the proclamation, as the legal effects of war
date from the first act of hostilities if the proclamation
does not fix an earlier date. The constitution of a state,

[1] Prize Cases, 2 Black, U. S. 635.
[2] Takahashi, 38 et seq.
[3] Calvo, § 1910.

written or unwritten, determines in what hands the right to declare war shall rest, *e.g.* in the United States in Congress.

By act of the United States Congress of April 25, 1898,[1] it was declared : —

"First, That war be, and the same is hereby, declared to exist, and that war has existed since the twenty-first day of April, *Anno Domini* eighteen hundred and ninety eight, including said day, between the United States of America and the Kingdom of Spain.

"Second, That the President of the United States be, and he hereby is, directed and empowered to use the entire land and naval forces of the United States, and to call into the actual service of the United States the militia of the several States, to such extent as may be necessary to carry this Act into effect."[2]

§ 97. Object

The object of war may be considered from two points of view, the political and the military. International law cannot determine the limits of just objects for which a state may engage in war. Politically the objects have covered a wide range, though there is a growing tendency to limit the number of objects for which a state may go to war. It is generally held that self-preservation is a proper object, but as each state must decide for itself what threatens its existence and well-being, even this object may be very broadly interpreted. History shows that it has not been difficult

[1] 30 U. S. Sts. at Large, 364.

[2] The French declaration of war against Prussia in 1870 is given in 2 Lorrimer, 443.

from the political point of view to find an object of war when the inclination was present in the state. The nominal are often not the real objects, and the changing conditions during the progress of the war may make the final objects quite different from the initial objects. The simple cost of carrying on hostilities sometimes changes the conditions upon which peace can be made. The classification of causes and objects formerly made have little weight in determining whether a state will enter upon war. The questions of policy and conformity to current standards are the main ones at the present time.

The object of war in the military sense "is a renewed state of peace,"[1] or as stated in the English manual, "to procure the complete submission of the enemy at the earliest possible period with the least possible expenditure of men and money." The "Institute of International Law," Oxford session of 1880, gave as a general principle that the only legitimate end that a state may have in war is to weaken the military strength of the enemy.[2]

§ 98. General Effects

The general and immediate effects of war are : —

(a) To suspend all non-hostile intercourse between the states parties to the war.

(b) To suspend the ordinary non-hostile intercourse between the citizens of the states parties to the war.

(c) To introduce new principles in the intercourse of the states parties to the war with third states. These impose new duties upon neutrals and allies.

[1] Inst. U. S. Armies, § 29; Appendix p. 338. [2] Appendix, p. 369.

(*d*) To abrogate or suspend certain treaties : —

(1) To abrogate those treaties which can have force only in time of peace, *e.g.* of amity, commerce, navigation, etc.

(2) To suspend those treaties which are permanent and naturally revive at the end of the war, *e.g.* of boundaries, public debts, etc.

(3) To bring into operation treaties concerning the conduct of hostilities.

The Convention with Respect to the Laws and Customs of War on Land, signed at the Hague on July 29, 1899, and proclaimed for the United States, April 11, 1902, in a measure supplants all other codifications and rules upon this subject. In cases for which the Convention provides the signatory powers are thereby bound ;

" in cases not included in the Regulations adopted by them populations and belligerents remain under the protection and empire of the principles of international law as they result from the usages established between civilized nations, from the laws of humanity, and the requirement of the public conscience." [1]

The provisions are to become binding upon the contracting states, and are to be made the regulations for their armed land forces. Non-signatory states may adhere to the Convention upon giving proper notification.[2] This Convention has been so widely adopted that it may be said to be generally binding for the subjects of which it treats.[3] Earlier codes and orders must be consulted for subjects not contained in the Hague Convention. These will be found in the Appendices.

[1] Preliminary Declaration, Appendix, p. 464.   [2] *Ibid.*, p. 465.
        [3] List of Signatory States, *ibid.*, p. 465.

CHAPTER XVII

§ 99. Persons affected by War

(*a*) By the strict theory of war "the **subjects of enemy states** are enemies."[1] The treatment of the subjects of enemy states is not, however, determined by the allegiance alone, but in part by conduct and in part by domicile of the subject.

(*b*) The **subjects of neutral states** are affected by their relations to the hostile states as established by their own government, as determined by their conduct, and as determined by their domicile.

(*c*) By conduct persons are divided into **combatants** and **non-combatants,** according as they do or do not participate in the hostilities. The status of such persons may be further modified by domicile or by political allegiance.

§ 100. Combatants

Combatants in the full sense are the regularly authorized military and naval forces of the states. They are liable to the risks and entitled to the immunities of warfare, and if captured become prisoners of war.

[1] Hall, § 126, p. 405; Instr. U. S. Armies, §§ 20, 21, 22; **Appendix,** pp. 336, 337.

(*a*) The **status of combatants** is also **allowed** to two classes which engage in defensive hostilities : —

(1) The officers and crew of a merchant vessel which defends itself by force are liable to capture as prisoners of war.

(2) With regard to *levies en masse* much difference of opinion exists. Article 10 of the Declaration of Brussels, 1874, was adopted at the Hague Conference in 1899, and may be considered as representing a generally accepted position, namely, " The population of a non-occupied territory, who, on the approach of the enemy, of their own accord take up arms to resist the invading troops, without having had time to organize themselves in conformity with Article 9 [providing for responsible leader, uniform, etc.], shall be considered as belligerents, if they respect the laws and customs of war." [1]

(*b*) The **status of combatants** is **not allowable** for those who, without state authorization, engage in aggressive hostilities.

(1) When in the time of war the officers and crew of a merchant vessel attack another merchant vessel, they are liable to punishment according to the nature of their acts, and the state to which they owe allegiance is only indirectly responsible, nor can they claim its protection.

(2) When bands of men without state authorization and control, such as guerrilla troops or private persons, engage in offensive hostilities, they are liable to the same treatment as above mentioned.

(3) Spies are those who, acting secretly or under

[1] See Appendix, p. 386.

false pretenses, collect or seek to collect information in the districts occupied by the enemy, with the intention of communicating it to the opposing force.[1] Such agents are not forbidden, but are liable to such treatment as the laws of the capturing army may prescribe. This may be death by hanging. The office of spy is not necessarily dishonorable.

§ 101. Non-combatants

Non-combatants include those who do not participate in the hostilities. In practice this status is generally conceded to women, children, clergy, scientists, artists, professional men, laborers, etc., who make no resistance, whether subjects of the state or not. These are, of course, liable to the hardships consequent upon war.

(a) When the armed forces of one state obtain authority over territory previously occupied by the other state, the non-combatant population is free from all violence or constraint other than that required by military necessity. They are liable, however, to the burdens imposed by civilized warfare.

(b) Subjects of one of the belligerent states sojourning within the jurisdiction of the other were in early times detained as prisoners. While Grotius (1625) allows this on the ground of weakening the forces of the enemy,[2] and while Ayala had earlier (1597) sanctioned it,[3] Bynkershoek, writing in 1737, mentions it as a right seldom used. The detention of English tourists by

[1] Appendix, pp. 353, 372, 388.
[2] "De Jure Belli," III., ix., 4.
[3] "De Jure et Officiis Bellicis," I., v., 25.

Napoleon in 1803 was not in accord with modern usage. During the eighteenth century, the custom was to secure, by treaty stipulation, a fixed time after the outbreak of hostilities during which enemy subjects might withdraw. While similar provisions are inserted in many treaties of the nineteenth century, the practice may be said to be so well established that, in absence of treaty stipulations, a reasonable time would be allowed for withdrawal. A large number of treaties of the nineteenth century have provisions to the effect of Article XXVI. of the treaty between the United States and Great Britain of 1795 : " The merchants and others of each of the two nations residing in the dominions of the other shall have the privilege of remaining and continuing their trade, so long as they live peaceably and commit no offense against the laws ; and in case their conduct should render them suspected, and their respective Governments should think proper to order them to remove, the term of twelve months from the publication of the order shall be allowed them for that purpose, to remove with their families, effects, and property." This custom of allowing enemy subjects to remain during good behavior has become common, but can hardly be called a rule of international law. Persons thus allowed to remain are generally treated as neutrals, though in the case of Alcinous v. Nigreu[1] it was held that an enemy subject, residing in England without a license, could not maintain an action for breach of contract, though the contract which had been entered into before the war was valid and might be enforced when peace was restored.

[1] 4 Ellis and Blackburn's Reports, 217.

CHAPTER XVIII

§ 102. Public Property of the Enemy

Formerly the public property of the enemy, whatever its nature, was regarded as hostile, and liable to seizure. Practice of modern times has gradually become less extreme, and the attitude of the powers in restoring the works of art which Napoleon had brought to Paris shows the sentiment early in the nineteenth century. The practice in regard to public property of the enemy has now become fairly defined.

The public property of one belligerent state within the territory of the other at the outbreak of war, if real property, may be administered during the war for the benefit of the local state ; if movable, it is liable to confiscation. Works of art, scientific and educational property, and the like are, however, exempt.[1] The Treaty of Aug. 20, 1890, between Great Britain and France, exempts public vessels employed in the postal service.

In case one belligerent by military occupation acquires authority over territory formerly within the

---

[1] Appendix, pp. 340, 385.

jurisdiction of the other, the rules of the Hague Conference of 1899 provide as follows : —

"ART. 53. An army of occupation can only take possession of the cash, funds, and property liable to requisition belonging strictly to the State, depots of arms, means of transport, stores and supplies, and generally, all movable property of the State which may be used for military operations.

"Railway plant, land telegraphs, telephones, steamers, and other ships, apart from cases governed by maritime law, as well as depots of arms and, generally, all kinds of war material, even though belonging to Companies or to private persons, are likewise material which may serve for military operations, but they must be restored at the conclusion of peace, and indemnities paid for them."

"ART. 55. The occupying state shall only be regarded as administrator and usufructuary of public buildings, real property, forests, and agricultural works belonging to the hostile State, and situated in the occupied country. It must protect the capital of these properties, and administer it according to the rules of usufruct.

"ART. 56. The property of communes, that of religious, charitable, and educational institutions, and those of arts and science, even when State property, shall be treated as private property.

"All seizure of, and destruction or intentional damage done to such institutions, to historical monuments, works of art or science, is prohibited, and should be made the subject of proceedings." [1]

§ 103. Real Property of Enemy Subjects

The real property of the subject of one belligerent situated within the territory of the other belligerent was in early times appropriated by the state, later prac-

[1] Holls, "Hague Peace Conference," 451, and Appendix, p. 477.

tice administered it during the war, for the benefit of the state; but at present it is treated as the real property of any non-hostile foreigner.

It is generally conceded that real property of the subjects of either state is unaffected by hostile occupation by the forces of the other state, except so far as the necessities of warfare may require.[1]

§ 104. Personal Property of Enemy Subjects

The *movable property* of the subject of one of the belligerent states in the territory of the other belligerent state was until comparatively recent times appropriated. In the case of Brown *v.* United States,[2] in 1814, the Supreme Court held that the "existence of war gave the right to confiscate, yet did not of itself and without more, operate as a confiscation of the property of an enemy," though it further held that the court could not condemn such property unless there was a legislative act authorizing the confiscation. Many modern treaties provide that in case of war between the parties to the treaties subjects of each state may remain in the other, "and shall be respected and maintained in the full and undisturbed enjoyment of their personal liberty and property so long as they conduct themselves peaceably and properly, and commit no offense against the laws."[3] The most recent practice has been to exempt personal property of the subject of one belligerent state from all molestation, even though it was within the territory of the other at the outbreak

[1] Appendix, pp. 339, 385.   [2] 8 Cr., 110.
[3] See Index U. S. Treaties, " Reciprocal Privileges of Citizens."

R

of war.   Of course, such property is liable to the taxes,
etc., imposed upon others not enemy subjects.

In case of hostile occupation, the Hague Conference
of 1899 summarized the rules as follows : —

"ART. 46. Private property cannot be confiscated.

"ART. 47. Pillage is formally prohibited.

"ART. 48. If, in the territory occupied, the occupant collects the taxes, dues, and tolls imposed for the benefit of the
State, he shall do it, so far as possible, in accordance with
the rules in existence and the assessment in force. . . .

"ART. 49. If . . . the occupant levies other money taxes
in the occupied territory, this can only be for military
necessities or the administration of such territory."

Articles 50, 51, 52, provide that burdens due to military
occupation shall be as equable as possible, and that payment
shall be made for contributions.[1]

The practice now is to exempt private property so
far as possible from the consequences of hostile occupation, and to take it only on the ground of reasonable
military necessity.[2]

With regard to one particular form of property, modern commercial relations as influenced by state credit
have been more powerful than theory or country.   The
stock in the *public debt* held by an enemy subject is
wholly exempt from seizure or sequestration, and practice even demands that interest must be paid to enemy
subjects during the continuance of the war.[3]

In case of belligerent occupation, contributions, requisitions, and other methods are sometimes resorted to in
supplying military needs.

[1] Holls, "Hague Peace Conference," 447, and Appendix, pp. 475, 476.
[2] Appendix, pp. 339, 377.
[3] Lawrence, § 198.

Contributions are money exactions in excess of taxes.[1] Contributions should be levied only by the general-in-chief.

Requisitions consist in payment in kind of such articles as are of use for the occupying forces, as food, clothes, horses, boats, compulsory labor, etc. Requisitions may be levied by subordinate commanders when there is immediate need, otherwise by superior officers. Such requisitions should not be in excess of need or of the resources of the region.

Receipts for the value of both contributions and requisitions should be given, in order that subsequent impositions may not be made without due knowledge, and in order that the sufferers may obtain due reparation from their own state on the conclusion of peace.

In naval warfare " reasonable requisitions for provisions and supplies essential at the time "[2] is allowed. Such requisitions may be enforced by bombardment if necessary. Contributions, however, cannot be exacted unless after actual and complete belligerent occupation, as by land forces. Contributions in the form of ransom to escape bombardment cannot be levied, as in such cases occupation is not a fact.[3]

Foraging is resorted to in cases where lack of time makes it inconvenient to obtain supplies by the usual process of requisition, and consists in the actual taking of provisions for men and animals by the troops themselves.

[1] 8 Whart., § 339.
[2] U. S. Naval War Code, Art. 4.   See Appendix, p. 401.
[3] Appendix, p. 401.

Booty commonly applies to military supplies seized from the enemy. In a more general sense it applies to all property of the enemy which is susceptible of appropriation. Such property passes to the state of the captor, and its disposition should be determined by that state.

CHAPTER XIX

§ 105. Vessels

Vessels may be classed as public, belonging to the state, and private, belonging to citizens of the state.

(a) **Public vessels** of a belligerent are liable to capture in any port or sea except in territorial waters of a neutral. The following public vessels are, however, exempt from capture unless they perform some hostile act : —

(1) Cartel ships commissioned for the exchange of prisoners.

(2) Vessels engaged exclusively in non-hostile scientific work and in exploration.[1]

(3) Hospital ships, properly designated and engaged exclusively in the care of the sick and wounded.

(b) **Private vessels** of the enemy are liable to capture in any port or sea except in territorial waters of a

---

[1] Appendix, p. 404.

245

neutral. The following private vessels are, however, exempt from capture unless they perform some hostile act: —

(1) Cartel ships.

(2) Vessels engaged in explorations and scientific work.

(3) Hospital ships.

(4) Small coast fishing vessels. This exemption is not allowed to deep sea fishing vessels.[1]

(5) Vessels of one of the belligerents in the ports of the other at the outbreak of hostilities are usually allowed a specified time in which to take cargo and depart. In the war between the United States and Spain, 1898, Spanish vessels were allowed thirty days in which to depart and were to be exempt on homeward voyage. Vessels sailing from Spain for the United States ports before the declaration of war were to be allowed to continue their voyages.[2] Spain allowed vessels of the United States five days in which to depart.[3] It did not prohibit the capture of such ships after departure. No provision was made for vessels sailing from the United States for Spanish ports before the declaration of war.

In the Prize Law of Japan, 1898, the following exemptions of enemy's vessels are made: —

" (1) Boats engaged in coast fisheries.

" (2) Ships engaged exclusively on a voyage of scientific discovery, philanthropy, or religious mission.

---

[1] Appendix, p. 404.   [2] Proclamation of April 26, 1898.
[3] Decree of April 23, 1898.

" (3) Vessels actually engaged in cartel service, and this even when they actually have prisoners on board.

" (4) Boats belonging to lighthouses." [1]

§ 106. Goods

In general all public goods found upon the seas outside of neutral jurisdiction are liable to capture. Works of art, historical and scientific collections are sometimes held to be exempt, and probably would not be captured.

Private hostile property at sea and not under the flag of a neutral is liable to capture unless such property consist of vessels, etc., exempt under § 105, (b).

Contraband of war under any flag, outside of neutral territory, and destined for the enemy, is liable to capture.

Neutral goods in the act of violating an established blockade may be captured.

Previous to the Treaty of Paris in 1856 great diversity in the treatment of maritime commerce prevailed. This treaty provided that : —

" The neutral flag covers enemy's goods, with the exception of contraband of war," and

" Neutral goods, with the exception of contraband of war, are not liable to capture under the enemy's flag." [2]

Nearly all the important states of the world acceded to these provisions except the United States

1 Takahashi, p. 178.   2 Appendix, p. 398.

... powers formally pro-
... these provisions in

... Telegraphic Cables

... telegraphic cables has
... great importance. Such a
... instrument of value in the
... of war. A convention of
... important states of the world
... agreed upon rules for the
... cables.[?] Article XV. of this
... "It is understood that the
... shall in no wise affect
... belligerents." The princi-
... seem to accord with Article 5
... Code of the United States, which

... are to be followed with regard to
... cables in time of war irrespective of

... telegraphic cables between points in the
... between the territory of the United
... enemy, are subject to such treatment
... war may require.
... telegraphic cables between the territory
... territory may be interrupted within
... jurisdiction of the enemy.

S. Proclamation, April 26, 1898; Spain, Decree of April 23,

Treaties U. S., p. 1170 ff.

" (c) Submarine telegraphic cables between two neutral territories shall be held inviolable and free from interruption." [1]

There is reason to believe that a submarine cable connecting the enemy's country with a neutral country is liable to such censorship as will render it neutral; and if this cannot be secured, it is liable to interruption outside of neutral jurisdiction, otherwise it might become a most dangerous organ of unneutral service.[2]

[1] U. S. Naval War Code, Art. 5. Appendix, p. 402.

[2] Captain C. H. Stockton, "Submarine Telegraph Cables in Time of War," Proceed. U. S. Naval Inst., Vol. XXIV., p. 451.

See discussion, Wilson, "Submarine Telegraphic Cables in their International Relations," Lectures U. S. Naval War College, 1901, also "The Report of the Inter-Departmental Committee on Cable Communication" to British Parliament, March, 1902.

CHAPTER XX[1]

§ 108. Belligerent Occupation

This is defined by the "Institute of International Law," Oxford, 1880, as follows : —

[1] For the discussion of the laws and customs of war, at The Hague Peace Conference, see Holls, 134 *et seq.*

" A territory is considered to be occupied, when, as the result of its invasion by an enemy's force, the State to which it belongs has ceased, in fact, to exercise its ordinary authority within it, and the invading State is alone in a position to maintain order. The extent and duration of the occupation are determined by the limits of space and time within which this state of things exists." [1]

The sovereignty of the occupied territory does not pass to the occupying state, but only the right to exercise the authority necessary for safety and operations of war. Belligerent occupation was formerly held to carry with it the right to full disposition of whatever appertained to the territory. During the nineteenth century it has been given a clearer definition. Belligerent occupation is a fact impairing the usual jurisdiction, but it does not transfer sovereignty.

In general the civil laws of the invaded state continue in force in so far as they do not affect the hostile occupant unfavorably. The regular judicial tribunals continue to act in cases not affecting the military occupation. Administrative officers continue to perform their functions in absence of orders to the contrary, though of course purely political officers would be limited in the exercise of their functions ; e.g. registrars of marriages, births, and deaths might act as usual, while the authority of a governor might be suspended. There is no doubt that the freedom of the press cannot be claimed, as this might bring grave consequences upon the occupying force.

The belligerent occupant may destroy or appropriate public property which may have a hostile purpose, as

[1] See Appendix, p. 375 ; also Hague Convention, p. 475.

forts, arms, armories, etc. The occupying force may enjoy the income from the public sources. Strictly private property should be inviolable, except so far as the necessity of war requires contrary action.

Means of transportation, railways, boats, etc., as of direct use in military operations, can be appropriated for the use of the invader. "Their destruction is forbidden, unless it be required by the necessities of war. They are restored, at the peace, in the state in which they then are."[1]

The invader is bound to give such measure of protection to the inhabitants of the occupied territory as he is able.[2]

Belligerent occupation begins when an invaded territory is effectively held by a military force.

§ 109. Forbidden Methods

In the conduct of hostilities certain methods of action and certain instruments are generally forbidden.

Deceit involving perfidy is forbidden.[3] As there are certain conventional agreements held to exist even between enemies, violations of these agreements remove from the violator the protection of the laws of war. On land it is not permitted to use the flag or uniform of the enemy for purposes of deceit.[4] Article 7 of the Naval War Code of the United States provides that "The use of false colors in war is forbidden, and when summoning a vessel to lie to, or before firing a

---

[1] Oxford Manual, 51 ; Appendix, p. 377.

[2] Appendix, pp. 341, 369, 391, 475, 476.

[3] Appendix, p. 370.

[4] Appendix, pp. 370, 387, 472.

gun in action, the national colors should be displayed by vessels of the United States."[1] Not all authorities agree in regard to the provision forbidding false colors, though agreeing upon the other provisions. The use of the conventional flag of truce, a white flag, or of the hospital flag, red cross on white ground, to cover military operations or supplies is forbidden.[2] Stratagems, such as feigned attacks, ambush, and deceit not involving perfidy are allowed.[3] Assassination by treachery is forbidden.[4]

"The bombardment, by a naval force, of unfortified and undefended towns, villages, or buildings is forbidden, except when such bombardment is incidental to the destruction of military or naval establishments, public depots of munitions of war, or vessels of war in port, or unless reasonable requisitions for provisions and supplies essential at the time to such naval vessel or vessels are forcibly withheld, in which case due notice of bombardment shall be given. The bombardment of unfortified and undefended towns and places for the non-payment of ransom is forbidden."[5]

By the declaration of the Hague Conference of 1898, "the contracting parties agree to prohibit, for a term of five years, the launching of projectiles and explosives from balloons or by other new methods of a similar nature."[6]

The use of poison, of projectiles or weapons inflicting unnecessary suffering, is prohibited.[7] The Hague Conference also declared against the "use of projectiles,

[1] Appendix, p. 402. [2] Appendix, pp. 370, 387.
[3] Appendix, p. 387. [4] Appendix, p. 364.
[5] U. S. Naval War Code, Art. 4; Appendix, p. 401.
[6] Holls, "Hague Peace Conference," 93 et seq., 455.
[7] Appendix, pp. 348, 370, 386, 387, 401.

the object of which is the diffusion of asphyxiating or deleterious gases."[1]

Retaliation, devastation, refusal of quarter, and other severe methods once resorted to are now generally forbidden, except as punishment for violation of the laws of war.

§ 110. Privateers

A private armed vessel owned and manned by private persons and under a state commission called a "letter of marque,"[2] is a privateer.

This method of carrying on hostilities has gradually met with less and less of favor.[3] From the early days of the fifteenth century neutrals were given commissions. Toward the end of the eighteenth century treaties and domestic laws gradually provided against this practice, though letters of marque were offered to foreigners by Mexico in 1845, and by the Confederate States in 1861–1865. These were not accepted, however, as such action had then come to be regarded as piracy by many states. Privateering of any kind, as Kent said, "under all the restrictions which have been adopted, is very liable to abuse. The object is not fame or chivalric warfare, but plunder and profit. The discipline of the crews is not apt to be of the highest order, and privateers are often guilty of enormous excesses, and become the scourge of neutral commerce. . . .

[1] See Holls, "Hague Peace Conference," 93 *et seq.*, 461.

[2] For form, see United States *v.* Baker, 5 Blatchford, 6 ; 2 Halleck, 110.

[3] See article of Dr. Stark on "Privateering," in Columbia University Publications (1897), Vol. VIII., No. 3.

Under the best regulations, the business tends to blunt the sense of private right, and to nourish a lawless and fierce spirit of rapacity."[1] The granting of letters of marque to private persons of either of the belligerent states was attended with grave evils, and, by the Declaration of Paris, 1856, "Privateering is, and remains, abolished."[2] This declaration was agreed to by the leading states of the world, with the exception of the United States, Spain, Mexico, Venezuela, and China. In the Spanish-American War of 1898 the United States formally announced that it would not resort to privateering.[3] Spain, while maintaining her right to issue letters of marque, declared the intention to organize for the present (May 8, 1898) a service of "auxiliary cruisers of the navy." The importance of the subject of privateering is now largely historical, as it is doubtful whether any civilized state would resort to this method of carrying on maritime war.

§ 111. Voluntary and Auxiliary Navy

The relations of private vessels to the state in time of war, which had been settled by the Declaration of Paris in 1856, was again made an issue by the act of Prussia in the Franco-German War. By a decree of July 24, 1870, the owners of vessels were invited to equip them for war and place them under the naval discipline. The officers and crews were to be furnished by the owners of the vessels, to wear naval uniform, to sail under the North-German flag, to take oath to the articles of war, and to receive certain premiums for

---

[1] 1 Kent Com., 97.   [2] Appendix, p. 398.
[3] Proclamation and Decrees (April 25, 1898), p. 77.

capture or destruction of the enemy's ships. The French authorities complained to the British that this was privateering in disguise and a violation of the Declaration of Paris. The law officers of the crown declared that there was a "substantial difference" between such a volunteer navy and a system of privateering, and that the action of Prussia was not contrary to the Declaration of Paris. With this position some authorities agree, while others dissent.[1] The weight of the act as a precedent is less on account of the fact that no ships of this navy ever put to sea. Similarly, the plan of Greece for a volunteer navy in 1897 was never put into operation.[2]

Russia, in view of possible hostilities with England in 1877–1878, accepted the offer of certain citizens to incorporate into the navy during the war vessels privately purchased and owned. Such vessels are still numbered in the "volunteer fleet," and though privately owned and managed are, since 1886, under the Admiralty. These vessels may easily be converted into cruisers, and are, so far as possible, favored with government service. There seems to be little question as to the propriety of such a relationship between the state and the vessels which may be used in war.

Still less open to objection is the plan adopted by Great Britain in 1887 and by the United States in 1892, by which these governments, through agreements with certain of their great steamship lines, could hire or purchase at a fixed price specified vessels for use in case of war. The construction of such vessels is subject to government approval, and certain subsidies are granted

[1] Hall, p. 547, § 181.   [2] R. D. I., IV., 695.

to these companies. In time of war both officers and men must belong to the public forces. The plans of Russia, Great Britain, and the United States have met with little criticism.[1]

§ 112. Capture and Ransom

For more than one hundred years the capture of private property at sea has been regarded with disfavor both on the continent of Europe and in America.

The attitude of the United States is shown by the provision in the Treaty with Prussia of 1785, whereby merchant vessels of either state are to pass "free and unmolested."[2] John Quincy Adams, in 1823, asked England, France, and Russia to exempt hostile private property from capture. The proposition was not accepted.[3] The United States withheld its approval of the Declaration of Paris of 1856 because private property was not exempted from capture. The resolution in the United States House of Representatives of Mr. Gillett of Massachusetts, of April 25, 1898, exempting merchant ships from capture, failed to pass, the argument being advanced that Spain had shown a lack of reciprocity. States in practice have attempted to introduce the principle of exemption of private property from capture, as at the inception of the Franco-German War in 1870. The voice of the publicists seems to be strongly in favor of exemption. By international law private property cannot be said to be exempt, though the feeling in favor of exemption is growing.

[1] See Act of May 10, 1892 ; 27 U. S. Sts. at Large, 27.
[2] Treaties of U. S., pp. 905, 906. [3] 3 Whart., § 342.

Article 11 of the Naval War Code of the United States provides that " The personnel of a merchant vessel of an enemy captured as a prize can be held, at the discretion of the captor, as witnesses, or as prisoners of war when by training or enrollment they are immediately available for the naval service of the enemy, or they may be released from detention or confinement." [1]

Passengers on such vessels should be treated with consideration and landed at a convenient port.[2]

Capture is complete when the hope of recovery has ceased and surrender has taken place. It was long held that twenty-four hours of possession constituted valid capture. In earlier times the capture was complete when the property seized was brought within the firm possession of the captor, as within a camp, fortress, fleet, etc. This rule seems to be more equable, as the effective possession is a better ground than the lapse of time.

The evidence of intention to capture must be shown by some act, such as the placing of a prize crew or prize master on board a captured vessel, though the vessel has been held to be under the control of the captor, even when by reason of the weather no one has been placed on board.[3]

The captor should bring his prize into port for adjudication by the court. The title to the prize immediately vests in the state, and is to be disposed of only by state authority. However, an enemy's vessel may be destroyed when it is no longer seaworthy, when it impedes unduly the progress of the capturing force, when

---

[1] Appendix, 403.   [2] Ibid.
[3] The " Grotius," 9 Cr., 368, 370.

its recapture is threatened by the enemy, when the capturing force is unable to place a sufficient prize crew on board without impairing too much its own efficiency, and when a port of the capturing force to which the prize may be brought is too far away.[1] The United States, in the War of 1812, directed its officers to destroy all the enemy's vessels captured, unless very valuable and near a port. This was necessary on account of the fewness of its forces.

Sometimes the original owner is allowed to ransom by repurchase property which has been captured. In such case the transaction is embodied in a "ransom bill," by which the master agrees that the owner will pay to the captor a certain sum of money. A duplicate copy of this bill serves as a safe-conduct for the ransomed vessel so long as there is no departure from its terms in regard to the course to be sailed, the ports to be entered, the time of sailing, etc. The contract is not violated when the ransomed vessel is driven from her course by stress of weather or by circumstances beyond her control.

The captor takes from the captured vessel a hostage for the fulfillment of the ransom contract. Should the captor's vessel be taken with the hostage and ransom bill on board by a vessel of the enemy, the ransom bill is discharged. The captor may bring suit in the courts of the captured vessel's state usually, though in England the process is by action of the imprisoned hostage to recover his freedom. Some of the European states forbid the practice, others limit it, and others, like the United States, allow ransom.

[1] See rules of the "Inst. of Int. Law," 1882; "Annuaire," 1883, p. 221.

§ 113. Postliminium

The word "postliminium" is derived from the Roman
Law idea that a person who had been captured and
afterwards returned within the boundaries of his own
state was restored to all his former rights, for *jus postliminium* supposes that the captive has never been absent.[1]
The attempt to incorporate this fiction into international law has obscured the fact for which it stands.
The fact is that the rights of an owner are suspended
by hostile occupation or capture. These rights revive
when the occupation or capture ceases to be effective.
The consequences of acts of the enemy involving the
capture while in the enemy's possession are not necessarily invalidated if these acts were within his competence by the laws recognized by civilized states. Thus
taxes paid during a hostile occupation or penalties for
crime imposed by the invader are held to discharge the
obligation as if imposed by the regular authorities.

When the restoration of the property or territory
which has been in the captor's possession is accomplished
by a party other than the owner, the service of restoration should receive proper acknowledgment as in other
cases of service. If territory is restored through the
coöperation of an ally, the conditions of the alliance will
determine the obligation of the original possessor.

Most states have definite rules as to the restoration
of ships, as well as other property, and the granting of
salvage. The United States provides that when any
vessel or other property already captured shall be recaptured, the same not having been condemned as prize

[1] Justinian, I., xii., 5.

before recapture, the court shall award salvage according to the circumstances of the case. If the captured property belonged to the United States, salvage and expenses shall be paid from the treasury of the United States; if to persons under the protection of the United States, salvage and expenses shall be paid by them on restoration; if to a foreigner, restoration shall be made upon such terms as by the law of his country would be required of a citizen of the United States under like circumstances of recapture; but, if there be no law, it shall be restored upon the payment of such salvage and expenses as the court may order. But these rules are not to contravene any treaty.[1] When the original crew of the vessel arise and take the vessel from their captors, it is called a rescue and the crew is not entitled to salvage. When an American ship, on a voyage to London in 1799, was captured by the French and afterward rescued by her crew, the British sailors working their passage to London in the ship were allowed salvage.[2]

While Prussia was in possession of a portion of France during the Franco-Prussian War of 1870, Prussia contracted with certain persons for a sale of a portion of the public forests in France. The purchasers paid for the privilege of felling the forests, but had not completed the cutting of the trees when the Prussian occupation ceased. The purchasers claimed that they had the right to complete their contract, but France maintained that her rights revived when the Prussian occupation ceased, and this position was accepted by

[1] U. S. Rev. Sts., § 4652.
[2] The "Two Friends," 1 C. Rob., 271.

Prussia in an additional article to the treaty of peace of Dec. 11, 1871.

§ 114. Prisoners and · their Treatment

" A prisoner of war is a public enemy armed or attached to the hostile army for active aid, who has fallen into the hands of the captor, either fighting or wounded, on the field, or in the hospital, by individual surrender, or capitulation. . . .   Citizens who accompany an army for whatever purpose, such as sutlers, editors, or reporters of journals, or contractors, if captured, may be made prisoners of war, and be detained as such." " All persons who are of particular and singular use and benefit to the hostile army or its government "[1] are liable to capture. Levies *en masse* are now treated as public enemies. Within recent years persons who by reason of their trades or training may be of special use to the enemy are included among those liable to capture ; as the personnel of captured merchantmen.[2]

It is now a fundamental principle of law that the treatment of a prisoner of war is not to be penal, unless the penalty is imposed for some act committed after his capture. A prisoner of war is subject to such restraint as is necessary for his safe custody. A prisoner of war may be killed while attempting to escape, but if recaptured no punishment other than such confinement as is necessary for his safe keeping is allowable.

[1] Instr. U. S. Armies, 50 ; Appendix, p. 344, 345.
[2] Appendix, pp. 403, 468.

(a) The refusal of **quarter** to prisoners of war is not now allowed. Those who have violated the laws of war or the principles of humanity are liable to **retaliation** as a measure of protective retribution only. It "shall only be resorted to after careful inquiry into the real occurrence, and the character of the misdeeds that may demand retribution." [1]

(b) **Internment.** "Prisoners of war may be interned in a town, fortress, camp, or any other locality, and bound not to go beyond certain fixed lines; but they can only be confined as an indispensable measure of safety." [2]

(c) **Employment.** "The state may utilize the labor of prisoners of war according to their rank and aptitude. Their tasks shall not be excessive and shall have nothing to do with the military operations. . . . The wages of the prisoners shall go towards improving their position, and the balance shall be paid them at the time of their release, after deducting the cost of their maintenance." [3]

(d) The **exchange** of prisoners of war is purely a voluntary act on the part of the states at war. This takes place under an agreement called a "cartel." The exchange is usually rank for rank, number for number, value for value, though it is sometimes necessary to agree upon certain conventional values where those of the same rank are not among the captives, as in 1862, when the United States exchanged a captain in the army for six privates, etc.

(e) Prisoners of war may be released **on parole,** which is a promise to do or to refrain from doing certain acts in consideration of the grant of freedom in

---

[1] Instr. U. S. Armies, 28. See Appendix, p. 338.
[2] Hague Convention, pp. 468, 477.   [3] *Ibid.*, p. 468.

other respects. The punishment for breach of parole is death if the person is again captured.[1]

(*f*) The **sick and wounded** taken in the field become prisoners of war. Their treatment is now generally determined by the provisions of the Geneva Convention of 1864. This convention provides for the neutralizing and protection of hospitals, ambulances, and those engaged in the care of the sick and wounded, and for distinctive marks for this service, particularly the Red Cross.[2]

(*g*) The Hague Convention provides for a **Bureau of Information** to answer inquiries, to preserve property found on battlefields or left by prisoners, etc.[3]

§ 115. Non-hostile Relations of Belligerents

(*a*) In time of war it is necessary that belligerents should have certain relations not strictly hostile. Negotiations are often opened under a **flag of truce.** In regard to this the Brussels Code, Article 43, provides: —

"An individual authorized by one of the belligerents to confer with the other on presenting himself with a white flag, accompanied by a trumpeter (bugler or drummer), or also by a flag-bearer, shall be recognized as the bearer of a flag of truce. He as well as the trumpeter (bugler or drummer), and the flag-bearer, who accompanies him, shall have the right of inviolability."

He may be accompanied, "if necessary, by a guide and an interpreter." A commander is not obliged to

[1] Instr U. S. Armies, 124. See, as to prisoners of war, Appendix, pp. 359, 381, 390.

[2] For details, see Geneva Convention, Appendix, p. 395; Holls, "Hague Peace Conference," 120 *et seq.* ; U. S. Naval War Code, Appendix, p. 406.

[3] Appendix, p. 470.

receive the bearer of a flag of truce, and may take necessary measures to prevent injury on account of his presence. He may be blindfolded, detained at an outpost, or be put under other restrictions. If the bearer take advantage of his privilege to spy upon the enemy, he is liable to treatment as a spy, though he may report such military information as he may acquire without effort on his own part. If a bearer present himself during active operations, firing need not necessarily cease, and the bearer is liable to such consequences as his act may bring upon himself.

"In operations afloat the senior officer alone is authorized to dispatch or to admit communication by flag of truce; a vessel in position to observe such a flag should communicate the fact promptly. The firing of a gun by the senior officer's vessel is generally understood as a warning not to approach nearer. The flag of truce should be met at a suitable distance by a boat or vessel in charge of a commissioned officer, having a white flag plainly displayed from the time of leaving until her return."[1]

(b) **Cartels** are agreements made to regulate intercourse during war. Such conventions may regulate postal and telegraphic communication, the reception of flags of truce, the exchange of prisoners, the care and treatment of the same and of the sick and wounded.

A cartel ship is a vessel sailing under a safe-conduct for the purpose of carrying exchanged prisoners. When thus employed the vessel is not subject to seizure, although this exemption does not extend to a voyage from one port to another in her own state for the sake of taking on prisoners. The immunity is lost if the

[1] "International Law," Naval War College, 2d ed., p. 93.

vessel departs from the strict line of service by engaging in ordinary commerce, transportation, or hostile acts.[1] Such a vessel may carry one gun for the purpose of salutes.

(c) **Passports, safe-conducts, and safeguards** are sometimes given in time of war.

A passport is a written permission given by the belligerent government or by its authorized agent to the subject of the enemy state to travel generally in belligerent territory.

A safe-conduct is a pass given to an enemy subject or to an enemy vessel, allowing passage between defined points. Safe-conducts are granted either by the government or by the officer in command of the region within which it is effective.[2]

A safeguard is a protection granted by a commanding officer either to person or property within his command. "Sometimes they are delivered to the parties whose persons or property are to be protected; at others they are posted upon the property itself, as upon a church, museum, library, public office, or private dwelling."[3] When the protection is enforced by a detail of men, this guard must use extreme measures, if necessary to fulfill their trust, and are themselves exempt from attack or capture by the enemy.

(d) **A license to trade** is a permission given by competent authority to the subject of that authority or to another to carry on trade even though there is a state of war. These licenses may be general or special. A general license grants to all the subjects of the

---

[1] The "Venus," 4 C. Rob., 355.   [2] Appendix, p. 352.
[3] 2 Halleck (3d ed.), 325.

enemy state or to all its own subjects the right to trade in specified places or in specified articles. A special license grants to a certain person the right to trade in the manner specified in his license. Neutrals may receive a license to trade in lines which otherwise would not be open to them.

A general license is granted by the head of the state. A special license may be granted by a subordinate, valid in the region which he commands so far as his subordinates are concerned. His superior officers are not necessarily bound by his act, however.[1]

It is held that a license must receive a reasonable construction. In general, fraud vitiates a license; it is not negotiable unless expressly made so; a fair compliance in regard to the terms as to goods is sufficient; a deviation from the prescribed course invalidates the license unless caused by stress of weather or by accident; and a delay in completing a voyage within the specified time invalidates the license unless caused by enemy or the elements.[2] When a license becomes void, the vessel is liable to the penalties which would fall upon it if it had committed the act without license.

(e) **The cessation of hostilities** for a time is sometimes brought about by agreement between the parties to the conflict. When this cessation is for a temporary or military end, and for a short time or within a limited area, it is usually termed a suspension of hostilities. When the cessation is quite general, for a considerable time, or for a political end, it is usually termed a truce or armistice.

[1] The "Sea Lion," 5 Wall., 630.　[2] Hall, § 196, pp. 575-578.

Acts of hostility done in ignorance of the existence of the cessation of hostilities are not violations of the agreement unless there has been negligence in conveying the information to the subordinates. Prisoners and property captured after the cessation in a given region must be restored. During the period of the truce, the commercial and personal intercourse between the opposing parties is under the same restrictions as during the active hostilities, unless there is provision to the contrary in the agreement. The relative position of the parties is supposed to be the same at the end of the truce as at the beginning.

Hall says, "The effect of truces and like agreements is therefore not only to put a stop to all directly offensive acts, but to interdict all acts tending to strengthen a belligerent which his enemy, apart from the agreement, would have been in a position to hinder."[1] Acts which the enemy would not have been in a position to hinder, even in the absence of a truce, are not necessarily interrupted by the agreement.[2]

The provisioning of a besieged place during a truce has been the subject of some difference of opinion. If the conditions of the truce are to be fair to the besieged party, that party must be allowed to bring in a supply of provisions equal to the consumption during the continuance of the truce.[3] At the present time this matter is usually provided for in the terms of the truce.

A truce or other form of cessation of hostilities, if for a definite time, comes to an end by the expiration of the

[1] § 192, p. 565.   [2] 2 Halleck (3d ed.), 314 et seq.
[3] Calvo, "Droit Int.," §§ 2440-2446.

time limit; if for an indefinite time, by notice from one party to the other, or is terminated by the violation of the conditions by either of the parties. A violation of a truce by an individual renders him liable to such punishment as his state may prescribe.[1]

(*f*) **A capitulation** is an agreement defining the conditions of surrender of military forces, places, or districts within the command of an officer. Such agreements are purely military and can have no political force. The capitulation agreed upon between Generals Sherman and Johnston, in 1865, was not sanctioned because it involved political provisions. By the capitulation of Santiago, July, 1898, the American commander agreed to transport the Spanish troops to Spain. The conditions involved in a capitulation may vary greatly, but at the present time it is usually possible to obtain the sanction of the political authority before entering upon an agreement, owing to the improved methods of communication. It is therefore hardly probable that the terms of capitulations will be set aside, as in the celebrated case of El Arisch, in 1800.[2] Agreements made by officers not possessing proper authority or made in excess of authority, are called *sponsions* or *sub spe rati*, and require ratification or acceptance by the state to render them effective.[3]

[1] 2 Halleck (3d ed.), 310 *et seq.*   [2] Lawrence, p. 453.
[3] See 1 Halleck (3d ed.), 277.

CHAPTER XXI

§ 116. Methods of Termination

War may come to an end, (1) by the complete submission of one of the parties to the conflict or by conquest, (2) by the cessation of hostilities between the parties to the conflict, or (3) by a treaty of peace duly concluded.[1]

The object of war in early times was often conquest, and the conflict ended only with the submission of one of the parties. This end is at present usually disavowed, and the object of war is proclaimed to be some purpose that will meet with as little disapproval as possible.[2] The conditions under which the war will be brought to an end will be in some measure determined by the object for which the war was undertaken.

§ 117. By Conquest

Conquest in the complete sense, as in the case of the *debellatio* of the Romans, is not now common. This

---

[1] Heffter-Geffcken, "Droit Int.," II., §§ 176–190.
[2] See above, § 97.

implies a submission of one of the parties without condition.   There have been examples of absorption of the sovereignty of the vanquished state in recent times, as in the Prussian Decree of Sept. 20, 1866, by which conquered Hanover, Hesse, Nassau, and Frankfort were incorporated into the Prussian state.   Similarly, some of the Italian states were absorbed by the kingdom of Italy after the Treaty of Villafranca, 1859, and Madagascar became a part of France in 1896.

Conquest is held to be complete when the fact is evident from actual, continued, and recognized possession. All of these evidences may not be present in a given case, but if the intention and the fact of the conquest and the submission are fully shown, it is sufficient to constitute validity.[1]

§ 118. By Cessation of Hostilities

Certain wars have terminated by the simple cessation of hostilities.   Cases of such termination are rare. Such a method leaves in doubt the relations of the parties to the conflict, and occasions inconvenience to all states which may have intercourse with the contestants.   The war between Sweden and Poland in 1716, and also the war between France and Spain in 1720, came to an end in this way.   The war between Spain and her American colonies ceased in 1825, but no diplomatic relations were established with them till 1840, and the independence of Venezuela was not recognized till 1850.   After the hostilities between France and Mexico, 1862–1867, no diplomatic relations were

[1] Case of Hesse Cassel, Hall, § 204, p. 588.

entered into till 1881. It is only fair to neutrals that a declaration of the conclusion of hostilities should be made.

§ 119. By Treaty of Peace

War is most often terminated by a treaty of peace, which is usually a diplomatic agreement upon the manner of cessation of hostilities and upon the conditions of the reëstablishment of friendly relations. In recent years such treaties have often been preceded by preliminary agreements. These are sometimes preceded by an armistice in order that the terms may not be changed from day to day by the current fortunes of war, as was the case in the discussions pending the Treaty of Westphalia in 1648. In the war between China and Japan, in 1894–1895, an agreement for the suspension of hostilities was made on March 30, 1895, but the treaty of peace was not signed till April 17th. These preliminary agreements may sometimes be made through the friendly offices of a third power, as in the protocol of Aug. 12, 1898, in regard to the suspension of hostilities between Spain and the United States. The ambassador of France acted for Spain.[1] These preliminary agreements can be concluded only by those persons delegated for the purpose, and they are as binding as any international agreement in the matters upon which they touch.

A treaty of peace usually covers, (1) the cessation of hostilities, (2) the subjects which have led to war,[2]

[1] 30 U. S. Sts. at Large, 1742.

[2] The Treaty of Ghent, Dec. 24, 1814, between U. S. and Great Britain is a marked exception. See Treaties of U. S., 399; Wheaton, "Hist. Int. Law," 585; Schurz, "Henry Clay," I., pp. 105 *et seq.*

(3) agreements for immunity for acts done during the war without sufficient authority or in excess of authority. Such acts might otherwise become bases for civil or criminal process. Acts not consequent upon the existence of war, but such as are actionable under the ordinary laws of the state, as for violation of private contract, ordinary debts, etc., are not included unless there is a direct stipulation to that effect. This immunity is commonly called amnesty. (4) Provision for the release of the prisoners of war is often included. (5) The renewal of former treaties is provided for in many peace agreements. (6) Special provision may be made for cession of territory, indemnity, boundaries, or other contingent points.[1]

A treaty of peace is usually held to be effective from the date of signature, or from the date set in the treaty. Provisions fixing the time at which hostilities shall cease at different points are common. Acts of war committed after the conclusion of peace or after the official notice of the termination of hostilities, are void.[2] The Treaty of Frankfort, 1871, provides that maritime captures not condemned at the conclusion of the war are not good prize.

" The general effect of a treaty of peace is to replace the belligerent countries in their normal relation to each other."[3] In case of no stipulations to the contrary, the doctrine of *uti possidetis* applies, by which the

[1] Treaty between Spain and U. S., Dec. 10, 1898; 30 U. S. Sts. at Large, 1754.

[2] Case of Swineherd, 1801, 1 Kent Com., 173, note (b); " Sophie," 1 Kent Com., 174; 6 C. Rob., 138.

[3] Hall, § 198, p. 579.

T

property and territory in the actual possession of either of the belligerents at the conclusion of the war vests in the one having possession.

Private rights suspended during the war revive on the conclusion of peace. Though it was once held that debts could be confiscated during war, this is now nowhere maintained.[1] In such cases the obligation revives on the conclusion of peace, and by the Statute of Limitations the period of the war is not reckoned in the time specified as the period at which debts become outlawed.[2]

[1] Treaties of U. S., 386. [2] Lawrence, § 239.

PART V

INTERNATIONAL LAW OF NEUTRALITY

CHAPTER XXII

DEFINITION AND HISTORY

§ 120. Definition

Neutrality is the relation which exists between states which take no part in the war and the belligerents. Impartial treatment of the belligerents is not necessarily neutrality. The modern idea of neutrality demands an entire absence of participation, direct or indirect, however impartial it may be.

§ 121. Forms of Neutrality and of Neutralization

The first form of neutrality is what was formerly known as perfect neutrality, in distinction from imperfect neutrality, which allowed a state to give to one of the belligerents such aid as it might have promised by treaty entered into before and without reference to the war. At the present time the only neutrality that is recognized is perfect, *i.e.* an entire absence of participation in the war. A second form of neutrality is commonly known as armed neutrality. This implies the existence of an understanding, on the part of some of the states not parties to the contest, in accordance with which they will resist by force certain acts which a belligerent may claim the right to perform. The armed neutralities of Feb. 28, 1780, and of Dec. 16, 1800, defended the principle of " free ships, free goods." [1]

Neutralization is an act by which, through a conventional agreement, the subject of the act is deprived of belligerent capacity to a specified extent. Neutralization may apply in various ways.

(1) *Neutralized states are bound to refrain from offensive hostilities,* and in consequence cannot make agreements which may demand such action. Thus it was recognized that Belgium itself, a neutralized state, could not guarantee the neutrality of Luxemburg in the Treaty of London, in 1867. Belgium is, however, a party to the Treaty of Berlin of 1885, agreeing to respect the neutrality of the Congo State. This agreement " to respect " does not carry with it the obligation to defend the neutrality of the Congo State.

The important instances of neutralization are those agreed upon by European powers. By the declaration signed at Vienna, March 20, 1815, the powers (Austria, France, Great Britain, Prussia, and Russia) " acknowledged that the general interest demands that the Helvetic States should enjoy the benefits of perpetual neutrality," and declared " that as soon as the Helvetic Diet should accede to the stipulations " prescribed, her

[1] Lawrence, p. 566.

neutrality should be guaranteed.[1] The Swiss Confederation acceded on the 27th of May, 1815, and the guaranteeing powers gave their acknowledgment on the 20th of November, 1815.[2] The powers also guaranteed the neutrality of a part of Savoy at the same time. The neutralization of Belgium is provided for by Article VII. of the Treaty of London, of Nov. 15, 1831, "Belgium, within the limits specified in Articles I., II., and IV., shall form an independent and perpetually Neutral State. It shall be bound to observe such Neutrality towards all other States."[3]

(2) *A portion of a state may be the subject of an act of neutralization*, as in the case of the islands of Corfu and Paxo by the Treaty of London, of March 29, 1864. By Article II., "The Courts of Great Britain, France, and Russia, in their character of Guaranteeing Powers of Greece declare, with the assent of the Courts of Austria and Prussia, that the Islands of Corfu and Paxo, as well as their Dependencies, shall, after their Union to the Hellenic Kingdom, enjoy the advantages of perpetual Neutrality. His Majesty the King of the Hellenes engages, on his part, to maintain such Neutrality."[4]

(3) *The neutralization of certain routes of commerc·* has often been the subject of convention. The United States guaranteed the "perfect neutrality" o· means of trans-isthmian transit when the State c· isw

---

[1] 1 Hertslet, 64.

[2] *Ibid.*, 370 ; see also "La Neutralité de Suisse" h. iw II., 636.

[3] 2 Hertslet, 863.

[4] Art. XXXV., Treaty of Dec. 12, 1846 :

Granada controlled the Isthmus of Panama in 1846. By the Treaty of 1867 with Nicaragua the United States guarantees "the neutrality and innocent use" of routes of communication across the state of Nicaragua.[1] The Nine Powers by the Convention of Constantinople, of Oct. 29, 1888, Great Britain making certain reservations, agree, by a conventional act upon "a definite system destined to guarantee at all times, and for all the powers, the free use of the Suez Maritime Canal."[2] Full provisions for the maintenance of the neutrality of the canal were adopted at this time also.

(4) *The Geneva Convention of* 1864 *neutralized persons and things* employed in the amelioration of the condition of the sick and wounded in the time of war.[3] At the present time hospital ships properly certified and designated by flags and by bands of color on the outside are neutralized by general practice.[4]

§ 122. History

Neutrality as now understood is of recent growth. In early times, and in general throughout the Middle Ages, the fear of retaliation alone deterred states from hostile action against belligerent states with which they were formally at peace. A belligerent in the prosecution of war might disregard the territorial, personal, or property rights in a neutral state without violation of the principles of public law then accepted.

[1] Art. XV., Treaty of Jan. 21, 1867 ; Treaties of U. S., 1784.
[2] Parl. Papers, 1889, Commercial, No. 2. See also Holland, "Studies in Int. Law," p. 216.
[3] Articles I. and II.; Appendix, pp. 395, 396.
[4] U. S. Naval War Code, § IV.; Appendix, p. 870.

A gradual formulation of principles which gave the basis of a more equable practice came through the custom of making treaty provisions in regard to the conduct of one of the parties when the other was at war with a third state. Thus it was usually provided that no aid should be given to the third state. By the end of the seventeenth century that which had formerly been a matter of treaty stipulation became quite generally accepted as a rule of action. Grotius, in 1625, gives only about a fourth of a short chapter to the consideration of the duties of the neutral toward the belligerents and the balance of the same chapter to the duties of belligerents toward those not parties to the war. Grotius maintains that " it is the duty of those who have no part in the war to do nothing which may favor the party having an unjust cause, or which may hinder the action of the one waging a just war, . . . and in a case of doubt to treat both belligerents alike, in permitting transit, in furnishing provisions to the troops, in refraining from assisting the besieged." [1] In Barbeyrac's note to Pufendorf, 1706, the discussion shows that the idea of neutrality is clearer, but still confused by the attempt to admit a variety of qualified forms by which a state may be neutral in some respects and not in others.[2] Bynkershoek in 1737 said, " I call those *non hostes* who are of neither party." [3] This statement of Bynkershoek furnishes a convenient starting-point for his successors. Vattel, in 1758, accepting this definition, also says that a state

[1] " De Jure Belli ac Pacis," Lib. III., C. XVI., iii., 1.
[2] " Le Droit de la Nature et des Gens," Liv. VIII., C. VI., vii., n. 2.
[3] " Quaestiones Juris Publici," I., ix.

may give such aid as has been promised in a treaty of alliance previously made with one of the states, and still preserve exact neutrality toward the other state.[1]

By Article XVII. of the Treaty of Amity and Commerce between the United States and France, in 1778, " It shall be lawful for the ships of war of either party, and privateers, freely to carry whithersoever they please the ships and goods taken from their enemies ; . . . on the contrary, no shelter or refuge shall be given in their ports to such as shall have made prize of the subjects, people or property of either of the parties," except when driven in by stress of weather. By Article XXII. of the same treaty, foreign privateers were not allowed to be fitted out or to sell their prizes in the ports of either party. In 1793 M. Genêt, the French minister, began to fit out privateers, to give commissions to citizens of the United States to cruise in the service of France against the British, and to set up prize courts in the French consulates. He justified himself under the provisions of the Treaty of 1778. His action threatened to bring the United States into war with Great Britain and led to the enunciation of the principles by the United States authorities, of which Canning in 1823 said, " If I wished for a guide in a system of neutrality, I should take that laid down by America in the days of the presidency of Washington and the secretaryship of Jefferson." [2] The President's Proclamation of Dec. 3, 1793, declares that, in the war of France and the European powers, " the duty and interest of the United States require that they should with sincerity and good faith adopt and pursue a con-

[1] " Droit des Gens," III., viii.   [2] 5 Speeches, 50.

duct friendly and impartial toward the belligerent powers."[1] While the Proclamation does not mention "neutrality," the orders and instructions issued in accordance with it use the word. By the Act of Congress of June 5, 1794, and by subsequent acts codified in 1818,[2] the United States assumed a position which marks an epoch in the history of neutrality. The principles then enunciated are the generally accepted rules of the present day. Great Britain passed similar enactments in 1819, and made these more definite and stringent by the Foreign Enlistment Act of 1870.[3]

§ 123. Declaration

In recent years it has become customary to issue proclamations of neutrality, or to make known the attitude of the state by some public announcement. This method publishes to other states and to the subjects of the state issuing the announcement the position which the state will take during the hostilities. Ordinarily some specifications as to what may be done during the war accompany the proclamation.

In the war between the United States and Spain in 1898, practically all the leading states of the world made known their neutrality. Germany, according to the custom in that state for twenty years preceding, made no public proclamation, but the neutrality of the Empire was announced less formally by the Emperor in a speech before the Reichstag. The British proclamation of April

---

[1] 1 Messages and Papers of the Presidents, 156.

[2] U. S. Rev. Sts., §§ 5281–5291, see Appendix, p. 417. For cases, see 1 Gould and Tucker, 990, and 2 *ibid.*, 627.

[3] 33 and 34 Vict., c. 90, p. 560. See also 2 Lorimer, 490.

23, 1898, is, however, a very full statement of the principles which are to be observed during the hostilities.[1]

A clause from the Russian Declaration of April 18, 1898, is an example of the announcement of the general fact of neutrality: "It is with keen regret that the Imperial Government witnesses an armed conflict between two states to which it is united by old friendship and deep sympathy. It is firmly resolved to observe with regard to these two belligerents a perfect and impartial neutrality."[2]

§ 124. Divisions

The relations between neutrals and belligerents naturally fall into two divisions : —

1. The relations between neutral states and belligerent states as states. These relations are determined by the respect for sovereignty, by international usage, and by treaties.

2. Relations between the states and individuals. These relations involve : —

> (1) Ordinary commerce.
> (2) Contraband.
> (3) Unneutral service.
> (4) Visit and search.
> (5) Convoy.
> (6) Blockade.
> (7) Continuous voyage.
> (8) Prize and prize courts.

[1] Proc. and Decrees during the war with Spain, p. 31.

[2] Proc. and Decrees during the war with Spain, p. 63. President Cleveland's neutrality proclamations as to the late war in Cuba are given in 29 U. S. Sts. at Large, 870, 881.

CHAPTER XXIII

RELATIONS OF NEUTRAL STATES AND BELLIG___
STATES

§ 125. General Principles of the ____ ____ ·States

Of the general principle W ____
of every independent state ____
other states are engaged ____
attribute of sovereignty ____
the right of a belligerent ____

¹ W____ ____

imminent danger is, however, not to be denied; otherwise these waters are open to belligerent ships of war only on condition that they observe the regulations prescribed by the neutral. Such regulations must of course be impartial. These regulations are now often announced in the proclamations of neutrality, as was the case in the war of the United States and Spain in 1898.

(d) Neutral territory may not be used as the base of military operations or for the organization or fitting out of warlike expeditions.

Sir W. Scott said in the case of the *Twee Gebroeders* that, "no proximate acts of war are in any manner to be allowed to originate on neutral grounds." [1] This would without doubt apply to filibustering expeditions. Many acts are of such nature as to make it impossible to determine whether this principle is violated until the actor is beyond the jurisdiction of the neutral. In such cases the neutral sovereignty is "violated constructively." [2] A second act of this kind might constitute the neutral territory a base of military operations.

It is difficult to distinguish in some cases between those expeditions which have a warlike character and those which cannot at the time of departure be so classed.

In 1828, during the revolution in Portugal, certain troops took refuge in England. In 1829 these men, unarmed but under military command, set out from Plymouth in unarmed vessels, ostensibly for Brazil. Arms for their use had been shipped elsewhere as merchandise. Off the island of Terceira, belonging to Portugal, they were stopped by English vessels within

[1] 3 C. Rob., 164.   [2] Hall, § 221, p. 627.

Portuguese waters, and taken back to a point a few hundred miles from the English Channel. The Portuguese then put into a French port. Most authorities are agreed that the expedition was warlike, but that the British ministers should have prevented the departure of the expedition from British waters where they had jurisdiction, instead of coercing it in Portuguese waters.[1]

During the Franco-German War of 1870 a large body of Frenchmen left New York in French vessels bound for France. These vessels also carried large quantities of rifles and cartridges. The Frenchmen were not organized, the arms were proper articles of commerce, and the two were not so related as to render them immediately effective for war. The American Secretary held that this was not a warlike expedition. In discussing this case Hall says, "The uncombined elements of an expedition may leave a neutral state in company with one another, provided they are incapable of proximate combination into an organized whole."[2]

In order, therefore, that an expedition may be warlike there must be an organized body of men, under military or naval direction, and intending to engage in war in the near future.

§ 127. Regulation of Neutral Relations

The relations between the belligerent and the neutral may in some respects be regulated by the neutral. Such regulations find expression in neutrality laws, in

[1] 3 Phillimore, 287-299.

[2] Hall, § 222, p. 631. For the case of the "Caroline," see Appendix, p. 434.

U

proclamations of neutrality, and in special regulations issued under exceptional circumstances or by joint agreement of several states.

(a) While it is admitted that the **belligerent troops** may not use the land of a neutral, yet the neutral is under obligation to offer asylum to those seeking refuge to escape death or captivity. It is the duty of a neutral state, within whose territory commands, or individuals, have taken refuge, to intern them at points as far removed as possible from the theater of war. Interned troops may be guarded in camps, or fortified places. The expenses occasioned by the internment are reimbursed to the neutral state by the belligerent state to whom the interned troops belong.[1]

(b) In general a belligerent vessel has the **right of asylum** in a neutral port. It may enter to escape the perils of the sea or to purchase provisions, and to make repairs indispensable to the continuance of the voyage. A vessel entering a neutral port after defeat by the enemy is not disarmed, as would be the case with land forces under similar conditions, though the neutral may prescribe the conditions of its sojourn and departure.[2]

(c) **Ordinary entry** depends upon the will of the neutral, and is subject to conditions imposed upon all belligerents alike.[3] These conditions usually allow a vessel to take on necessary provisions and supplies to enable her to reach the nearest home port. A regula-

[1] Appendix, pp. 357, 477.

[2] Perels, "Droit Maritime," § 39, p. 244. The Netherlands Proclamation of Neutrality prescribed, in 1898, that "If ships of war, pursued by the enemy, seek refuge within our territory, they shall liberate their prizes."

[3] 7 Attorney-generals' Opinions, 122.

tion of the Netherlands as to the vessels of the Spanish-American War of 1898 prescribes that "Coal shall not be supplied them so long as they are in possession of prizes," otherwise a supply sufficient to bring the vessel to a home port or to the port of an ally was allowed.

(*d*) **The time of sojourn** is usually limited to twenty-four hours, unless a longer time is necessary for taking on supplies, completing necessary repairs, or from stress of weather.   Regulations as to the time of departure of hostile vessels from a neutral port were quite fully outlined in President Grant's proclamations of Aug. 22 and of Oct. 8, 1870, during the Franco-Prussian War.[1] He declared that no vessel of war of either belligerent should leave the

"waters subject to the jurisdiction of the United States from which a vessel of the other belligerent . . . shall have previously departed, until after the expiration of at least twenty-four hours from the departure of such last-mentioned vessel beyond the jurisdiction of the United States. If any ship of war or privateer of either belligerent shall, after the time this notification takes effect, enter any . . . waters of the United States, such vessel shall be required . . . to put to sea within twenty-four hours after her entrance into such . . . waters, except in case of stress of weather or of her requiring provisions or things necessary for the subsistence of her crew, or for repairs; in either of which cases the authorities . . . shall require her to put to sea as soon as possible after the expiration of such period of twenty-four hours, without permitting her to take in supplies beyond what may be necessary for her immediate use ; and no such vessel . . . shall continue within such . . . waters . . . for a longer period than twenty-four hours

[1] As to the British Neutrality Regulations, see 2 Ferguson, Appendix F, p. 77 ; 2 Lorimer, 446.

after her necessary repairs shall have been completed, unless within such twenty-four hours a vessel . . . of the other belligerent, shall have departed therefrom, in which case the time limited for the departure . . . shall be extended so far as may be necessary to secure an interval not less than twenty-four hours between such departure and that of any . . . ship of the other belligerent which may have previously quit the same . . . waters. No ship of war . . . of either belligerent shall be detained in any . . . waters of the United States more than twenty-four hours, by reason of the successive departures from such . . . waters of more than one vessel of the other belligerent. But if there be several vessels of each or either of the two belligerents in the same . . . waters, the order of their departure therefrom shall be so arranged as to afford the opportunity of leaving alternately to the vessels of the respective belligerents, and to cause the least detention consistent with the objects of this proclamation. No ship of war . . . of either belligerent shall be permitted, while in any . . . waters within the jurisdiction of the United States, to take in any supplies except provisions and such other things as may be requisite for the subsistence of her crew, and except so much coal only as may be sufficient to carry such vessel, if without sail power, to the nearest European port of her own country; or in case the vessel is rigged to go under sail, and may also be propelled by steam power, then with half the quantity of coal which she would be entitled to receive if dependent upon steam alone; and no coal shall be again supplied to any such ship of war . . . in the same or in any other . . . waters of the United States, without special permission, until after the expiration of three months from the time when such coal may have been last supplied to her within the waters of the United States, unless such ship of war . . . shall, since last supplied, have entered a European port of the government to which she belongs." [1]

[1] 8 Whart., § 402; U. S. For. Rel., 1870.

The tendency at the present time is to make regulations which shall guard most effectively against any possible use of neutral maritime jurisdiction for hostile purposes. In the Spanish-American War of 1898, Brazil provided that in case of two belligerent vessels : — "If the vessel leaving, as well as that left behind, be a steamer, or both be sailing vessels, there shall remain the interval of twenty-four hours between the sailing of one and the other. If the one leaving be a sailing vessel and that remaining a steamer, the latter may only leave seventy-two hours thereafter."[1] Many states have adopted the practice of absolutely refusing entrance within their waters to belligerent vessels with prizes, except in case of distress. Some states prescribe that, in such cases, the prizes should be liberated. There are examples of this refusal in the neutrality proclamations of 1898. All forms of sale or disposal of prize in neutral jurisdiction is of course generally forbidden.

§ 128. No Direct Assistance by the Neutral

The neutral state may not furnish to a belligerent any assistance in military forces, supplies of war, loans of money, or in any similar manner.

(a) Formerly military assistance was often furnished to one of the belligerents by a state claiming to be neutral on the ground that such action was justified by a treaty obligation entered into before the war could be foreseen. This position was supported by

[1] Proc. and Decrees of the war with Spain, Brazil, XVI, p. 15.

some of the ablest of the authorities of the nineteenth century,[1] but is denied by the latest writers.

(b) It is generally held that a neutral state may not furnish to one or both of the belligerents **supplies of war**. As Hall says, "The general principle that a mercantile act is not a violation of a state of neutrality, is pressed too far when it is made to cover the sale of munitions or vessels of war by a state."[2]

A case that aroused discussion was occasioned by the action of the authorities of the United States conformably to a joint resolution of Congress of July 20, 1868, by which the Secretary of War was to cause " to be sold, after offer at public sale on thirty days' notice, . . . the old cannon, arms, and other ordnance stores . . . damaged or otherwise unsuitable for the United States military service, etc."[3] Complaint was made that sales made under this act during the time of the Franco-German War were in violation of neutrality. A committee appointed by the United States Senate to investigate these charges reported that sales " were not made under such circumstances as to violate the obligations of our government as a neutral power; and this, to recapitulate, for three reasons: (1) The Remingtons [the alleged purchasing agents of the French government] were not, in fact, agents of France during the time when sales were made to them; (2) if they were such agents, such fact was neither known nor suspected by our government at the time the sales were made; and (3) if they had been such

---

[1] Wheat., D., § 425; Dana, *contra*, note 208; 1 Kent Com., pp. 49, 116; Bluntschli, § 759; Woolsey, § 165.

[2] Hall, § 217, p. 621.   [3] 15 U. S. Sts. at Large, 259.

agents, and that fact had been known to our government, or if, instead of sending agents, Louis Napoleon or Frederick William had personally appeared at the War Department to purchase arms, it would have been lawful for us to sell to either of them, in pursuance of a national policy adopted by us prior to the commencement of hostilities."[1] This last statement does not accord with the best opinion and doubtless would not be maintained at the present time. The first and second claims might justify the sale, though it would be in better accord with a strict neutrality for a state to refrain from all sale of supplies of war during the period of war between two states, toward which states it professes to maintain a neutral attitude. This, of course, does not affect the rights of commerce in arms on the part of the citizens of a neutral state.

(c) The authorities are practically agreed that **loans of money** to a belligerent state may not be made or guaranteed by a neutral state. This does not, however, affect the commerce in money which may be carried on by the citizens of a neutral state.

(d) A neutral may not permit the **enlistment of troops** for belligerent service within its jurisdiction. This applies to such action as might assume the proportions of recruiting. The citizens or subjects of a neutral state may enter the service of one of the belligerents in a private manner.

§ 129. Positive Obligations of a Neutral State

Not only must a neutral state refrain from direct assistance of either belligerent, but it must also put

[1] 3 Whart., § 391.

forth positive efforts to prevent acts which would assist
a belligerent.   If a state has neutrality laws, it is under
obligations to enforce these laws, and is also under
obligation to see that the principles generally recognized by international law are observed.   Most states
make provision for the enforcement of neutrality.   In
the United States the President is authorized to employ
the land and naval forces or militia to execute the law.[1]
Jefferson said that, " If the United States have a right
to refuse the permission to arm vessels and raise men
within their ports and territories, they are bound by
the laws of neutrality to exercise that right, and to
prohibit such armaments and enlistments."[2]   There can
be no difference of opinion upon the proposition that
a neutral state is bound to restrain within its jurisdiction all overt acts of a character hostile to either
belligerent.

There are, however, many acts which in themselves
have no necessarily warlike character.   Whether such
acts are in violation of neutrality must be determined
by inference as to their purpose.   By such acts, as
Hall says, " the neutral sovereignty is only violated
constructively."[3]   These acts vary so much in character
and are of so wide a range that the determination of
their true nature often imposes severe burdens upon
the neutral attempting to prevent them.   The destination of a vessel that is in the course of construction
may determine its character so far as the laws of
neutrality are concerned.   If it is for a friendly state
which is at peace with all the world, no objection to

[1] U. S. Rev. Sts., § 5288.   [2] 1 Amer. State Papers, 116.
[3] p. 627, § 221.

its construction and sale can be raised. If a subject of a neutral state builds a vessel for one of the belligerents, such an act has sometimes been regarded as a legitimate business transaction, at other times as an act in violation of neutrality. As a business transaction, the vessel after leaving neutral territory is liable to the risk of seizure as contraband. As an act in violation of neutrality, the neutral state is bound to prevent the departure of the vessel by a reasonable amount of care. The line of demarcation which determines what acts a neutral state is under obligation to prevent, and what acts it may allow its subjects to perform at their own risk, is not yet clearly drawn. It is certain that a state is bound to use " due diligence " to prevent the violation of its neutrality. In the case of the *Alabama*,[1] this phrase was given different meanings by the representatives of the United States and Great Britain. The arbitrators declared that " due diligence " should be " in exact proportion to the risks to which either of the belligerents may be exposed from a failure to fulfil the obligations of neutrality on their part."[2] This definition is not satisfactory, and the measure of care required still depends upon the circumstances of each individual case, and is therefore a matter of doubt.

[1] See Appendix, p. 435.   [2] 3 Whart., § 402 *a*, p. 632.

CHAPTER XXIV

NEUTRAL RELATIONS BETWEEN STATES AND INDIVIDUALS

130. ORDINARY COMMERCE.
  (a) Destination.
  (b) Ownership of goods.
  (c) Nationality of vessel.
  (d) Declaration of Paris.

131. CONTRABAND.

132. PENALTY FOR CARRYING CONTRABAND.

133. UNNEUTRAL SERVICE.

134. VISIT AND SEARCH.
  (a) Right.
  (b) Object.
  (c) Method.
  (d) Ship's papers.
  (e) Grounds of seizure.
  (f) Seizure.

135. CONVOY.

136. BLOCKADE.
  (a) Historical.
  (b) Conditions of existence.
  (c) A war measure.
  (d) Who can declare.
  (e) Notification.
  (f) Must be effective.
  (g) Cessation.

137. VIOLATION OF BLOCKADE.

138. CONTINUOUS VOYAGES.

139. PRIZE AND PRIZE COURTS.

§ 130. Ordinary Commerce

As a general principle, subjects of a neutral state may carry on commerce in the time of war as in the time of peace. At the same time, owing to the fact of war, a belligerent has the right to take measures to reduce his opponent to subjection. The general right of the neutral and the special right of the belligerent come into opposition. The problem becomes one of "taking into consideration the respective rights of the belligerents and of the neutrals; rights of the belligerents to place their opponent beyond the power of resistance, but respecting the liberty and independence of the neutral in doing this; rights of the neutrals to maintain with each of the belligerents free commercial relations, without injury to the opponent of either."[1]

In regard to commerce in the time of war, the matters of destination, ownership of goods, and the nationality of the vessel have been the facts ordinarily determining the treatment by the belligerent. If there is nothing hostile in the destination of the commercial undertaking, in the nature of the goods, or in the means of transport, the commerce is free from interruption by the belligerent.

(a) The questions arising in regard to **destination** will naturally be treated under the subjects of blockade and continuous voyage.

(b) **The ownership of goods** has usually been a fact determining their liability to capture.

[1] Bonfils, "Droit Int. Public," § 1494 ff.; Despagnet, "Droit Int. Public," § 682 ff.; Investigation Chalmette Supply Camp, House Doc. 568, 57th Cong. U. S., 1902.

The rules of the *Consolato del Mare*, compiled in the thirteenth or fourteenth century, looked to the protection of the neutral vessel and the neutral goods on the one hand, and to the seizure of the enemy vessel and of the enemy goods on the other hand. The goods of an enemy could be seized under a neutral flag, and the goods of a neutral were free even though under an enemy flag. This doctrine considered mainly the character of the goods. These rules were held in favor till the sixteenth century, from which time the practice varied greatly, sometimes being regulated by treaty. In the sixteenth century France advanced the doctrine of *hostile contagion*, maintaining the principle of " enemy ships, enemy goods," and " enemy goods, enemy ships." [1] The practice of states was far from uniform in the various wars.

(*c*) **The nationality of the vessel** has been sometimes regarded as the sole fact determining liability of goods to capture, and at other times affecting only the vessel itself.

Under the rules of the *Consolato*, the flag determined the liability of the vessel only. Under the French ordinances, the flag contaminated the goods. From 1778, the doctrine that the neutral flag covered enemy goods became more commonly accepted. This was especially emphasized by the armed neutrality of 1780.

Some of the agreements of the United States will show the variety of practice even in recent times. By Art. XXIII. of the Treaty of 1778 with France it is provided, " that free ships shall also give a freedom to goods, and that everything shall be deemed to be free and exempt which shall be found on board the ships belonging

[1] Walker, " Science of Int. Law," p. 296.

to the subjects of either of the confederates, although
the whole lading or any part thereof should appertain to
the enemies of either, contraband goods being always
excepted." In the Treaty of 1785 with Prussia occurs
the following: "free vessels making free goods, inso-
much that all things shall be adjudged free which shall
be on board any vessel belonging to the neutral party,
although such things belong to an enemy of the other."
In the Treaty of 1795 with Spain is a similar provision,
excepting, however, contraband of war. It is asserted
in the Treaty of 1799 with Prussia that as the doctrine
of "free ships make free goods" has not been respected
"during the two last wars," and in the one "which
still continues," the contracting parties propose "after
the return of a general peace" to confer with other
nations and meantime to observe "the principles and
rules of the law of nations generally acknowledged."
The Treaty of 1819 with Spain interprets the clause of
the Treaty of 1795, in which it is stipulated that the
flag shall cover the property, by saying, "that this shall
be so understood with respect to those Powers who
recognize this principle; but if either of the two contracting parties shall be at war with a third party, and
the other neutral, the flag of the neutral shall cover
the property of enemies whose Government acknowledges this principle, and not of others." The Treaty
of 1794 with Great Britain expressly provides that
property of an enemy on a neutral vessel shall be good
prize. In 1887 it was agreed in the treaty with Peru
"that the stipulation in this article declaring that the
flag shall cover the property shall be understood as
applying to those nations only who recognize this prin-

ciple ; but if either of the contracting parties shall be
at war with a third, and the other shall remain neutral.
the flag of the neutral shall cover the property of enemies whose Governments acknowledge this principle,
and not that of others."[1]   In spite of these variations,
the practice of the United States has been much more
uniform than that of the states in which the foreign
relations have exercised a more direct influence.

(d) Since 1856 the principles enunciated in the
Declaration of Paris have generally prevailed.   The
provisions in regard to the flag and goods are : —

"2. The neutral flag covers enemy's goods, with the exception of contraband of war.

"3. Neutral goods, with the exception of contraband of
war, are not liable to capture under the enemy's flag."[2]

This agreement bound only those states which signed
it.   A few states, including the United States, Spain,
Mexico, Venezuela, and China, did not accede to these
provisions.   The United States declined because the
government desired a provision exempting all private
property at sea from capture.[3]   In the War of 1898, the
United States announced that the rules of the Declaration of Paris would be observed, and Spain made a similar announcement except as to the clause in regard to
privateering.[4]   Spain did not, however, make use of
privateers.   The goods of a neutral embarked in a
belligerent carrying vessel are liable to the damages

[1] See Treaties of U. S. under respective dates.

[2] See Appendix, p. 398.

[3] For the discussion of "the immunity of private property on the
high seas," at the Hague Peace Conference, see Holls, 306 *et seq*.

[4] Proclamations and Decrees during the war with Spain, pp. 77, 98.

or destruction which may be the consequence of necessary acts of war. Destruction not the result of such necessary acts would be in violation of the spirit of the Declaration of Paris, and the neutral might justly demand reparation.

The rules of the Declaration of Paris have been so generally accepted in practice that there is little possibility that they will be disregarded by the civilized states of the world.

§ 131. Contraband

Contraband is the term applied to those articles which from their usefulness in war a neutral cannot transport without risk of seizure. While a state is under obligation to prevent the fitting out of hostile expeditions and to refrain from furnishing belligerent ships warlike material, a state is not bound to prevent the traffic of its citizens or subjects in contraband of war. Such articles as are contraband may be seized on the high seas,[1] and by the Declaration of Paris are not protected by the neutral flag.[2]

Of the articles of commerce themselves, Grotius makes three general classes : —

"1. Those which have their sole use in war, such as arms."

"2. Those which have no use in war, as articles of luxury."

"3. Those which have use both in war and out of war, as money, provisions, ships, and those things appertaining to ships."[3]

[1] 3 Whart., § 391. [2] Appendix, p. 365.
[3] "De Jure Belli," Bk. III., Ch. i., 5; The "Petershoff," 5 Wall., 28, 58.

Grotius regards articles of the first class as hostile, of the second as not a matter of complaint, and of the third as of ambiguous use (*usus ancipitis*), of which the treatment is to be determined by their relation to the war.

While the general principle may be clear, the application of the principle is not simple. Those articles whose sole use is in war are, without question, contraband. Articles exclusively for peaceful use are not contraband. Between these two classes are many articles in regard to which both practice and theory have varied most widely.[1] The theorists have usually endeavored to give the neutral the largest possible liberty in commerce, on the ground that those who were not parties to the war should not bear its burdens. This has been the opinion most approved by the jurists of Continental Europe. Great Britain and the United States have been inclined to extend the range of articles which might on occasion be classed as contraband.

The attitude of the United States may be seen from the following enumeration of articles, which is practically the same as was declared contraband in the Spanish War of 1898 : —

"ABSOLUTELY CONTRABAND. —Ordnance; machine guns and their appliances and the parts thereof; armor plate and whatever pertains to the offensive and defensive armament of naval vessels; arms and instruments of iron, steel, brass, or copper, or of any other material, such arms and instruments being specially adapted for use in war by land or sea; torpedoes and their appurtenances; cases for mines, of whatever material; engineering and transport materials, such as gun carriages, caissons, cartridge boxes, campaign-

---

[1] Woolsey, "Int. Law," § 194.

ing forges, canteens, pontoons; ordnance stores; portable range finders; signal flags destined for naval use; amunition and explosives of all kinds and their component parts; machinery for the manufacture of arms and munitions of war; saltpeter; military accouterments and equipments of all sorts; horses and mules."

"CONDITIONALLY CONTRABAND. — Coal, when destined for a naval station, a port of call, or a ship or ships of the enemy; materials for the construction of railways or telegraphs: and money, when such materials or money are destined for the enemy's forces; provisions, when actually destined for the enemy's military or naval forces." [1]

The range of articles classed as contraband will naturally vary from time to time as changes in the method of carrying on war occur. Horses have usually been regarded as contraband by France, England, and the United States, except in their dealings with Russia, which state has always opposed this inclusion. The increasing importance of coal during the latter half of the nineteenth century has led to the policy of determination of its character by its destination. Provisions are in practically the same position as coal. [2] In the war with Spain in 1898, the United States included as absolute contraband, horses, and as conditionally contraband, coal, money, and provisions, which Spain did not mention. Spain mentioned by name sulphur, which the United States did not specify, though it might be included in some of the general classes. "As the supply of sulphur is chiefly obtained from Sicily, the Spanish government would have had a rare opportunity

---

[1] U. S. Naval War Code, Arts. 34, 36; Appendix, p. 412; see Propositions Institute Int. Law, Cambridge, 1895, §§ 3 and 4.

[2] The "Commercen," 1 Wheat., 382.

x

to seize and confiscate it as it passed through the Straits
of Gibraltar. But upon the request of the Italian government it . . . refrained from treating sulphur as contraband." [1]

§ 132. Penalty for Carrying Contraband

No penalty attaches to the simple act of transportation of contraband.   It is the hostile destination of the
goods that renders them liable to penalty and the
vessel liable to delay or other consequences according
to circumstances.

The general rules are as follows : —

1. When the ship and the contraband cargo belong to
the same owner, both are liable to be condemned.

2. When the ship and the contraband cargo belong
to different owners, the cargo only is liable to be
condemned.

3. When the owner of the cargo is also part owner
of the ship, it has been held that his part of the ship is
also liable to be condemned.[2]

4. When non-contraband goods on the ship belong
to the same owner with the contraband goods, it
has been held that these goods are also liable to be
condemned.   " To escape from the contagion of contraband, the innocent articles must be the property of a
different owner." [3]

5. A vessel which would otherwise be free when
carrying contraband may become liable to condemna-

[1] See article of John Bassett Moore in *Review of Reviews*, May,
1899.

[2] The " Jonge Tobias," 1 C. Rob. 329.

[3] The " Staadt Embden," 1 C. Rob. 26 ; Takahashi, p. 94.

tion on account of fraud. Such fraud may consist in bearing false papers or claiming a false destination.

6. In certain instances, vessels have been held liable to condemnation because carrying articles which by treaty between the state of the captor and the state of the carrier are specially forbidden.

As Perels maintains, it is difficult to see how the fourth rule can be enforced consistently with the Declaration of Paris, by which they would be exempt even if belonging to the enemy.[1]

The neutral carrier loses freight on the contraband goods and suffers such inconvenience and delay as the bringing in of the contraband and its adjudication in a proper court may entail.

Under special circumstances goods have been treated as liable to preëmption instead of absolute seizure. Of this Hall says, "In strictness every article which is either necessarily contraband, or which has become so from the special circumstances of war, is liable to confiscation; but it is usual for those nations who vary their list of contraband to subject the latter class to preëmption only, which by the English practice means purchase of the merchandise at its mercantile value, together with a reasonable profit, usually calculated at ten per cent on the amount."[2] This practice is not viewed with favor upon the Continent as indicating a departure from the generally accepted practice.[3]

[1] Perels, "Manuel Droit Maritime," § 46, p. 283.

[2] p. 690, § 247.

[3] In some cases, belligerents exercise the so-called right of using or destroying neutral property on the plea of necessity, giving compensation. This practice is called "angary" or "prestation," and is by most jurists either condemned or regarded with disfavor. An illustra-

§ 133. Unneutral Service

Unneutral service differs from the carriage of contraband, particularly in being hostile in its nature and involving a participation in the contest.   Such service involves assistance in the performance of warlike acts. While the destination is a question of vital importance in the case of contraband, the intent of the act is a matter of highest importance in cases of unneutral service.

.The acts generally regarded as in the category of unneutral service are : —

1. The carriage of enemy dispatches.

2. The carriage of certain belligerent persons.

3. Aid by auxiliary coal, repair, supply, or transpoi ships.

4. Knowing coöperation in the transmission of cer tain messages and information to the belligerent.

(1) Of the *carriage of dispatches*, in the case of tht *Atalanta*, Lord Stowell said : —

" How is the intercourse between the mother country and the colonies kept up in the time of peace ? By ships of war or by packets in the service of the state. If a war intervenes, and the other belligerent prevails to interrupt that communication, any person stepping in to lend himself to

tion is the sinking, during the Franco-Prussian War of 1870, by the Germans, of several British merchant ships in the Seine to prevent French gunboats from going up the river.   During the same war; the Germans seized in Alsace. for military purposes. certain railway carriages of the Central Swiss Railway and certain Austrian rolling stock, all of which remained in the possession of the Germans for some time. See Lawrence, § 252 ; Hall, p. 765, § 278. See Appendix, p. 402.

effect the same purpose, under the privilege of an ostensible neutral character, does in fact place himself in the service of the enemy state." [1]

"A neutral vessel carrying hostile dispatches, when sailing as a dispatch vessel practically in the service of the enemy, is liable to seizure. Mail steamers under neutral flags carrying dispatches in the regular and customary manner, either as a part of their mail in their mail bags, or separately as a matter of accommodation and without special arrangement or remuneration, are not liable to seizure and should not be detained, except upon clear grounds of suspicion of a violation of the laws of war with respect to contraband, blockade, or unneutral service, in which case the mail bags must be forwarded with seals unbroken." [2]

Regular diplomatic and consular correspondence is not regarded as hostile unless there is some special reason for such belief.

(2) The limitation in regard to the *carriage of certain belligerent persons* applies to those who travel in such manner as to make it evident that they travel in the military or naval service of the belligerent state. If the carriage of the person or persons is paid by the state, or is done under state contract, it is regarded as sufficient evidence of unneutral service.[3] The neutral carrier engaged in ordinary service is not obliged to investigate the character of persons who take passage in the usual way. The case of the *Trent* had no particular bearing upon this subject, as it merely emphasized an already settled principle "that a public ship, though of a nation at war, cannot take persons

---

[1] 6 C. Rob. 440, 454.
[2] U. S. Naval War Code, Art. 20 ; Appendix, p. 406.
[3] The "Orozembo," 6 C. Rob. 430.

out of a neutral vessel at sea, whatever may be the claim of her government on those persons." [1]

(3) *Auxiliary coal, repair, supply, or transport ships*, as, directly in the service of the belligerent, have an undoubted hostile character. [2]

(4) Knowing coöperation in the *transmission of certain messages* for the belligerent renders the ship liable to penalty. Such an act as the repetition of signals would fall in this class. Submarine telegraphic cables between a belligerent and a neutral state may become liable to censorship or to interruption beyond neutral jurisdiction if used for hostile purposes. A neutral vessel engaged in the laying, cutting, or repair of war telegraph cables is held to be performing unneutral service.

The general penalty for the performance of unneutral service is the forfeiture of the vessel so engaged.

§ 134. Visit and Search

(a) "The right of visiting and searching merchant ships upon the seas — whatever be the ships, whatever be the cargoes, whatever be the destinations — is an incontestable right of the lawfully commissioned cruisers of a belligerent nation." [3] is the statement of the general principle laid down in the case of the *Nereide*. Judge Story says that the right is "allowed by the general consent of nations in the time of war and limited to those occasions." [4] There is, however, a qualified right of search in the time of peace in case of vessels suspected of piracy or of slave trade. Under

[1] Wheat. D. p. 465. [2] The "Kwa-sung," Takahashi, 3a-5i.
[3] I. C. Rob. Adl. 540. [4] The "Marianna Flora," 11 Wheat. 1.

search. If the vessel be released, an entry in the log
book to that effect should be made by the boarding
officer." [1]

(d) **Ship's Papers.** The papers expected to be on
board as evidence of the character of the vessel are : —
    1. The register.
    2. The crew and passenger list.
    3. The log book.
    4. A bill of health.
    5. The manifest of cargo.
    6. A charter party, if the vessel is chartered.
    7. Invoices and bills of lading. [2]

(e) **Grounds of Seizure.** It is generally held that a
vessel may be seized in case of : —
    1. Resistance to visit and search.
    2. Clear evidence of attempt to avoid visit and
search by escape.
    3. Clear evidence of illegal acts on the part of
the neutral vessel.
    4. Absence of or defect in the necessary papers.
        (a) Fraudulent papers.
        (b) Destruction, defacement, or conceal-
           ment of papers.
        (c) Simple failure to produce regular
           papers.

(f) **Seizure.** In case of seizure it is held that the
neutral vessel and property vests in the neutral till
properly condemned by a duly authorized court. The
captor is therefore under obligation : —

[1] U. S. Naval War Code, Art. 32 : Appendix, p. 470.
[2] U. S. Naval War Code, Art. 33 : Appendix, p. 470. Most of the
forms are given in Glass's "Marine International Law."

1. To conduct the seizure with due regard to the person and property of the neutral.

2. To exercise reasonable diligence to bring the capture quickly to a port for its adjudication.

3. To guard the capture from injury so far as within his power.

Failure to fulfill these obligations renders the belligerent liable to damages.[1]

In the Chino-Japanese War of 1894, the Japanese war vessels visited eighty-one neutral vessels but only one was brought to the prize court.[2]

§ 135. Convoy

·A neutral merchant vessel is sometimes placed under the protection of a ship of war of its own state, and is then said to be under convoy.

It has been claimed by many authorities, particularly those of Continental Europe, that such a merchant vessel is exempt from visitation and search upon the declaration of the commander of the neutral ship of war that the merchantman is violating no neutral obligation. England has uniformly denied the validity of this claim.

Practice has been very divergent in most states. From the middle of the seventeenth century the right of convoy has been asserted. From the end of the eighteenth century the claim has gained in importance.[3] The United States has made many treaties directly

---

[1] Hall, p. 644, § 277.   [2] Takahashi, 16-28.

[3] Gessner, "Le droit des neutres sur mer," Ch. IV.; Perels, "Manuel Droit Maritime," § 56.

recognizing the practice, and instructs naval officers that, " Convoys of neutral merchant vessels, under escort of vessels of war of their own State, are exempt from the right of search, upon proper assurances, based on thorough examination, from the commander of the convoy." [1]

In the war of 1894, —

" Japan ordered naval officers to give credence to the declaration of a convoying officer. The idea was simply that, as generosity was the chief object of Japan, she did not wish to search and make actual inspection in order to verify the character of escorted merchantmen and goods, trusting to the honor of neutral officers. This was the main idea of the Japanese in adopting the Continental principle regarding convoy; but she was not, in actual cases, so lax as to admit exorbitant claims of the right of convoy, such as an English admiral made for all British ships in the China Sea." [2]

The present tendencies seem to indicate an inclination to admit the right of convoy within reasonable limits and under reasonable regulations. [3]

§ 136. Blockade

Blockade is the obstruction of communication with a place in the possession of one of the belligerents by the armed forces of the other belligerent. The form which blockade takes in most cases is that of obstruction of communication by water.

(a) Historical. In 1584 Holland declared the ports of Flanders blockaded. Holland did not, however, maintain this declaration by ships of war; indeed, in

---

[1] U. S. Naval War Code, Art. 30. [2] Takahashi, p. 13.
[3] Lawrence, § 268; Appendix, p. 409.

the early days there were no such ships as would make the maintenance of a blockade possible. Such paper blockades were common in the following centuries, and all the ports of a state were frequently proclaimed blockaded, even though there might be no force in the neighborhood to insure that the blockade would not be violated. Treaties of the eighteenth century show an inclination in the states to lessen the evils of blockade by proclamation. The growth of neutral trade led to the adoption of rules for its greater protection. The armed neutrality of 1780 asserted in its proclaimed principles that a valid blockade should involve such a disposition of the vessels of the belligerent proclaiming the blockade as to make the attempt to enter manifestly dangerous.[1] The armed neutrality of 1800 asserted that a notice from the commander of the blockading vessels must be given to the approaching neutral vessel. During the Napoleonic wars there was a return to the practice of issuing proclamations with the view to limiting neutral commerce. The English Orders in Council of 1806 and 1807, and the Berlin Decree of 1806, and the Milan Decree of 1807, by which Napoleon attempted to meet the English Orders, were the expression of the extremest belligerent claims in regard to the obstruction of neutral commerce. The treaties of 1815 said nothing in regard to blockade. The practice and theory varied till, by the Declaration of Paris in 1856, a fixed basis was announced in the provision that "Blockades, in order to be binding, must be effective."[2]

(b) **Conditions of Existence.** A blockade presupposes, —

---

[1] Walker, "Science of Int. Law," p. 304.　　[2] Appendix, p. 398.

1. A state of war.

2. Declaration by the proper authority.

3. Notification of neutral states and their subjects.

4. Effective maintenance.

(c) **Blockade a War Measure.** The so-called pacific blockade differs in its purpose and method to such an extent as to cause many to deny it any standing in international law. Only a belligerent can institute a blockade which other states are bound to respect, as, without war, there are no neutrals. The blockade may continue even until the conclusion of peace. The agreement to a truce or an armistice does not put an end to the blockade.

(d) **Declaration.** Blockade can be declared only by the proper authority.

As war is a state act, only the person or authority designated by the constitution or law of the state can declare a blockade. Such a declaration must, in general, come from the chief of the state. In certain cases a blockade declared by an officer in command of forces remote from the central government is held to be valid from the time of its proclamation, if the act of the commander receives subsequent ratification from the central authority.

(e) **Notification.** Neutrals must be notified of the existence of a blockade. This notification may be : —

1. By official proclamation announcing the place to be blockaded, and the time when the proclamation becomes effective.

2. By notification to vessels when they come near the place blockaded.

3. The use of both the above methods.

The theory of the American and English authorities has been to assume a knowledge of the blockade on the part of subjects if the political authority of their state had been informed of the existence of the blockade before the neutral vessel left port. In practice both powers have in recent years given a neutral vessel warning of the existence of blockade of a port before seizure.[1]

The French rule is to give in every instance an approaching neutral vessel warning of the existence of a blockade, and to consider the notification to the neutral state authorities as merely a diplomatic courtesy.

Sometimes local notification is made to port and consular authorities of the place blockaded.

In recent years the time allowed a vessel to discharge, reload, and to leave port has been specified.

In case of special notification by the officer in command of a blockading ship, the fact with particulars should be entered in the log of the neutral vessel over the officer's signature.

(*f*) **A Blockade must be Effective.** This principle applies both to the place and to the manner of enforcement.

    1. It must apply to a place which may be blockaded, *i.e.* to seaports, rivers, gulfs, bays, roadsteads, etc. A river which forms the boundary between one of the belligerent states and a neutral state may not be blockaded. Rivers flow-

---

[1] President McKinley's Proclamation of Blockade, during the war with Spain, is given in Proclamations and Decrees, p. 75, and President Lincoln's, during the war with the South, in 12 U. S. Sts. at Large, Appendix, ii, iii.

ing for a part of their course through belligerent territory but discharging through neutral territory may not be blockaded. Certain waters are not liable to blockade because exempt by agreement; as in the case of the Congo River by the Act of 1885.

2. "Blockades, in order to be binding, must be effective, that is to say, maintained by a force sufficient really to prevent access to the coast of the enemy." [1] This is interpreted in the United States Naval Code as a "force sufficient to render hazardous the ingress to or egress from a port." [2] The subject of the degree of effectiveness which is necessary has been much discussed, and can only be determined by the circumstances in a given case. [3] The English interpretation in the main agrees with that of the United States. The Continental states are inclined to give a more literal interpretation to the rule.

(*g*) **Cessation.** A blockade comes to an end : —

1. By the cessation of any attempt to render it effective.

2. By the repulse by force of the vessels attempting to maintain the blockade.

3. For a given neutral vessel when there is no evidence of a blockade, after due care to respect its existence. This may happen when the blockading force is absent in pursuit of an offending vessel, or for similar reason.

In this last case the Continental authorities hold that

---

[1] Declaration of Paris, Appendix, p. 398.
[2] Art. 37 ; see Appendix, 412.   [3] Calvo, § 2841.

the neutral is free to enter without question, as it is the duty of the belligerent to render the blockade at all times evident and effective. The English and American authorities generally consider such a case merely an interruption, and hold that it does not require that the blockade be proclaimed again. There is a general agreement that in the other cases it must be formally instituted again as it was in the beginning.

§ 137. Violation of Blockade

"A breach of blockade is not an offense against the laws of the country of the neutral owner or master. The only penalty for engaging in such trade is the liability to capture and condemnation by the belligerent."[1] The American and English practice is to regard as the breach of blockade the act of passing into or out of a blockaded place, unless by special privilege, or a manifestation of an intent to thus pass. The French courts impose a penalty only upon those who actually attempt to run the blockade. The American practice would make the vessel liable to penalty from the time of its departure from neutral jurisdiction with intent to enter the blockaded port until its return, unless the blockade is raised meantime.

Under proper regulations, certain vessels are usually allowed to pass a blockade without penalty : —

1. Neutral vessels in actual distress.

2. Neutral vessels of war strictly as a privilege.

3. Neutral vessels in the port at the time of the establishment of the blockade, provided they depart

---

[1] "International Law," Naval War College, p. 155.

within a reasonable time. In the War of 1898, the United States allowed thirty days after the establishment of the blockade to neutral vessels to load and to depart.

The penalty for the violation of blockade is forfeiture of vessel and cargo, although when vessel and cargo belong to different owners, and the owner of the cargo is an innocent shipper, it has been held that the cargo may be released. This may happen if a vessel deviates from her original destination to a blockaded port. Even though a vessel pass a blockade, she is liable to capture while at sea before the termination of the voyage, provided the blockade continues.[1] The crews of neutral vessels violating a blockade are not prisoners of war, but may be held as witnesses before a prize court.

§ 138. Continuous Voyages

The Rule of War of 1756 declared that during war neutrals were not permitted to engage with the colonies of a belligerent in a trade which was not permitted to foreigners in time of peace.[2] Ordinarily in the time of peace, trade between the mother country and the colony was restricted to domestic ships. This rule was adopted in order that a neutral might not, by undertaking trade denied him in time of peace, relieve one of the belligerents of a part of the burdens of war which the interruption of domestic commerce by the other belligerent had imposed. Trade with neutral ports was allowed in time of peace. Therefore, to avoid technical violation of the rule, neutral vessels sailing

---

[1] " Juffrow Maria Schroeder," 3 C. Rob., 147, 153, 154.
[2] See 3 Phillimore, Chap. XI.

from a port within belligerent jurisdiction, touched at a port within neutral jurisdiction, and in some cases landed and reshipped their cargoes. Lord Stowell decided that it was a settled principle "that the mere touching at any port without importing the cargo into the common stock of the country will not alter the nature of the voyage, which continues the same in all respects, and must be considered as a voyage to the country to which the vessel is actually going for the purpose of delivering her cargo at the ultimate port." [1] In the case of the *William* in 1806, Sir William Grant declared that "the truth may not always be discernible, but when it is discovered, it is according to the truth and not according to the fiction that we are to give to the transaction its character and denomination. If the voyage from the place of lading be not really ended, it matters not by what acts the party may have evinced his desire of making it appear to have ended. That those acts have been attended with trouble and expense cannot alter their quality or their effect." [2] The English authorities held that the visit to a neutral port did not constitute the trip two voyages, but that the voyage was continuous and the property liable to confiscation, though Hall says the "cargo was confiscated only when captured on its voyage from the port of colonial importation to the enemy country." [3] British cruisers, however, seized three German vessels, the *Bundesrath*, and the *General*, during the South African War of 1899–1900, while on a voyage to the neutral port of Lorenço Marques, which was the nearest port

---

[1] The "Maria," 5 C. Rob., 365.
[2] p. 695 n, § 247.

Y

of entry for Pretoria, the capital of the South African
Republic.   Germany protested.   The vessels were
released and the English authorities promised that in
the future they would refrain from searching vessels
until the vessels had passed beyond Aden, or any other
place, at the same distance from Delagoa Bay.

The American doctrine of continuous voyages is a
considerable extension of the English doctrine and has
met with severe criticism.   In the case of the *Bermuda*,
captured during the Civil War of 1861–1864, it was
held that : —

"Destination alone justifies seizure and condemnation of
ship and cargo in voyage to ports under blockade; and such
destination justifies equally seizure of contraband in voyage
to ports not under blockade; but in the last case the ship,
and cargo, not contraband, are free from seizure, except in
cases of fraud or bad faith." [1]

In the case of the *Stephen Hart*, a British schooner,
bound from London to Cuba with a cargo of war supplies, captured in 1862 off the coast of Florida, Judge
Betts condemned both vessel and cargo.   He maintained
that : —

"The commerce is in the destination and intended use of
the property laden on board of the vessel, and not in the
incidental, ancillary, and temporary voyage of the vessel,
which may be but one of many carriers through which the
property is to reach its true and original destination. . . .
If the guilty intention, that the contraband goods should
reach a port of the enemy, existed when such goods left
their English port, that guilty intention cannot be oblit-
erated by the innocent intention of stopping at a neutral port
on the way. . . . This court holds that, in all such cases,

[1] 3 Wall. 514.

the transportation or voyage of the contraband goods is to be considered as a unit, from the port of lading to the port of delivery in the enemy's country; that if any part of such voyage or transportation be unlawful, it is unlawful throughout; and that the vessel and her cargo are subject to capture; as well before arriving at the first neutral port at which she touches after her departure from England, as on the voyage or transportation by sea from such neutral port to the port of the enemy." [1]

This position of the United States, which has been so criticised, is liable to be abused to the disadvantage of neutral commerce. The absence of some such rule would open the door to acts which, though neutral in form, would be hostile in fact. The present tendency seems to be to allow the exercise of a certain amount of supervision over commerce of neutrals when it is destined to neutral ports having convenient communication with the enemy. This may extend to the seizure of neutral vessels bound for that port only in form, provided there is no doubt as to the true destination, but such seizure must be made with the greatest care not to violate the proper rights of neutrals. There is less reason for the general exercise of this supervision over vessels sailing to a neutral port which is separated from the belligerent territory by a considerable expanse of water, than for its exercise over vessels sailing to a port which is separated only by a narrow expanse of water. In cases where the neutral port is upon the same land area with the belligerent territory and has easy communication by rail or otherwise, so that it may become a natural port of entry for goods bound for one of the

[1] Blatchford's Prize Cases, 387, 405, 407; Snow's " Cases," p. 500.

belligerents, the other belligerent may properly exercise a greater degree of authority in the supervision of commerce than would ordinarily be allowable. It was on this ground that England could justify her action in the seizure of vessels bound for Delagoa Bay during the war in South Africa, in 1899–1900; and similarly Italy justified her seizure of the Dutch vessel, *Doelwyk*, in August, 1896, during the Abyssinian war. This vessel was bound for a friendly port, but a port from which its cargo of war supplies would pass overland to the enemy without difficulty.

§ 139. Prize and Prize Courts

Prize is the general term applied to captures made at sea. The ships and goods of an enemy liable to capture by the laws of war, and the ships and goods of a neutral when involved in acts forbidden by the laws of war, may be brought into port for adjudication and disposition. Enemy's goods, except contraband of war, are not liable to capture on neutral ships.[1] Certain ships engaged in charitable or scientific pursuits, and coast fishing vessels, are exempt from capture,[2] as are also certain specially exempted by treaty. In general other goods and vessels of the enemy are liable to capture. Contraband goods of a neutral, vessels attempting to violate blockade, vessels performing unneutral service, or goods or vessels otherwise involved in a way contrary to the laws of war are liable to capture.

A *prize court* is the tribunal which determines the rights of the parties concerned in the capture and the

[1] Appendix, p. 398.
[2] U. S. Naval War Code, Arts. 13, 14, 21.

disposition of the goods or vessel. All captures belong to the state in whose name they are made. An inchoate title to the prize is acquired by possession, but complete title is acquired only after condemnation by a properly constituted prize court.

A prize court may be established by the belligerent in its own state, in the territory where the belligerent has military jurisdiction or in the territory of an ally.[1] The establishment of a court in neutral jurisdiction is not permitted. When Genêt, the minister of France, tried, in 1793, to set up consular prize courts in the United States, Washington protested and Genêt was recalled. Takahashi says, "It is clear that if we admit the prevailing principle concerning the establishment of a prize court in a belligerent's own dominions or its ally's, or in occupied territory, we may infer that a court can be held on the deck of a man-of-war — a floating portion of a territorial sovereignty — lying in the abovementioned waters, provided the processes of procedure are followed."[2] He maintains, however, that a court might not be established on the high seas, as proper procedure for the interested parties would not be possible.

The tribunals which have jurisdiction of prize cases differ in the different countries. In the United States, the District Courts possess the powers of a prize court, and an appeal lies to the Supreme Court.[3]

The methods of procedure of prize courts are similar in different countries. The practice in the United States is as follows : —

---

[1] Lawrence, § 212.　　[2] Takahashi, p. 105.
[3] U. S. Rev. Sts., § 563, cl. 8 ; 18 St., 316, c. 80.

Dana calls the prize tribunal *an inquest by the state*, and regards it as the means by which the sovereign "desires and is required to inform himself, by recognized modes, of the lawfulness of the capture." The commanding officer of the capturing vessel, after securing the cargo and documents of the captured vessel, makes an inventory of the last named, seals them and sends them, together with the master, one or more of the other officers, the supercargo, purser, or agent of the prize, and also any one on board supposed to have information, under charge of a prize master and a prize crew, into port to be placed in the custody of the court. The prize master delivers the documents and the inventory to prize commissioners, who are appointed by the court, and reports to the district attorney, who files a libel against the prize property and sees " that the proper preparatory evidence is taken by the prize commissioners, and that the prize commissioners also take the depositions *de bene esse* of the prize crew, and of other transient persons cognizant of any facts bearing on condemnation or distribution."[1] The libel should "properly contain only a description of the prize, with dates, etc., for identification, and the fact that it was taken as prize of war by the cruiser, and brought to the court for adjudication, that is, of facts enough to show that it is a maritime cause of prize jurisdiction and not a case of municipal penalty or forfeiture."[2] Notice is then published that citizens or neutrals, but not enemies, interested in the prize property shall appear and enter their

[1] U. S. Rev. Sts., § 4618, also 1624, par. 16–17; 4615, 4617, 4621; The " Nassau," 4 Wall., 634.

[2] Wheat., D., n. 186, III.; U. S. Rev. Sts. § 4622.

claims. As there are no allegations in the libel, the answer of the claimant is only a general denial under oath. The prize commissioners then examine the witnesses privately ; and this evidence, which is kept in secret until complete, is called *in preparatorio*.[1] If the court is in doubt it will order " further proof," that is besides the ship, cargo, documents, and witnesses. The burden is on the claimant to prove title.[2] If the claimant's right is not sufficiently established, the property is condemned. The captors are, however, liable to damages if there is found no probable cause for the capture.[3]

It has been the general practice to distribute the proceeds, or a part of the proceeds, of a capture among the captors. This distribution is a matter of municipal law. In England the sum realized from the sale of the goods and vessel is distributed among the captors, though the crown reserves the right to decide what interest the captors shall have, if any.[4] By a royal decree of June 20, 1864, Prussia provided in detail what each of those participating in the capture should receive.[5] By the act of March 3, 1899, the United States provided that " all provisions of law authorizing

---

[1] Wheat., D., n. 186, III.; The " Springbok " 5 Wall., 1 ; The " Sir William Peel," *ibid.*, 517.

[2] Wheat., D., n. 186, III.

[3] The " La Manche," 2 Sprague, 207. The method of procedure *in* a prize court, in case of enemy property, is given in Appendix, p. 421 *et seq.* With a few changes, the same forms may be used in the case of neutral property. See further on the method of procedure in a prize court, Takahashi, pp. 11 *et seq.*, 73–107, 172–191.

[4] Lawrence, § 212.

[5] Perels, " Manuel Droit Maritime Int.," p. 457.

the distribution among captors of the whole, or any portion, of the proceeds of vessels, or any property hereafter captured, condemned as prize, or providing for the payment of bounty for the sinking or destruction of vessels of the enemy hereafter occurring in time of war, are hereby repealed." [1]

"If there are controlling reasons why vessels that are properly captured may not be sent in for adjudication — such as unseaworthiness, the existence of infectious disease, or the lack of a prize crew — they may be appraised and sold, and if this cannot be done, they may be destroyed. The imminent danger of recapture would justify destruction, if there should be no doubt that the vessel was a proper prize. But in all such cases all of the papers and other testimony should be sent to the prize court, in order that a decree may be duly entered." [2]

[1] 30 U. S. Sts. at Large, 1007.
[2] U. S. Naval War Code, Art. 50 ; Appendix, p. 415 ; U. S. Rev. Sts. §§ 4615, 4627, 4628.

APPENDIX

INSTRUCTIONS FOR THE GOVERNMENT OF ARMIES OF THE UNITED STATES IN THE FIELD

GENERAL ORDERS, }   WAR DEPARTMENT,
No. 100. }   ADJUTANT GENERAL'S OFFICE,
        Washington, April 24, 1863.

The following "Instructions for the Government of Armies of the United States in the Field," prepared by FRANCIS LIEBER, LL.D., and revised by a Board of Officers, of which Major General E. A. HITCHCOCK is president, having been approved by the President of the United States, he commands that they be published for the information of all concerned.

BY ORDER OF THE SECRETARY OF WAR:

E. D. TOWNSEND,
Assistant Adjutant General.

INSTRUCTIONS FOR THE GOVERNMENT OF ARMIES OF THE UNITED STATES IN THE FIELD

SECTION I

MARTIAL LAW — MILITARY JURISDICTION — MILITARY NECESSITY — RETALIATION

1

A place, district, or country occupied by an enemy stands, in consequence of the occupation, under the Martial Law of the invading or occupying army, whether any proclama-

tion declaring Martial Law, or any public warning to the
inhabitants, has been issued or not. Martial Law is the
immediate and direct effect and consequence of occupation
or conquest.

The presence of a hostile army proclaims its Martial Law.

2

Martial Law does not cease during the hostile occupation,
except by special proclamation, ordered by the commander
in chief; or by special mention in the treaty of peace concluding the war, when the occupation of a place or territory
continues beyond the conclusion of peace as one of the conditions of the same.

3

Martial Law in a hostile country consists in the suspension, by the occupying military authority, of the criminal
and civil law, and of the domestic administration and government in the occupied place or territory, and in the substitution of military rule and force for the same, as well as
in the dictation of general laws, as far as military necessity requires this suspension, substitution, or dictation.

The commander of the forces may proclaim that the administration of all civil and penal law shall continue either
wholly or in part, as in times of peace, unless otherwise
ordered by the military authority.

4

Martial Law is simply military authority exercised in
accordance with the laws and usages of war. Military
oppression is not Martial Law; it is the abuse of the power
which that law confers. As Martial Law is executed by
military force, it is incumbent upon those who administer
it to be strictly guided by the principles of justice, honor,
and humanity — virtues adorning a soldier even more than
other men, for the very reason that he possesses the power
of his arms against the unarmed.

5

Martial Law should be less stringent in places and countries fully occupied and fairly conquered. Much greater severity may be exercised in places or regions where actual hostilities exist, or are expected and must be prepared for. Its most complete sway is allowed — even in the commander's own country — when face to face with the enemy, because of the absolute necessities of the case, and of the paramount duty to defend the country against invasion.

To save the country is paramount to all other considerations.

6

All civil and penal law shall continue to take its usual course in the enemy's places and territories under Martial Law, unless interrupted or stopped by order of the occupying military power; but all the functions of the hostile government — legislative, executive, or administrative — whether of a general, provincial, or local character, cease under Martial Law, or continue only with the sanction, or, if deemed necessary, the participation of the occupier or invader.

7

Martial law extends to property, and to persons, whether they are subjects of the enemy or aliens to that government.

8

Consuls, among American and European nations, are not diplomatic agents. Nevertheless, their offices and persons will be subjected to Martial Law in cases of urgent necessity only: their property and business are not exempted. Any delinquency they commit against the established military rule may be punished as in the case of any other inhabitant, and such punishment furnishes no reasonable ground for international complaint.

9

The functions of Ambassadors, Ministers, or other diplomatic agents, accredited by neutral powers to the hostile government, cease, so far as regards the displaced government; but the conquering or occupying power usually recognizes them as temporarily accredited to itself.

10

Martial Law affects chiefly the police and collection of public revenue and taxes, whether imposed by the expelled government or by the invader, and refers mainly to the support and efficiency of the army, its safety, and the safety of its operations.

11

The law of war does not only disclaim all cruelty and bad faith concerning engagements concluded with the enemy during the war, but also the breaking of stipulations solemnly contracted by the belligerents in time of peace, and avowedly intended to remain in force in case of war between the contracting powers.

It disclaims all extortions and other transactions for individual gain; all acts of private revenge, or connivance at such acts.

Offenses to the contrary shall be severely punished, and especially so if committed by officers.

12

Whenever feasible, Martial Law is carried out in cases of individual offenders by Military Courts; but sentences of death shall be executed only with the approval of the chief executive, provided the urgency of the case does not require a speedier execution, and then only with the approval of the chief commander.

13

Military jurisdiction is of two kinds: First, that which is conferred and defined by statute; second, that which is derived from the common law of war.   Military offenses under the statute law must be tried in the manner therein directed; but military offenses which do not come within the statute must be tried and punished under the common law of war.   The character of the courts which exercise these jurisdictions depends upon the local laws of each particular country.

In the armies of the United States the first is exercised by courts-martial, while cases which do not come within the " Rules and Articles of War," or the jurisdiction conferred by statute on courts-martial, are tried by military commissions.

14

Military necessity, as understood by modern civilized nations, consists in the necessity of those measures which are indispensable for securing the ends of the war, and which are lawful according to the modern law and usages of war.

15

Military necessity admits of all direct destruction of life or limb of *armed* enemies, and of other persons whose destruction is incidentally *unavoidable* in the armed contests of the war; it allows of the capturing of every armed enemy, and every enemy of importance to the hostile government, or of peculiar danger to the captor; it allows of all destruction of property, and obstruction of the ways and channels of traffic, travel, or communication, and of all withholding of sustenance or means of life from the enemy; of the appropriation of whatever an enemy's country affords necessary for the subsistence and safety of the army, and of such deception as does not involve the breaking of good faith either positively pledged, regarding agreements entered into during the war, or supposed by the modern law of war to exist.   Men who take up arms against one another in public war do not cease on this account to be moral beings, responsible to one another and to God.

16

Military necessity does not admit of cruelty — that is, the infliction of suffering for the sake of suffering or for revenge, nor of maiming or wounding except in fight, nor of torture to extort confessions. It does not admit of the use of poison in any way, nor of the wanton devastation of a district. It admits of deception, but disclaims acts of perfidy; and, in general, military necessity does not include any act of hostility which makes the return to peace unnecessarily difficult.

17

War is not carried on by arms alone. It is lawful to starve the hostile belligerent, armed or unarmed, so that it leads to the speedier subjection of the enemy.

18

When a commander of a besieged place expels the noncombatants, in order to lessen the number of those who consume his stock of provisions, it is lawful, though an extreme measure, to drive them back, so as to hasten on the surrender.

19

Commanders, whenever admissible, inform the enemy of their intention to bombard a place, so that the noncombatants, and especially the women and children, may be removed before the bombardment commences. But it is no infraction of the common law of war to omit thus to inform the enemy. Surprise may be a necessity.

20

Public war is a state of armed hostility between sovereign nations or governments. It is a law and requisite of civilized existence that men live in political, continuous societies, forming organized units, called states or nations, whose constituents bear, enjoy, and suffer, advance and retrograde together, in peace and in war.

21

The citizen or native of a hostile country is thus an enemy, as one of the constituents of the hostile state or nation, and as such is subjected to the hardships of the war.

22

Nevertheless, as civilization has advanced during the last centuries, so has likewise steadily advanced, especially in war on land, the distinction between the private individual belonging to a hostile country and the hostile country itself, with its men in arms. The principle has been more and more acknowledged that the unarmed citizen is to be spared in person, property, and honor as much as the exigencies of war will admit.

23

Private citizens are no longer murdered, enslaved, or carried off to distant parts, and the inoffensive individual is as little disturbed in his private relations as the commander of the hostile troops can afford to grant in the overruling demands of a vigorous war.

24

The almost universal rule in remote times was, and continues to be with barbarous armies, that the private individual of the hostile country is destined to suffer every privation of liberty and protection, and every disruption of family ties. Protection was, and still is with uncivilized people, the exception.

25

In modern regular wars of the Europeans, and their descendants in other portions of the globe, protection of the inoffensive citizen of the hostile country is the rule; privation and disturbance of private relations are the exceptions.

z

26

Commanding generals may cause the magistrates and civil officers of the hostile country to take the oath of temporary allegiance or an oath of fidelity to their own victorious government or rulers, and they may expel every one who declines to do so. But whether they do so or not, the people and their civil officers owe strict obedience to them as long as they hold sway over the district or country, at the peril of their lives.

27

The law of war can no more wholly dispense with retaliation than can the law of nations, of which it is a branch. Yet civilized nations acknowledge retaliation as the sternest feature of war. A reckless enemy often leaves to his opponent no other means of securing himself against the repetition of barbarous outrage.

28

Retaliation will, therefore, never be resorted to as a measure of mere revenge, but only as a means of protective retribution, and moreover, cautiously and unavoidably ; that is to say, retaliation shall only be resorted to after careful inquiry into the real occurrence, and the character of the misdeeds that may demand retribution.

Unjust or inconsiderate retaliation removes the belligerents farther and farther from the mitigating rules of regular war, and by rapid steps leads them nearer to the internecine wars of savages.

29

Modern times are distinguished from earlier ages by the existence, at one and the same time, of many nations and great governments related to one another in close intercourse.

Peace is their normal condition ; war is the exception. The ultimate object of all modern war is a renewed state of peace.

The more vigorously wars are pursued, the better it is for humanity. Sharp wars are brief.

30

Ever since the formation and coexistence of modern nations, and ever since wars have become great national wars, war has come to be acknowledged not to be its own end, but the means to obtain great ends of state, or to consist in defense against wrong; and no conventional restriction of the modes adopted to injure the enemy is any longer admitted; but the law of war imposes many limitations and restrictions on principles of justice, faith, and honor.

SECTION II

PUBLIC AND PRIVATE PROPERTY OF THE ENEMY — PROTECTION OF PERSONS, AND ESPECIALLY OF WOMEN; OF RELIGION THE ARTS AND SCIENCES — PUNISHMENT OF CRIMES AGAINST THE INHABITANTS OF HOSTILE COUNTRIES

31

A victorious army appropriates all public money, seizes all public movable property until further direction by its government, and sequesters for its own benefit or of that of its government all the revenues of real property belonging to the hostile government or nation. The title to such real property remains in abeyance during military occupation, and until the conquest is made complete.

32

A victorious army, by the martial power inherent in the same, may suspend, change, or abolish, as far as the martial power extends, the relations which arise from the services due, according to the existing laws of the invaded country, from one citizen, subject, or native of the same to another.

The commander of the army must leave it to the ultimate treaty of peace to settle the permanency of thi͏.

33

It is no longer considered lawful — on the contrary, it is held to be a serious breach of the law of war — to force the subjects of the enemy into the service of the victorious government, except the latter should proclaim, after a fair and complete conquest of the hostile country or district, that it is resolved to keep the country, district, or place permanently as its own and make it a portion of its own country.

34

As a general rule, the property belonging to churches, to hospitals, or other establishments of an exclusively charitable character, to establishments of education, or foundations for the promotion of knowledge, whether public schools, universities, academies of learning or observatories, museums of the fine arts, or of a scientific character — such property is not to be considered public property in the sense of paragraph 31; but it may be taxed or used when the public service may require it.

35

Classical works of art, libraries, scientific collections, or precious instruments, such as astronomical telescopes, as well as hospitals, must be secured against all avoidable injury, even when they are contained in fortified places whilst besieged or bombarded.

36

If such works of art, libraries, collections, or instruments belonging to a hostile nation or government, can be removed without injury, the ruler of the conquering state or nation may order them to be seized and removed for the benefit of the said nation. The ultimate ownership is to be settled by the ensuing treaty of peace.

In no case shall they be sold or given away, if captured by the armies of the United States, nor shall they ever be privately appropriated, or wantonly destroyed or injured.

37

The United States acknowledge and protect, in hostile countries occupied by them, religion and morality; strictly private property; the persons of the inhabitants, especially those of women; and the sacredness of domestic relations. Offenses to the contrary shall be rigorously punished.

This rule does not interfere with the right of the victorious invader to tax the people or their property, to levy forced loans, to billet soldiers, or to appropriate property, especially houses, lands, boats or ships, and churches, for temporary and military uses.

38

Private property, unless forfeited by crimes or by offenses of the owner, can be seized only by way of military necessity, for the support or other benefit of the army or of the United States.

If the owner has not fled, the commanding officer will cause receipts to be given, which may serve the spoliated owner to obtain indemnity.

39

The salaries of civil officers of the hostile government who remain in the invaded territory, and continue the work of their office, and can continue it according to the circumstances arising out of the war — such as judges, administrative or police officers, officers of city or communal governments — are paid from the public revenue of the invaded territory, until the military government has reason wholly or partially to discontinue it. Salaries or incomes connected with purely honorary titles are always stopped.

40

There exists no law or body of authoritative rules of action between hostile armies, except that branch of the

law of nature and nations which is called the law and
usages of war on land.

41

All municipal law of the ground on which the armies
stand, or of the countries to which they belong, is silent
and of no effect between armies in the field.

42

Slavery, complicating and confounding the ideas of property (that is of a *thing*), and of personality (that is of
humanity), exists according to municipal or local law only.
The law of nature and nations has never acknowledged it.
The digest of the Roman law enacts the early dictum of
the pagan jurist, that "so far as the law of nature is concerned, all men are equal." Fugitives escaping from a
country in which they were slaves, villains, or serfs, into
another country, have, for centuries past, been held free and
acknowledged free by judicial decisions of European countries, even though the municipal law of the country in
which the slave had taken refuge acknowledged slavery
within its own dominions.

43

Therefore, in a war between the United States and a belligerent which admits of slavery, if a person held in bond-
age by that belligerent be captured by or come as a fugitive
under the protection of the military forces of the United
States, such person is immediately entitled to the rights
and privileges of a freeman. To return such person into
slavery would amount to enslaving a free person, and
neither the United States nor any officer under their
authority can enslave any human being. Moreover, a
person so made free by the law of war is under the shield
of the law of nations, and the former owner or State can
have, by the law of postliminy, no belligerent lien or claim
of service.

44

All wanton violence committed against persons in the invaded country, all destruction of property not commanded by the authorized officer, all robbery, all pillage or sacking, even after taking a place by main force, all rape, wounding, maiming, or killing of such inhabitants, are prohibited under the penalty of death, or such other severe punishment as may seem adequate for the gravity of the offense.

A soldier, officer or private, in the act of committing such violence, and disobeying a superior ordering him to abstain from it, may be lawfully killed on the spot by such superior.

45

All captures and booty belong, according to the modern law of war, primarily to the government of the captor.

Prize money, whether on sea or land, can now only be claimed under local law.

46

Neither officers nor soldiers are allowed to make use of their position or power in the hostile country for private gain, not even for commercial transactions otherwise legitimate. Offenses to the contrary committed by commissioned officers will be punished with cashiering or such other punishment as the nature of the offense may require; if by soldiers, they shall be punished according to the nature of the offense.

47

Crimes punishable by all penal codes, such as arson, murder, maiming, assaults, highway robbery, theft, burglary, fraud, forgery, and rape, if committed by an American soldier in a hostile country against its inhabitants, are not only punishable as at home, but in all cases in which d is not inflicted, the severer punishment shall be pre

SECTION III

DESERTERS — PRISONERS OF WAR — HOSTAGES — BOOTY ON THE
BATTLEFIELD

48

Deserters from the American Army, having entered the
service of the enemy, suffer death if they fall again into the
hands of the United States, whether by capture, or being
delivered up to the American Army; and if a deserter from
the enemy, having taken service in the Army of the United
States is captured by the enemy, and punished by them
with death or otherwise, it is not a breach against the law
and usages of war, requiring redress or retaliation.

49

A prisoner of war is a public enemy armed or attached to
the hostile army for active aid, who has fallen into the
hands of the captor, either fighting or wounded, on the
field or in the hospital, by individual surrender, or by
capitulation.

All soldiers, of whatever species of arms; all men who
belong to the rising *en masse* of the hostile country; all
those who are attached to the army for its efficiency and
promote directly the object of the war, except such as are
hereinafter provided for; all disabled men or officers on the
field or elsewhere, if captured; all enemies who have thrown
away their arms and ask for quarter, are prisoners of war,
and as such exposed to the inconveniences as well as
entitled to the privileges of a prisoner of war.

50

Moreover, citizens who accompany an army for whatever
purpose, such as sutlers, editors, or reporters of journals,
or contractors, if captured, may be made prisoners of war,
and be detained as such.

The monarch and members of the reigning hostile family, male or female, the chief, and chief officers of the hostile government, its diplomatic agents, and all persons who are of particular and singular use and benefit to the hostile army or its government, are, if captured, on belligerent ground, and if unprovided with a safe conduct granted by the captor's government, prisoners of war.

51

If the people of that portion of an invaded country which is not yet occupied by the enemy, or of the whole country, at the approach of a hostile army, rise, under a duly authorized levy, *en masse* to resist the invader, they are now treated as public enemies, and, if captured, are prisoners of war.

52

No belligerent has the right to declare that he will treat every captured man in arms of a levy *en masse* as a brigand or bandit.

If, however, the people of a country, or any portion of the same, already occupied by an army, rise against it, they are violators of the laws of war, and are not entitled to their protection.

53

The enemy's chaplains, officers of the medical staff, apothecaries, hospital nurses and servants, if they fall into the hands of the American Army, are not prisoners of war, unless the commander has reasons to retain them. In this latter case, or if, at their own desire, they are allowed to remain with their captured companions, they are treated as prisoners of war, and may be exchanged if the commander sees fit.

54

A hostage is a person accepted as a pledge for the fulfillment of an agreement concluded between belligerents during the war, or in consequence of a war. Hostages are rare in the present age.

55

If a hostage is accepted, he is treated like a prisoner of war, according to rank and condition, as circumstances may admit.

56

A prisoner of war is subject to no punishment for being a public enemy, nor is any revenge wreaked upon him by the intentional infliction of any suffering, or disgrace, by cruel imprisonment, want of food, by mutilation, death, or any other barbarity.

57

So soon as a man is armed by a sovereign government and takes the soldier's oath of fidelity, he is a belligerent; his killing, wounding, or other warlike acts are not individual crimes or offenses. No belligerent has a right to declare that enemies of a certain class, color, or condition, when properly organized as soldiers, will not be treated by him as public enemies.

58

The law of nations knows of no distinction of color, and if an enemy of the United States should enslave and sell any captured persons of their army, it would be a case for the severest retaliation, if not redressed upon complaint.

The United States can not retaliate by enslavement; therefore death must be the retaliation for this crime against the law of nations.

59

A prisoner of war remains answerable for his crimes committed against the captor's army or people, committed before he was captured, and for which he has not been punished by his own authorities.

All prisoners of war are liable to the infliction of retaliatory measures.

60

It is against the usage of modern war to resolve, in hatred and revenge, to give no quarter. No body of troops has the right to declare that it will not give, and therefore will not expect, quarter; but a commander is permitted to direct his troops to give no quarter, in great straits, when his own salvation makes it *impossible* to cumber himself with prisoners.

61

Troops that give no quarter have no right to kill enemies already disabled on the ground, or prisoners captured by other troops.

62

All troops of the enemy known or discovered to give no quarter in general, or to any portion of the army, receive none.

63

Troops who fight in the uniform of their enemies, without any plain, striking, and uniform mark of distinction of their own, can expect no quarter.

64

If American troops capture a train containing uniforms of the enemy, and the commander considers it advisable to distribute them for use among his men, some striking mark or sign must be adopted to distinguish the American soldier from the enemy.

65

The use of the enemy's national standard, flag, or other emblem of nationality, for the purpose of deceiving the enemy in battle, is an act of perfidy by which they lose all claim to the protection of the laws of war.

66

Quarter having been given to an enemy by American troops, under a misapprehension of his true character, he may, nevertheless, be ordered to suffer death if, within three days after the battle, it be discovered that he belongs to a corps which gives no quarter.

67

The law of nations allows every sovereign government to make war upon another sovereign state, and, therefore, admits of no rules or laws different from those of regular warfare, regarding the treatment of prisoners of war, although they may belong to the army of a government which the captor may consider as a wanton and unjust assailant.

68

Modern wars are not internecine wars, in which the killing of the enemy is the object. The destruction of the enemy in modern war, and, indeed, modern war itself, are means to obtain that object of the belligerent which lies beyond the war.

Unnecessary or revengeful destruction of life is not lawful.

69

Outposts, sentinels, or pickets are not to be fired upon, except to drive them in, or when a positive order, special or general, has been issued to that effect.

70

The use of poison in any manner, be it to poison wells, or food, or arms, is wholly excluded from modern warfare. He that uses it puts himself out of the pale of the law and usages of war.

71

Whoever intentionally inflicts additional wounds on an enemy already wholly disabled, or kills such an enemy, or who orders or encourages soldiers to do so, shall suffer death, if duly convicted, whether he belongs to the Army of the

United States, or is an enemy captured after having committed his misdeed.

72

Money and other valuables on the person of a prisoner, such as watches or jewelry, as well as extra clothing, are regarded by the American Army as the private property of the prisoner, and the appropriation of such valuables or money is considered dishonorable, and is prohibited.

Nevertheless, if *large* sums are found upon the persons of prisoners, or in their possession, they shall be taken from them, and the surplus, after providing for their own support, appropriated for the use of the army, under the direction of the commander, unless otherwise ordered by the government. Nor can prisoners claim, as private property, large sums found and captured in their train, although they have been placed in the private luggage of the prisoners.

73

All officers, when captured, must surrender their side arms to the captor. They may be restored to the prisoner in marked cases, by the commander, to signalize admiration of his distinguished bravery or approbation of his humane treatment of prisoners before his capture. The captured officer to whom they may be restored can not wear them during captivity.

74

A prisoner of war, being a public enemy, is the prisoner of the government, and not of the captor. No ransom can be paid by a prisoner of war to his individual captor or to any officer in command. The government alone releases captives, according to rules prescribed by itself.

75

Prisoners of war are subject to confinement or imprisonment such as may be deemed necessary on account of safety, but they are to be subjected to no other intentional suffering or indignity. The confinement and mode of treating a prisoner may be varied during his captivity according to the demands of safety.

76

Prisoners of war shall be fed upon plain and wholesome food, whenever practicable, and treated with humanity.

They may be required to work for the benefit of the captor's government, according to their rank and condition.

77

A prisoner of war who escapes may be shot or otherwise killed in his flight; but neither death nor any other punishment shall be inflicted upon him simply for his attempt to escape, which the law of war does not consider a crime. Stricter means of security shall be used after an unsuccessful attempt at escape.

If, however, a conspiracy is discovered, the purpose of which is a united or general escape, the conspirators may be rigorously punished, even with death; and capital punishment may also be inflicted upon prisoners of war discovered to have plotted rebellion against the authorities of the captors, whether in union with fellow prisoners or other persons.

78

If prisoners of war, having given no pledge nor made any promise on their honor, forcibly or otherwise escape, and are captured again in battle after having rejoined their own army, they shall not be punished for their escape, but shall be treated as simple prisoners of war, although they will be subjected to stricter confinement.

79

Every captured wounded enemy shall be medically treated, according to the ability of the medical staff.

80

Honorable men, when captured, will abstain from giving to the enemy information concerning their own army, and the modern law of war permits no longer the use of any violence against prisoners in order to extort the desired information or to punish them for having given false information.

SECTION IV

PARTISANS — ARMED ENEMIES NOT BELONGING TO THE HOSTILE ARMY — SCOUTS — ARMED PROWLERS — WAR-REBELS

81

Partisans are soldiers armed and wearing the uniform of their army, but belonging to a corps which acts detached from the main body for the purpose of making inroads into the territory occupied by the enemy. If captured, they are entitled to all the privileges of the prisoner of war.

82

Men, or squads of men, who commit hostilities, whether by fighting, or inroads for destruction or plunder, or by raids of any kind, without commission, without being part and portion of the organized hostile army, and without sharing continuously in the war, but who do so with intermitting returns to their homes and avocations, or with the occasional assumption of the semblance of peaceful pursuits, divesting themselves of the character or appearance of soldiers — such men, or squads of men, are not public enemies, and, therefore, if captured, are not entitled to the privileges of prisoners of war, but shall be treated summarily as highway robbers or pirates.

83

Scouts, or single soldiers, if disguised in the dress of the country or in the uniform of the army hostile to their own, employed in obtaining information, if found within or lurking about the lines of the captor, are treated as spies, and suffer death.

84

Armed prowlers, by whatever names they may be called, or persons of the enemy's territory, who steal within the lines of the hostile army for the purpose of robbing, killing, or of destroying bridges, roads, or canals, or of robbing or destroying the mail, or of cutting the telegraph wires, are not entitled to the privileges of the prisoner of war.

85

War-rebels are persons within an occupied territory who rise in arms against the occupying or conquering army, or against the authorities established by the same.   If captured, they may suffer death, whether they rise singly, in small or large bands, and whether called upon to do so by their own, but expelled, government or not.   They are not prisoners of war; nor are they if discovered and secured before their conspiracy has matured to an actual rising or armed violence.

SECTION V

SAFE-CONDUCT — SPIES — WAR-TRAITORS — CAPTURED MESSENGERS — ABUSE OF THE FLAG OF TRUCE

86

All intercourse between the territories occupied by belligerent armies, whether by traffic, by letter, by travel, or in any other way, ceases.   This is the general rule, to be observed without special proclamation.

Exceptions to this rule, whether by safe-conduct, or permission to trade on a small or large scale, or by exchanging mails, or by travel from one territory into the other, can take place only according to agreement approved by the government, or by the highest military authority.

Contraventions of this rule are highly punishable.

87

Ambassadors, and all other diplomatic agents of neutral powers, accredited to the enemy, may receive safe-conducts through the territories occupied by the belligerents, unless there are military reasons to the contrary, and unless they may reach the place of their destination conveniently by another route. It implies no international affront if the safe-conduct is declined. Such passes are usually given by the supreme authority of the State and not by subordinate officers.

88

A spy is a person who secretly, in disguise or under false pretense, seeks information with the intention of communicating it to the enemy.

The spy is punishable with death by hanging by the neck, whether or not he succeed in obtaining the information or in conveying it to the enemy.

89

If a citizen of the United States obtains information in a legitimate manner, and betrays it to the enemy, be he a military or civil officer, or a private citizen, he shall suffer death.

90

A traitor under the law of war, or a war-traitor, is a person in a place or district under martial law who, unauthorized by the military commander, gives information of any kind to the enemy, or holds intercourse with him.

91

The war-traitor is always severely punished. If his offense consists in betraying to the enemy anything concern-

2 A

ing the condition, safety, operations, or plans of the troops holding or occupying the place or district, his punishment is death.

92

If the citizen or subject of a country or place invaded or conquered gives information to his own government, from which he is separated by the hostile army, or to the army of his government, he is a war-traitor, and death is the penalty of his offense.

93

All armies in the field stand in need of guides, and impress them if they can not obtain them otherwise.

94

No person having been forced by the enemy to serve as guide is punishable for having done so.

95

If a citizen of a hostile and invaded district voluntarily serves as a guide to the enemy, or offers to do so, he is deemed a war-traitor, and shall suffer death.

96

A citizen serving voluntarily as a guide against his own country commits treason, and will be dealt with according to the law of his country.

97

Guides, when it is clearly proved that they have misled intentionally, may be put to death.

98

All unauthorized or secret communication with the enemy is considered treasonable by the law of war.

Foreign residents in an invaded or occupied territory, or foreign visitors in the same, can claim no immunity from this law. They may communicate with foreign parts, or with the inhabitants of the hostile country, so far as the military authority permits, but no further. Instant expulsion from the occupied territory would be the very least punishment for the infraction of this rule.

99

A messenger carrying written dispatches or verbal messages from one portion of the army, or from a besieged place, to another portion of the same army, or its government, if armed, and in the uniform of his army, and if captured, while doing so, in the territory occupied by the enemy, is treated by the captor as a prisoner of war. If not in uniform, nor a soldier, the circumstances connected with his capture must determine the disposition that shall be made of him.

100

A messenger or agent who attempts to steal through the territory occupied by the enemy, to further, in any manner, the interests of the enemy, if captured, is not entitled to the privileges of the prisoner of war, and may be dealt with according to the circumstances of the case.

101

While deception in war is admitted as a just and necessary means of hostility, and is consistent with honorable warfare, the common law of war allows even capital punishment for clandestine or treacherous attempts to injure an enemy, because they are so dangerous, and it is so difficult to guard against them.

102

The law of war, like the criminal law regarding other offenses, makes no difference on account of the difference of sexes, concerning the spy, the war-traitor, or the war-rebel.

103

Spies, war-traitors, and war-rebels are not exchanged according to the common law of war. The exchange of such persons would require a special cartel, authorized by the government, or, at a great distance from it, by the chief commander of the army in the field.

104

A successful spy or war-traitor, safely returned to his own army, and afterwards captured as an enemy, is not subject to punishment for his acts as a spy or war-traitor, but he may be held in closer custody as a person individually dangerous.

SECTION VI

EXCHANGE OF PRISONERS — FLAGS OF TRUCE — FLAGS OF PROTECTION

105

Exchanges of prisoners take place — number for number — rank for rank — wounded for wounded — with added condition for added condition — such, for instance, as not to serve for a certain period.

106

In exchanging prisoners of war, such numbers of persons of inferior rank may be substituted as an equivalent for one of superior rank as may be agreed upon by cartel, which requires the sanction of the government, or of the commander of the army in the field.

107

A prisoner of war is in honor bound truly to state to the captor his rank; and he is not to assume a lower rank than belongs to him, in order to cause a more advantageous exchange, nor a higher rank, for the purpose of obtaining better treatment.

Offenses to the contrary have been justly punished by the commanders of released prisoners, and may be good cause for refusing to release such prisoners.

108

The surplus number of prisoners of war remaining after an exchange has taken place is sometimes released either for the payment of a stipulated sum of money, or, in urgent cases, of provision, clothing, or other necessaries.

Such arrangement, however, requires the sanction of the highest authority.

109

The exchange of prisoners of war is an act of convenience to both belligerents. If no general cartel has been concluded, it can not be demanded by either of them. No belligerent is obliged to exchange prisoners of war.

A cartel is voidable as soon as either party has violated it.

110

No exchange of prisoners shall be made except after complete capture, and after an accurate account of them, and a list of the captured officers, has been taken.

111

The bearer of a flag of truce can not insist upon being admitted. He must always be admitted with great caution. Unnecessary frequency is carefully to be avoided.

112

If the bearer of a flag of truce offer himself during an engagement, he can be admitted as a very rare exception only. It is no breach of good faith to retain such flag of truce, if admitted during the engagement. Firing is not required t/ cease on the appearance of a flag of truce in battle.

113

If the bearer of a flag of truce, presenting himself during an engagement, is killed or wounded, it furnishes no ground of complaint whatever.

114

If it be discovered, and fairly proved, that a flag of truce has been abused for surreptitiously obtaining military knowledge, the bearer of the flag thus abusing his sacred character is deemed a spy.

So sacred is the character of a flag of truce, and so necessary is its sacredness, that while its abuse is an especially heinous offense, great caution is requisite, on the other hand, in convicting the bearer of a flag of truce as a spy.

115

It is customary to designate by certain flags (usually yellow) the hospitals in places which are shelled, so that the besieging enemy may avoid firing on them. The same has been done in battles, when hospitals are situated within the field of the engagement.

116

Honorable belligerents often request that the hospitals within the territory of the enemy may be designated, so that they may be spared.

An honorable belligerent allows himself to be guided by flags or signals of protection as much as the contingencies and the necessities of the fight will permit.

117

It is justly considered an act of bad faith, of infamy or fiendishness, to deceive the enemy by flags of protection. Such act of bad faith may be good cause for refusing to respect such flags.

118

The besieging belligerent has sometimes requested the besieged to designate the buildings containing collections of works of art, scientific museums, astronomical observatories, or precious libraries, so that their destruction may be avoided as much as possible.

SECTION VII

THE PAROLE

119

Prisoners of war may be released from captivity by exchange, and, under certain circumstances, also by parole.

120

The term "Parole" designates the pledge of individual good faith and honor to do, or to omit doing, certain acts after he who gives his parole shall have been dismissed, wholly or partially, from the power of the captor.

121

The pledge of the parole is always an individual, but not a private act.

122

The parole applies chiefly to prisoners of war whom the captor allows to return to their country, or to live in greater freedom within the captor's country or territory, on conditions stated in the parole.

123

Release of prisoners of war by exchange is the general rule; release by parole is the exception.

124

Breaking the parole is punished with death when the person breaking the parole is captured again.

Accurate lists, therefore, of the paroled persons must be kept by the belligerents.

125

When paroles are given and received there must be an exchange of two written documents, in which the name and rank of the paroled individuals are accurately and truthfully stated.

126

Commissioned officers only are allowed to give their parole, and they can give it only with the permission of their superior, as long as a superior in rank is within reach.

127

No noncommissioned officer or private can give his parole except through an officer. Individual paroles not given through an officer are not only void, but subject the individuals giving them to the punishment of death as deserters. The only admissible exception is where individuals, properly separated from their commands, have suffered long confinement without the possibility of being paroled through an officer.

128

No paroling on the battlefield; no paroling of entire bodies of troops after a battle; and no dismissal of large numbers of prisoners, with a general declaration that they are paroled, is permitted, or of any value.

129

In capitulations for the surrender of strong places or fortified camps the commanding officer, in cases of urgent necessity, may agree that the troops under his command shall not fight again during the war, unless exchanged.

130

The usual pledge given in the parole is not to serve during the existing war, unless exchanged.

This pledge refers only to the active service in the field, against the paroling belligerent or his allies actively engaged in the same war. These cases of breaking the parole are patent acts, and can be visited with the punishment of death; but the pledge does not refer to internal service, such as recruiting or drilling the recruits, fortifying places not besieged, quelling civil commotions, fighting against belligerents unconnected with the paroling belligerents, or to civil or diplomatic service for which the paroled officer may be employed.

131

If the government does not approve of the parole, the paroled officer must return into captivity, and should the enemy refuse to receive him, he is free of his parole.

132

A belligerent government may declare, by a general order, whether it will allow paroling, and on what conditions it will allow it. Such order is communicated to the enemy.

133

No prisoner of war can be forced by the hostile government to parole himself, and no government is obliged to parole prisoners of war, or to parole all captured officers, if it paroles any. As the pledging of the parole is an individual act, so is paroling, on the other hand, an act of choice on the part of the belligerent.

134

The commander of an occupying army may require of the civil officers of the enemy, and of its citizens, any pledge he may consider necessary for the safety or security of his army, and upon their failure to give it he may arrest, confine, or detain them.

SECTION VIII

ARMISTICE — CAPITULATION

135

An armistice is the cessation of active hostilities for a period agreed between belligerents. It must be agreed upon in writing, and duly ratified by the highest authorities of the contending parties.

136

If an armistice be declared, without conditions, it extends no further than to require a total cessation of hostilities along the front of both belligerents.

If conditions be agreed upon, they should be clearly expressed, and must be rigidly adhered to by both parties. If either party violates any express condition, the armistice may be declared null and void by the other.

137

An armistice may be general, and valid for all points and lines of the belligerents; or special, that is, referring to certain troops or certain localities only.

An armistice may be concluded for a definite time; or for an indefinite time, during which either belligerent may resume hostilities on giving the notice agreed upon to the other.

138

The motives which induce the one or the other belligerent to conclude an armistice, whether it be expected to be preliminary to a treaty of peace, or to prepare during the armistice for a more vigorous prosecution of the war, does in no way affect the character of the armistice itself.

139

An armistice is binding upon the belligerents from the day of the agreed commencement; but the officers of the armies are responsible from the day only when they receive official information of its existence.

140

Commanding officers have the right to conclude armistices binding on the district over which their command extends, but such armistice is subject to the ratification of the superior authority, and ceases so soon as it is made known to the enemy that the armistice is not ratified, even if a certain time for the elapsing between giving notice of cessation and the resumption of hostilities should have been stipulated for.

141

It is incumbent upon the contracting parties of an armistice to stipulate what intercourse of persons or traffic between the inhabitants of the territories occupied by the hostile armies shall be allowed, if any.

If nothing is stipulated the intercourse remains suspended, as during actual hostilities.

142

An armistice is not a partial or a temporary peace; it is only the suspension of military operations to the extent agreed upon by the parties.

143

When an armistice is concluded between a fortified place and the army besieging it, it is agreed by all the authorities on this subject that the besieger must cease all extension, perfection, or advance of his attacking works as much so as from attacks by main force.

But as there is a difference of opinion among martial jurists, whether the besieged have the right to repair breaches or to erect new works of defense within the place during an armistice, this point should be determined by express agreement between the parties.

144

So soon as a capitulation is signed, the capitulator has no right to demolish, destroy, or injure the works, arms, stores, or ammunition, in his possession, during the time which elapses between the signing and the execution of the capitulation, unless otherwise stipulated in the same.

145

When an armistice is clearly broken by one of the parties, the other party is released from all obligation to observe it.

146

Prisoners taken in the act of breaking an armistice must be treated as prisoners of war, the officer alone being responsible who gives the order for such a violation of an armistice. The highest authority of the belligerent aggrieved may demand redress for the infraction of an armistice.

147

Belligerents sometimes conclude an armistice while their plenipotentiaries are met to discuss the conditions of a treaty of peace; but plenipotentiaries may meet without a preliminary armistice; in the latter case, the war is carried on without any abatement.

SECTION IX

ASSASSINATION

148

The law of war does not allow proclaiming either an individual belonging to the hostile army, or a citizen, or a subject of the hostile government, an outlaw, who may be slain without trial by any captor, any more than the modern law of peace allows such intentional outlawry; on the contrary, it abhors such outrage. The sternest retaliation should follow the murder committed in consequence of such proclamation, made by whatever authority. Civilized nations look with horror upon offers of rewards for the assassination of enemies as relapses into barbarism.

SECTION X

INSURRECTION — CIVIL WAR — REBELLION

149

Insurrection is the rising of people in arms against their government, or a portion of it, or against one or more of its laws, or against an officer or officers of the government. It may be confined to mere armed resistance, or it may have greater ends in view.

150

Civil war is war between two or more portions of a country or state, each contending for the mastery of the whole, and each claiming to be the legitimate government. The term is also sometimes applied to war of rebellion, when the rebellious provinces or portion of the state are contiguous to those containing the seat of government.

151

The term "rebellion" is applied to an insurrection of large extent, and is usually a war between the legitimate government of a country and portions of provinces of the same who seek to throw off their allegiance to it and set up a government of their own.

152

When humanity induces the adoption of the rules of regular war toward rebels, whether the adoption is partial or entire, it does in no way whatever imply a partial or complete acknowledgment of their government, if they have set up one, or of them, as an independent and sovereign power.

Neutrals have no right to make the adoption of the rules of war by the assailed government toward rebels the ground of their own acknowledgment of the revolted people as an independent power.

153

Treating captured rebels as prisoners of war, exchanging them, concluding of cartels, capitulations, or other warlike agreements with them; addressing officers of a rebel army by the rank they may have in the same; accepting flags of truce; or, on the other hand, proclaiming martial law in their territory, or levying war-taxes or forced loans, or doing any other act sanctioned or demanded by the law and usages of public war between sovereign belligerents, neither proves nor establishes an acknowledgment of the rebellious people, or of the government which they may have erected, as a public or sovereign power. Nor does the adoption of the rules of war toward rebels imply an engagement with them extending beyond the limits of these rules. It is victory in the field that ends the strife and settles the future relations between the contending parties.

154

Treating, in the field, the rebellious enemy according to the law and usages of war has never prevented the legitimate government from trying the leaders of the rebellion or chief rebels for high treason, and from treating them accordingly, unless they are included in a general amnesty.

155

All enemies in regular war are divided into two general classes — that is to say, into combatants and noncombatants, or unarmed citizens of the hostile government.

The military commander of the legitimate government, in a war of rebellion, distinguishes between the loyal citizen in the revolted portion of the country and the disloyal citizen. The disloyal citizens may further be classified into those citizens known to sympathize with the rebellion without positively aiding it, and those who, without taking up arms, give positive aid and comfort to the rebellious enemy without being bodily forced thereto.

156

Common justice and plain expediency require that the military commander protect the manifestly loyal citizens, in revolted territories, against the hardships of the war as much as the common misfortune of all war admits.

The commander will throw the burden of the war, as much as lies within his power, on the disloyal citizens, of the revolted portion or province, subjecting them to a stricter police than the noncombatant enemies have to suffer in regular war; and if he deems it appropriate, or if his government demands of him that every citizen shall, by an oath of allegiance, or by some other manifest act, declare his fidelity to the legitimate government, he may expel, transfer, imprison, or fine the revolted citizens who refuse to pledge themselves anew as citizens obedient to the law and loyal to the government.

Whether it is expedient to do so, and whether reliance can be placed upon such oaths, the commander or his government has the right to decide.

157

Armed or unarmed resistance by citizens of the United States against the lawful movements of their troops is levying war against the United States, and is therefore treason.

APPENDIX II

MANUAL OF THE LAWS OF WAR ON LAND

PREPARED BY THE INSTITUTE OF INTERNATIONAL
LAW, AND UNANIMOUSLY ADOPTED AT ITS MEET-
ING AT OXFORD ON SEPTEMBER 9, 1880 [1]

PART I. GENERAL PRINCIPLES

1. The state of war admits of the performance of acts of
violence on the part only of the armed forces of the belligerent states.

Persons not forming part of a belligerent armed force
must abstain from the performance of such acts.

A distinction being implied in the above rule between the individuals of whom the armed force of a state is composed and other
subjects of a State, it becomes necessary to define an "armed force."

2. The armed force of a state comprehends —
   § 1. The army properly so called, including militia.
   § 2. National Guards Landsturm, and all corps which
      satisfy the following requirements:
      (a) That of being under the direction of a respon-
         sible leader.
      (b) That of wearing a uniform or a distinctive
         mark, which latter must be fixed, and
         capable of being recognized at a distance.
      (c) That of bearing arms openly.
   § 3. Crews of vessels of war, and other members of the
      naval forces of the country.
   § 4. Inhabitants of a territory not militarily occupied

[1] This translation is by W. E. Hall, member of the Institute.

by the enemy, who, on the approach of his army, take up arms spontaneously and openly for the purpose of combating it. Such persons form part of the armed force of the State, even though, owing to want of time, they have not organized themselves militarily.

3. Every belligerent armed force is bound to conform to the laws of war.

The sole object during war to which states can legitimately direct their hostilities being the enfeeblement of the military strength of the enemy. (Declaration of St. Petersburg of the 4/16th November, 1868.)

4. The laws of war do not allow belligerents an unlimited freedom of adopting whatever means they may choose for injuring their enemy. Especially they must abstain from all useless severity, and from disloyal, unjust, or tyrannical acts.

5. Military conventions made between belligerents during war — such as armistices and capitulations — must be scrupulously observed and respected.

6. No invaded territory is considered to be conquered until war is ended. Until then the occupying state only exercises a *de facto* control of an essentially provisional nature.

PART II. APPLICATION OF THE GENERAL PRINCIPLES

I. Of Hostilities

A. RULES OF CONDUCT WITH RESPECT TO PERSONS

(a) *Of the inoffensive population*

Acts of violence being permissible only between armed forces (Art. 1),

7. It is forbidden to maltreat the inoffensive portion of the population.

2 B

(b) *Of means of injuring the enemy*

Loyalty of conduct being enjoined (Art. 4),

8. It is forbidden:—

 (a) To employ poison in any form.

 (b) To endeavor to take the life of an enemy in a traitorous manner, — *e.g.* by employing assassins, or by simulating surrender.

 (c) To attack the enemy while concealing the distinctive marks of an armed force.

 (d) To make improper use of the national flag, of signs of military ranks, or of the uniform of the enemy, of a flag of truce, or of the protective marks prescribed by the Convention of Geneva. (See Arts. 17 and 40.)

It being obligatory to abstain from useless severities (Art. 4),

9. It is forbidden : —

 (a) To use arms, projectiles, or substances calculated to inflict superfluous suffering, or to aggravate wounds, particularly projectiles which, being explosible, or charged with fulminating or inflammable substances, weigh less than four hundred grams. (Declaration of St. Petersburg.)[1]

 (b) To mutilate or kill an enemy who has surrendered at discretion, or is disabled, and to declare that quarter will not be given, even if the force making such declaration does not claim quarter for itself.

(c) *Of wounded, sick, and the hospital staff*

The wounded, the sick, and the hospital staff are exempted from unnecessary severities, which might otherwise touch them, by the following rules (Arts. 10 to 18), drawn from the Convention of Geneva.

10. Wounded and sick soldiers must be brought in and cared for, to whatever nation they belong.

11. When circumstances permit, officers commanding in chief, immediately after a combat, may send in enemy

---

[1] See Holls, " Hague Peace Conference," 457.

soldiers wounded during it to the advanced. posts of the
enemy, with the consent of the latter.

12. The operation of moving sick and wounded is a
neutral act, and the staff engaged in it is neutral.

13. The staff of the hospitals and ambulances — namely,
surgeons, clerks, hospital orderlies, and other persons employed in the sanitary, administrative, and transport departments, as well as chaplains, and members and agents of
societies duly authorized to assist the official hospital staff
— is considered to be neutral while exercising its functions,
and so long as there are wounded to remove or succor.

14. The staff specified in the preceding Article must continue after occupation by an enemy has taken place to give
its attention to the sick and wounded, to such extent as may
be needful, in the ambulance or hospital which it serves.

15. When such staff applies for leave to retire, it falls to
the officer commanding the occupying troops to fix the date
of departure. After request, however, has been made, the
departure of the staff can only be postponed for a short
time, and for reasons of military necessity.

16. Measures must, if possible, be taken to secure to the
neutralized staff fitting maintenance and allowance when it
falls into the hands of the enemy.

17. The neutralized hospital staff must wear a white armlet with a red cross on it. The armlet can be issued only
by the military authorities.

18. It is the duty of the generals of the belligerent Powers
to appeal to the humanity of the inhabitants of the country
in which they are operating, for the purpose of inducing
them to succor the wounded, pointing out to them at the
same time the advantages which result to themselves therefrom (Arts. 36 and 59). Those who respond to any such
appeal are entitled to special protection.

(d) Of the dead

19. It is forbidden to strip and mutilate th
on the field of battle.

20. The dead must never be buried before such indications of their identity (especially "livrets, numeros," etc.) as they may have upon them have been collected. The indications thus gathered upon enemy dead are communicated to their army or government.

(e) *Who can be made prisoners of war*

21. Persons forming part of the armed force of belligerents, on falling into the power of the enemy, must be treated as prisoners of war, conformably to Article 61, and those following it.

This rule applies to messengers openly carrying official dispatches, and to civil aëronauts employed to observe the enemy or to keep up communication between different parts of the army or territory.

22. Persons who follow an army without forming part of it, such as correspondents of newspapers, sutlers, contractors, etc., on falling into the power of the enemy, can only be detained for so long a time as may be required by military necessity.

(f) *Of spies*

23. Persons captured as spies cannot demand to be treated as prisoners of war.

But

24. Persons belonging to a belligerent armed force are not to be considered spies on entering, without the cover of a disguise, within the area of the actual operations of the enemy. Messengers, also, who openly carry official dispatches, and aëronauts (Art. 21) are not to be considered spies.

To guard against the abuses to which accusations of acting as a spy give rise in time of war, it must clearly be understood that

25. No person accused of being a spy can be punished without trial.

It is moreover admitted that

26. A spy who succeeds in quitting a territory occupied

by the enemy, cannot be held responsible for acts done before so leaving, if he afterwards falls into the enemy's hands.

(g) Of flags of truce

27. A person who is authorized by one of the belligerents to enter communication with the other belligerent, and presents himself to the latter with a white flag, is inviolable.

28. He may be accompanied by a trumpeter or drummer, by a flag-bearer, and, if necessary by a guide, and an interpreter, all of whom are also inviolable.

The necessity of this privilege is evident, especially as its exercise is frequently required in the simple interests of humanity. It must not, however, be so used as to be prejudicial to the opposite party.

Hence,

29. The commander to whom a flag of truce is sent is not obliged to receive its bearer under all circumstances.

Besides,

30. The commander who receives a flag of truce has the right to take all necessary measures to prevent the presence of an enemy within his lines from being prejudicial to him.

The bearer of a flag of truce, and those who accompany him, are bound to act with good faith toward the enemy who receives them (Art. 4).

31. If the bearer of a flag of truce abuse the confidence which is accorded to him, he may be temporarily detained; and if it be proved that he has made use of his privileges to suborn to traitorous practices, he loses his right of inviolability.

B. RULES OF CONDUCT WITH REGARD TO THINGS

(a) Of the means of exercising violence. Of bombardment

Mitigations of the extreme rights of violence are necessarily consequent upon the rule that useless severity shall not be indulged (Art. 4). It is thus that

32. It is forbidden

(a) To pillage, even in the case of town assault.

(b) To destroy public or private property, unless its destruction be required by an imperative necessity of war.

(c) To attack and bombard undefended places.

The right of belligerents to have recourse to bombardment against fortresses and other places in which the enemy is intrenched is not contestable, but humanity requires that this form of violence shall be so restrained as to limit as much as possible its effects to the armed forces of the enemy and to their defenses.

Hence,

33. The commander of an attacking force must do everything in his power to intimate to the local authorities his intention of bombarding, before the bombardment commences, except when bombardment is coupled with assault.

34. In cases of bombardment, all necessary measures ought to be taken to spare, so far as possible, buildings devoted to religion, the arts, sciences, and charity, hospitals, and places in which sick and wounded are kept; provided always that such buildings are not at the same time utilized, directly or indirectly, for defense.

It is the duty of the besieged to indicate these buildings by visible signs, notified to the besieger beforehand.

(b) Of the sanitary matériel

The rules (Arts. 10 and those following) for the protection of the wounded would be insufficient if special protection were not also given to hospitals. Consequently, in accordance with the Convention of Geneva,

35. The ambulances and hospitals used by armies are recognized as being neutral, and must be protected and respected as such by the belligerents, so long as there are sick and wounded in them.

36. A like rule applies to private buildings, or parts of private buildings, in which sick and wounded are collected and cared for.

Nevertheless,

37. The neutrality of ambulances and hospitals ceases to

exist if they are guarded by a military force, a police post being alone permissible.

38. The *matériel* of military hospitals remains subject to the laws of war; persons attached to the hospitals can only, therefore, carry away their private property on leaving. Ambulances, on the other hand, preserve their *matériel*.

39. Under the circumstances contemplated in the foregoing paragraph, the term "ambulance" is applicable to field hospitals and other temporary establishments which follow the troops to the field of battle for the purpose of receiving sick and wounded.

40. A distinctive flag and uniform, bearing a red cross upon a white ground, is adopted for hospitals, ambulances, and things and persons connected with the movement of sick and wounded. It must always be accompanied by the national flag.

II. OF OCCUPIED TERRITORY

A. DEFINITION

41. A territory is considered to be occupied when, as the result of its invasion by an enemy's force, the State to which it belongs has ceased, in fact, to exercise its ordinary authority within it, and the invading State is alone in a position to maintain order. The extent and duration of the occupation are determined by the limits of space and time within which this state of things exists.

B. RULES OF CONDUCT WITH REGARD TO PERSONS

Since new relations arise from the provisional change of government,

42. It is the duty of the occupying military authority to inform the inhabitants of the occupied territory as soon as possible of the powers which it exercises and the local extent of the occupation.

43. The occupier must take all reestablish and to preserve pub

With this object

44. The occupier must, so far as possible, retain the laws which were in vigor in the country in time of peace, modifying, suspending, or replacing them only in case of necessity.

45. The civil functionaries of every kind who consent to continue the exercise of their functions are under the protection of the occupier. They may be dismissed, and they may resign at any moment. For failing to fulfill the obligations freely accepted by them, they can only be subjected to disciplinary punishment. For betraying their trust, they may be punished in such manner as the case may demand.

46. In emergencies the occupier may require the inhabitants of an occupied district to give their assistance in carrying on the local administration.

As occupation does not entail a change of nationality on the part of the inhabitants,

47. The population of an occupied country cannot be compelled to take an oath of fidelity or obedience to the enemy's power. Persons doing acts of hostility directed against the occupier are, however, punishable (Art. 1).

48. Inhabitants of an occupied territory who do not conform to the orders of the occupier can be compelled to do so.

The occupier cannot, however, compel the inhabitants to assist him in his works of attack or defense, nor to take part in military operations against their own country (Art. 4).

Moreover,

49. Human life, female honor, religious beliefs, and forms of worship must be respected. Interference with family life is to be avoided (Art. 4).

C. RULES OF CONDUCT WITH RESPECT TO THINGS

(a) *Public property*

Although an occupier, for the purpose of governing the occupied territory, takes the place, in a certain sense, of the legitimate government, he does not possess unrestricted powers. So long as the ultimate fate of the territory is undecided — that is to say, until the conclusion of peace — the occupier is not at liberty to dispose freely of such property of his enemy as is not immediately serviceable for the operations of war.

Hence,

50. The occupier can appropriate only money and debts (including negotiable instruments) belonging to the State, arms, stores, and, in general, such movable property of the State as can be used for the purposes of military operations.

51. Means of transport (State railways and their rolling stock, State vessels, etc.), as well as land telegraphs and landing cables, can only be sequestrated for the use of the occupier. Their destruction is forbidden, unless it be required by the necessities of war. They are restored at the peace in the state in which they then are.

52. The occupier can only enjoy the use of, and do administrative acts with respect to immovable property, such as buildings, forests, and agricultural lands belonging to the enemy State (Art. 6).

Such property cannot be alienated, and must be maintained in good condition.

53. The property of municipal and like bodies, that of religious, charitable, and educational foundations, and that appropriated to the arts and sciences, are exempt from seizure.

All destruction or intentional damage of buildings devoted to the above purposes, of historical monuments, of archives, and of works of art or science, is forbidden, unless it be imperatively demanded by the necessities of war.

(b) Private property

If the powers of an occupier are limited with respect to the property of the enemy state, a fortiori they are limited with respect to the property of private persons.

54. Private property, whether held by individuals or by corporations, companies, or other bodies, must be respected, and cannot be confiscated except in the cases mentioned in the following Articles.

55. Means of transport (railways and their rolling stock, vessels, etc.), telegraphs, stores of arms and munitions of war, may be seized by the occupier, notwithstanding that they belong to individuals or companies; but they must be restored if possible at the conclusion of peace, and compensation for the loss inflicted on their owners must be provided.

56. Supplies in kind (requisitions) demanded from districts or individuals must correspond to the generally recognized necessities of war, and must be proportioned to the resources of the country.

Requisitions can only be made by express authorization of the officer commanding in the occupied locality.

57. The occupier can only levy such taxes and duties as are already established in the occupied State. He uses them to satisfy the expenses of administration to the extent that they have been so used by the legitimate government.

58. The occupier can only levy contributions in money as the equivalent of unpaid fines, or unpaid taxes, or of supplies in kind, which have not been duly made.

Contributions in money can only be imposed by the order, and on the responsibility, of the general in chief or of the supreme civil authority established in the occupied territory; and their incidence must as far as possible correspond to that of the taxes already in existence.

59. In apportioning the burdens arising from the billeting of troops and contributions of war, zeal shown by individuals in caring for the wounded is to be taken into consideration.

60. Receipts are to be given for the amount of contributions of war, and for articles requisitioned when payment for them is not made. Measures must be taken to secure that these receipts shall be given always, and in proper form.

III. Of Prisoners of War

A. THE STATE OF CAPTIVITY

Captivity is neither a punishment inflicted on prisoners of war (Art. 21) nor an act of vengeance; it is merely a temporary detention which is devoid of all penal character. In the following Articles, regard is had both to the consideration due to prisoners of war and to the necessity of keeping them in safe custody.

61. Prisoners of war are at the disposal of the enemy government, not of the individuals or corps which have captured them.

62. They are subjected to the laws and rules in force in the enemy army.

63. They must be treated with humanity.

64. All that belongs to them personally, except arms, remains their property.

65. Prisoners are bound to state, if asked, their true name and rank. If they do not do so, they can be deprived of all or any of the mitigations of imprisonment enjoyed by other prisoners circumstanced like themselves.

66. Prisoners can be subjected to internment in a town, fortress, camp, or any other place, definite bounds being assigned which they are not allowed to pass; but they can only be confined in a building when such confinement is indispensable for their safe detention.

67. Insubordination justifies whatever measures of severity may be necessary for its repression.

68. Arms may be used against a fugitive prisoner after summons to surrender.

If he is retaken before he has rejoined his army, or has escaped from the territory under the control of his captor, he may be punished, but solely in a disciplinary manner, or he may be subjected to more severe surveillance than that to which prisoners are commonly subjected. But if he be captured afresh, after having accomplished his escape, he is not punishable unless he has given his parole not to escape, in which case he may be deprived of his rights as prisoner of war.

69. The government detaining prisoners is charged with their maintenance.

In default of agreement between the belligerents on this point, prisoners are given such clothing and rations as the troops of the capturing State receive in time of peace.

70. Prisoners cannot be compelled to take part in any manner in the operations of the war, nor to give information as to their country or army.

71. They may be employed upon public works which have no direct relation to the operations carried on in the theater of war, provided that labor be not exhausting in kind or degree, and provided that the employment given to them is neither degrading with reference to their military rank, if they belong to the army, nor to their official or social position, if they do not so belong.

72. When permission is given to them to work for private employers, their wages may be received by the detaining government, which must either use it in procuring comforts for them, or must pay it over to them on their liberation, the cost of their maintenance being if necessary first deducted.

B. TERMINATION OF CAPTIVITY

The reasons which justify the detention of a captured enemy last only during the continuance of war.

Consequently,

73. The captivity of prisoners of war ceases as of course on the conclusion of peace ; but the time and mode of their actual liberation is a matter for agreement between the governments concerned.

In virtue of the Convention of Geneva,

74. Captivity ceases as of course, before the date fixed upon for general liberation, in the case of wounded or sick prisoners who, after being cured, are found to be incapable of further service.

The captor must send these back to their country so soon as their incapacity is established.

During the war

75. Prisoners can be released by means of a cartel of exchange negotiated between the belligerent parties.

Even without exchange

76. Prisoners can be set at liberty on parole, if the laws of their country do not forbid it. The conditions of their parole must be clearly stated. If so set at liberty, they are bound, on their honor, to fulfill scrupulously the engagements which they have freely entered into. Their government, on its part, must neither require nor accept from them any service inconsistent with their pledged word.

77. A prisoner cannot be compelled to accept his liberty on parole. In the same way the enemy government is not obliged to accede to a request made by a prisoner to be released on parole.

78. Prisoners liberated on parole and retaken in arms against the government to which they are pledged, can be deprived of the rights of prisoners of war, unless they have been included among prisoners exchanged unconditionally under a cartel of exchange negotiated subsequently to their liberation.

IV. Persons Interned in Neutral Territory

It is universally admitted that a neutral State cannot lend assistance to belligerents, and especially cannot allow them to make use of its territory without compromising its neutrality. Humanity, on the other hand, demands that a neutral State shall not be obliged to repel persons who beg refuge from death or captivity. The following rules are intended to reconcile these conflicting requirements :

79. The neutral State within the territory of which bodies of troops or individuals belonging to the armed force of the belligerents take refuge, must intern them at a place as distant as possible from the theater of war. It must do the same with persons using its territory as a means of carrying on military operations.

80. Interned persons may be kept in camps, or may be shut up in fortresses or other places of safety. The neutral State decides whether officers may be left free on parole on an engagement being entered into by them not to leave the neutral territory without authorization.

- 81. In default of special convention regulating the maintenance of interned persons, the neutral State supplies them with rations and clothes, and bestows care upon them in other ways to such extent as is required by humanity.

It also takes care of the *matériel* of war which the interned persons may have had with them on entering the neutral territory.

On the conclusion of peace, or sooner if possible, the expenses occasioned by the internment are repaid to the neutral State by the belligerent State to which the interned persons belong.

82. The provisions of the Convention of Geneva of the 22d August, 1864 (see above, Articles 10 to 18, 35 to 40, and 74) are applicable to the hospital staff, as well as to the sick and wounded who have taken refuge in, or been carried into, neutral territory.

Especially,

83. Sick and wounded who are not prisoners may be moved across neutral territory, provided that the persons accompanying them belong solely to the hospital staff, and that any *matériel* carried with them is such only as is required for the use of sick and wounded. The neutral State, across the territory of which sick and wounded are moved, is bound to take whatever measures of control are required to secure the strict observance of the above conditions.

PART III. PENAL SANCTION

When infractions of the foregoing rules take place, the guilty persons should be punished, after trial, by the belligerent within whose power they are.

84. Persons violating the laws of war are punishable in such way as the penal law of the country may prescribe.

But this mode of repressing acts contrary to the laws of war being only applicable when the guilty person can be reached, the injured party has no resource other than the use of reprisals when the guilty person cannot be reached, if the acts committed are sufficiently serious to render it urgently necessary to impress respect for the law upon the enemy. Reprisals, the occasional necessity of which is to be deplored, are an exceptional practice, at variance with the general principles that the innocent must not suffer for the guilty, and that every belligerent ought to conform to the laws of war, even without reciprocity on the part of the enemy. The right to use reprisals is tempered by the following restrictions : —

85. Reprisals are forbidden whenever the wrong which has afforded ground of complaint has been repaired.

86. In the grave cases in which reprisals become an imperative necessity, their nature and scope must never exceed the measure of the infraction of the laws of war committed by the enemy.

They can only be made with the authorization of the commander in chief.

They must, in all cases, be consistent with the rules of humanity and morality.

APPENDIX .III

CONFERENCE AT BRUSSELS, 1874, ON THE RULES OF MILITARY WARFARE[1]

SECTION I

OF THE RIGHTS OF BELLIGERENTS ONE TOWARD THE OTHER

CHAPTER I. *Of Military Authority over the Hostile State*

ARTICLE 1. A territory is considered as occupied when it is actually placed under the authority of the hostile army.

The occupation only extends to those territories where this authority is established and can be exercised.

ART. 2. The authority of the legal power being suspended, and having actually passed into the hands of the occupier, he shall take every step in his power to reëstablish and secure, as far as possible, public safety and social order.

ART. 3. With this object he will maintain the laws which were in force in the country in time of peace, and will only modify, suspend, or replace them by others if necessity obliges him to do so.

ART. 4. The functionaries and officials of every class who, at the instance of the occupier, consent to continue to perform their duties, shall be under his protection. They shall not be dismissed or be liable to summary punishment unless they fail in fulfilling the obligations they have undertaken, and shall be handed over to justice only if they violate those obligations by unfaithfulness.

[1] The modified text alone is given. The entire report of the proceedings by Sir A. Horsford will be found in 2 Lorimer, 337 *et seq.*

ART. 5. The army of occupation shall only levy such taxes, dues, duties, and tolls as are already established for the benefit of the State, or their equivalent if it be impossible to collect them, and this shall be done as far as possible in the form of and according to existing practice. It shall devote them to defraying the expenses of the administration of the country to the same extent as was obligatory on the legal Government.

ART. 6. The army occupying a territory shall take possession only of the specie, the funds, and bills, etc., which are the actual property of the state; the depots of arms, means of transport, magazines, and supplies, and, in general, all the personal property of the State, which may be of service in carrying on the war.

Railway plant, land telegraphs, steam and other vessels, not included in cases regulated by maritime law, as well as depots of arms, and generally every kind of munitions of war, although belonging to companies or to private individuals, are to be considered equally as means of aid in carrying on a war, which cannot be left at the disposal of the enemy. Railway plant, land telegraphs, as well as the steam and other vessels above mentioned, shall be restored, and indemnities be regulated on the conclusion of peace.

ART. 7. The occupying state shall only consider itself in the light of an administrator and usufructuary of the public buildings, real property, forests, and agricultural works belonging to the hostile state, and situated in the occupied territory. It is bound to protect these properties, and to administer them according to the laws of usufruct.

ART. 8. The property of parishes, of establishments devoted to religion, charity, education, arts, and sciences, although belonging to the State, shall be treated as private property.

Every seizure, destruction of, or willful damage to such establishments, historical monuments, or works of art, or of science, should be prosecuted by the competent authorities.

2c

CHAPTER II. *Of those who are to be recognized as Belligerents; of Combatants and Non-combatants*

ART. 9. The laws, rights, and duties of war are applicable not only to the army, but likewise to militia and corps of volunteers complying with the following conditions: •

1. That they have at their head a person responsible for his subordinates;

2. That they wear some settled, distinctive badge, recognizable at a distance;

3. That they carry arms openly; and

4. That, in their operations, they conform to the laws and customs of war.

In those countries where the militia form the whole or part of the army, they shall be included under the denomination of "army."

ART. 10. The population of a non-occupied territory, who, on the approach of the enemy, of their own accord take up arms to resist the invading troops, without having had time to organize themselves in conformity with Article 9, shall be considered as belligerents, if they respect the laws and customs of war.

ART. 11. The armed forces of the belligerents may be composed of combatants and non-combatants. In the event of being captured by the enemy, both one and the other shall enjoy the rights of prisoners of war.

CHAPTER III. *Of the Means of injuring the Enemy; of those which are permitted or should be forbidden*

ART. 12. The laws of war do not allow to belligerents an unlimited power as to the choice of means of injuring the enemy.

ART. 13. According to this principle are strictly forbidden:

(*a*) The use of poison or poisoned weapons.

(*b*) Murder by treachery of individuals belonging to the hostile nation or army.

(c) Murder of an antagonist who, having laid down his arms, or having no longer the means of defending himself, has surrendered at discretion.

(d) The declaration that no quarter will be given.

(e) The use of arms, projectiles, or substances which may cause unnecessary suffering, as well as the use of the projectiles prohibited by the declaration of St. Petersburg in 1868.[1]

(f) Abuse of the flag of truce, the national flag, or the military insignia or uniform of the enemy, as well as the distinctive badges of the Geneva Convention.

(g) All destruction or seizure of the property of the enemy which is not imperatively required by the necessity of war.

ART. 14. Stratagems and the employment of means necessary to procure intelligence respecting the enemy or the country (subject to the provisions of Art. 36), are considered as lawful means.

CHAPTER IV. *Of Sieges and Bombardments*

ART. 15. Fortified places are alone liable to be besieged. Towns, agglomerations of houses or villages, which are open and undefended, cannot be attacked or bombarded.

ART. 16. But if a town or fortress, agglomeration of houses, or village be defended, the commander of the attacking forces should, before commencing a bombardment, and except in the case of surprise, do all in his power to warn the authorities.

ART. 17. In the like case all necessary steps should be taken to spare, as far as possible, buildings devoted to religion, arts, sciences, and charity, hospitals and places where sick and wounded are collected, on condition that they are not used at the same time for military purposes.

It is the duty of the besieged to indicate these buildings by special visible signs to be notified beforehand by the besieged.

[1] See Glenn, 373; Holls, " Hague Peace Conference," 457.

ART. 18. A town taken by storm should not be given up to the victorious troops to plunder.

CHAPTER V. *Of Spies*

ART. 19. No one shall be considered as a spy but those who, acting secretly or under false pretenses, collect, or try to collect information in districts occupied by the enemy with the intention of communicating it to the opposing force.

ART. 20. A spy, if taken in the act, shall be tried and treated according to the laws in force in the army which captures him.

ART. 21. If a spy, who rejoins the army to which he belongs, is subsequently captured by the enemy, he is to be treated as a prisoner of war, and incurs no responsibility for his previous acts.

ART. 22. Military men who have penetrated within the zone of operations of the enemy's army, with the intention of collecting information, are not considered as spies if it has been possible to recognize their military character.

In like manner military men (and also non-military persons carrying out their mission openly), charged with the transmission of dispatches either to their own army or to that of the enemy, shall not be considered as spies if captured by the enemy.

To this class belong also, if captured, individuals sent in balloons to carry dispatches, and generally to keep up communications between the different parts of an army, or of a territory.

CHAPTER VI. *Of Prisoners of War*

ART. 23. Prisoners of war are lawful and disarmed enemies. They are in the power of the enemy's Government but not of the individuals or of the corps who made them prisoners.

They should be treated with humanity.

Every act of insubordination authorizes the necessary measures of severity to be taken with regard to them.

All their personal effects, except their arms, are considered to be their own property.

ART. 24. Prisoners of war are liable to internment in a town, fortress, camp, or in any locality whatever, under an obligation not to go beyond certain fixed limits; but they may not be placed in confinement unless absolutely necessary as a measure of security.

ART. 25. Prisoners of war may be employed on certain public works which have no immediate connection with the operations on the theater of war, provided the employment be not excessive nor humiliating to their military rank, if they belong to the army, or to their official or social position if they do not belong to it.

They may also, subject to such regulations as may be drawn up by the military authorities, undertake private work.

The pay they receive will go towards ameliorating their position, or will be put to their credit at the time of their release. In this case the cost of their maintenance may be deducted from their pay.

ART. 26. Prisoners of war cannot be compelled in any way to take any part whatever in carrying on the operations of the war.

ART. 27. The Government in whose power are the prisoners of war, undertakes to provide for their maintenance.

The conditions of such maintenance may be settled by a mutual understanding between the belligerents.

In default of such an understanding, and as a general principle, prisoners of war shall be treated, as regards food and clothing, on the same footing as the troops of the Government who made them prisoners.

ART. 28. Prisoners of war are subject to the laws and regulations in force in the army in whose power they are.

Arms may be used, after summoning, against a prisoner attempting to escape. If retaken, he is subject to summary punishment or to a stricter surveillance.

If after having escaped he is again made prisoner, he is not liable to any punishment for his previous escape.

ART. 29. Every prisoner is bound to declare, if interrogated on the point, his true names and rank; and in the case of his infringing this rule, he will incur a restriction of the advantages granted to the prisoners of the class to which he belongs.

ART. 30. The exchange of prisoners of war is regulated by mutual agreement between the belligerents.

ART. 31. Prisoners of war may be released on parole if the laws of their country allow of it; and in such a case they are bound on their personal honor to fulfill scrupulously, as regards their own Government, as well as that which made them prisoners, the engagements they have undertaken.

In the same case their own Government should neither demand nor accept from them any service contrary to their parole.

ART. 32. A prisoner of war cannot be forced to accept release on parole, nor is the enemy's Government obliged to comply with the request of a prisoner claiming to be released on parole.

ART. 33. Every prisoner of war liberated on parole, and retaken carrying arms against the Government to which he had pledged his honor, may be deprived of the rights accorded to prisoners of war, and may be brought before the tribunals.

ART. 34. Persons in the vicinity of armies, but who do not directly form part of them, such as correspondents, newspaper reporters, *vivandiers*, contractors, etc., may also be made prisoners of war.

These persons should, however, be furnished with a permit, issued by a competent authority, as well as with a certificate of identity.

CHAPTER VII. *Of Non-combatants and Wounded*

ART. 35. The duties of belligerents, with regard to the treatment of sick and wounded, are regulated by the Convention of Geneva of the 22d August, 1864, subject to the modifications' which may be introduced into that Convention.

SECTION II

OF THE RIGHTS OF BELLIGERENTS WITH REFERENCE TO PRIVATE INDIVIDUALS

CHAPTER I. *Of the Military Power with respect to Private Individuals*

ART. 36. The population of an occupied territory cannot be compelled to take part in military operations against their own country.

ART. 37. The population of occupied territories cannot be compelled to swear allegiance to the enemy's power.

ART. 38. The honor and rights of the family, the life and property of individuals, as well as their religious convictions and the exercise of their religion, should be respected.

ART. 39. Pillage is expressly forbidden.

CHAPTER II. *Of Requisitions and Contributions*

ART. 40. As private property should be respected, the enemy will demand from parishes or the inhabitants, only such payments and services as are connected with the necessities of war generally acknowledged in proportion to the resources of the country, and which do not imply, with regard to the inhabitants, the obligation of taking part in the operations of war against their own country.

ART. 41. The enemy, in levying contributions, whether as equivalent for taxes (see Art. 5), or for payments which should be made in kind, or as fines, will proceed, as far as possible, according to the rules of the distribution and assessment of the taxes in force in the occupied territory.

The civil authorities of the legal Government will afford their assistance, if they have remained in office.

Contributions can be imposed only on the order and on the responsibility of the General in chief, or of the superior civil authority established by the enemy in the occupied territory.

For every contribution a receipt shall be given to the person furnishing it.

ART. 42. Requisitions shall be made only by the authority of the commandant of the locality occupied.

For every requisition an indemnity shall be granted, or a receipt given.

SECTION III

OF RELATIONS BETWEEN BELLIGERENTS

CHAPTER I. *Of Modes of Communication and Envoys*

ART. 43. An individual authorized by one of the belligerents to confer with the other, on presenting himself with a white flag, accompanied by a trumpeter (bugler or drummer), or also by a flag-bearer, shall be recognized as the bearer of a flag of truce. He, as well as the trumpeter (bugler or drummer), and the flag-bearer, who accompanies him, shall have the right of inviolability.

ART. 44. The commander, to whom a bearer of a flag of truce is dispatched, is not obliged to receive him under all circumstances and conditions.

It is lawful for him to take all measures necessary for preventing the bearer of the flag of truce taking advantage of his stay within the radius of the enemy's position, to the prejudice of the latter; and if the bearer of the flag of truce is found guilty of such a breach of confidence, he has the right to detain him temporarily.

He may equally declare beforehand that he will not receive bearers of flags of truce during a certain period. Envoys presenting themselves after such a notification from the side to which it has been given, forfeit their right of inviolability.

ART. 45. The bearer of a flag of truce forfeits his right of inviolability, if it be proved in a positive and irrefutable manner that he has taken advantage of his privileged position to incite to, or commit an act of treachery.

CHAPTER II. *Of Capitulations*

ART. 46. The conditions of capitulations shall be settled by the contracting parties.

These conditions should not be contrary to military honor.

When once settled by a convention they should be scrupulously observed by both sides.

CHAPTER III. *Of Armistices*

ART. 47. An armistice suspends warlike operations by a mutual agreement between the belligerents. Should the duration thereof not be fixed, the belligerents may resume operations at any moment, provided, however, that proper warning be given to the enemy, in accordance with the conditions of the armistice.

ART. 48. An armistice may be general or local. The former suspends all warlike operations between the belligerents; the latter only those between certain portions of the belligerent armies, and within a fixed radius.

ART. 49. An armistice should be notified officially and without delay to the competent authorities, and to the troops. Hostilities are suspended immediately after the notification.

ART. 50. It rests with the contracting parties to define in the clauses of the armistice the relations which shall exist between the populations.

ART. 51. The violation of the armistice by either of the parties gives to the other the right of terminating it.

ART. 52. The violation of the clauses of an armistice by private individuals, on their own personal initiative, only affords the right of demanding the punishment of the guilty persons, and, if there is occasion for it, an indemnity for losses sustained.

CHAPTER IV. *Of Belligerents interned, and of Wounded treated, in Neutral Territory*

ART. 53. The neutral State receiving in its territory troops belonging to the belligerent armies, will intern them, so far as it may be possible, away from the theater of war.

They may be kept in camps, or even confined in fortresses, or in places appropriated to this purpose.

It will decide whether the officers may be released on giving their parole not to quit the neutral territory without authority.

ART. 54. In default of a special agreement, the neutral State which receives the belligerent troops will furnish the interned with provisions, clothing, and such aid as humanity demands.

The expenses incurred by the internment will be made good at the conclusion of peace.

ART. 55. The neutral State may authorize the transport across its territory of the wounded and sick belonging to the belligerent armies, provided that the trains which convey them do not carry either the *personnel* or *matériel* of war.

In this case the neutral State is bound to take the measures necessary for the safety and control of the operation.

ART. 56. The Convention of Geneva is applicable to the sick and wounded interned on neutral territory.

APPENDIX IV

AMELIORATION OF THE CONDITION OF THE WOUNDED IN WAR

CONVENTION FOR THE AMELIORATION OF THE CONDITION OF THE WOUNDED IN ARMIES IN THE FIELD BETWEEN SWITZERLAND, BADEN, BELGIUM, DENMARK, SPAIN, FRANCE, HESSE, ITALY, NETHERLANDS, PORTUGAL, PRUSSIA, WÜRTEMBURG, AND ACCEDED TO BY SWEDEN AND NORWAY, GREECE, GREAT BRITAIN, MECKLENBURG-SCHWERIN, TURKEY, BAVARIA, AUSTRIA, RUSSIA, ROUMANIA, PERSIA, SALVADOR, MONTENEGRO, SERVIA, BOLIVIA, CHILI, ARGENTINE REPUBLIC, PERU, AND JAPAN.

Concluded August 22, 1864; ratifications exchanged at Geneva, June 22, 1865; acceded to by the United States, March 1, 1882; accession of United States accepted by Switzerland, on behalf of the Powers, June 9, 1882; proclaimed as to the original convention, but with reserve as to the additional articles, July 26, 1882.

After reciting the desire of the different governments "to soften, as much as depends on them, the evils of warfare, to suppress its useless hardships and improve the fate of wounded soldiers on the field of battle," the Convention names the negotiators,

Who, after having exchanged their powers and found them in good and due form, agree to the following articles:

ARTICLE 1. Ambulances and military hospitals shall be acknowledged to be neuter, and as such, shall be protected and respected by belligerents so long as any sick or wounded may be therein.

Such neutrality shall cease if the ambulances or hospitals should be held by a military force.

ART. 2. Persons employed in hospitals and ambulances, comprising the staff for superintendence, medical service, administration, transport of wounded, as well as chaplains, shall participate in the benefit of neutrality, whilst so employed, and so long as there remain any wounded to bring in or to succor.

ART. 3. The persons designated in the preceding article may, even after occupation by the enemy, continue to fulfill their duties in the hospital or ambulance which they serve, or may withdraw in order to rejoin the corps to which they belong.

Under such circumstances, when these persons shall cease from their functions, they shall be delivered by the occupying army to the outposts of the enemy.

ART. 4. As the equipment of military hospitals remains subject to the laws of war, persons attached to such hospitals cannot, in withdrawing, carry away any articles but such as are their private property.

Under the same circumstances an ambulance shall, on the contrary, retain its equipment.

ART. 5. Inhabitants of the country who may bring help to the wounded, shall be respected and shall remain free. The generals of the belligerent Powers shall make it their care to inform the inhabitants of the appeal addressed to their humanity, and of the neutrality which will be the consequence of it.

Any wounded man entertained and taken care of in a house shall be considered as a protection thereto. Any inhabitant who shall have entertained wounded men in his house shall be exempted from the quartering of troops, as well as from a part of the contributions of war which may be imposed.

ART. 6. Wounded or sick soldiers shall be entertained and taken care of, to whatever nation they may belong.

Commanders in chief shall have the power to deliver immediately to the outposts of the enemy soldiers who have been wounded in an engagement, when circumstances permit this to be done, and with the consent of both parties.

Those who are recognized, after their wounds are healed, as incapable of serving, shall be sent back to their country. The others may also be sent back, on condition of not again bearing arms during the continuance of the war.

Evacuations, together with the persons under whose directions they take place, shall be protected by an absolute neutrality.

ART. 7. A distinctive and uniform flag shall be adopted for hospitals, ambulances, and evacuations. It must, on every occasion, be accompanied by the national flag. An arm badge (brassard) shall also be allowed for individuals neutralized, but the delivery thereof shall be left to military authority.

The flag and the arm badge shall bear a red cross on a white ground.

ART. 8. The details of execution of the present convention shall be regulated by the commanders in chief of belligerent armies, according to the instructions of their respective governments, and in conformity with the general principles laid down in this convention.

ART. 9. The high contracting Powers have agreed to communicate the present convention to those Governments which have not found it convenient to send plenipotentiaries to the International Conference at Geneva, with an invitation to accede thereto ; the protocol is for that purpose left open.

ART. 10. The present convention shall be ratified, and the ratifications shall be exchanged at Berne in four months, or sooner if possible.

[Additional articles, extending to naval forces the advantages of the above convention, were concluded Oct. 20, 1868, by most of the powers of Europe, and later acceded to by the United States; but they have never been ratified. See U. S. Treaties, p. 1153.] [1]

---

[1] See Holls, " Hague Peace Conference," 121 *et seq.*

APPENDIX V

DECLARATION OF PARIS

The Plenipotentiaries who signed the Treaty of Paris of the thirtieth of March, one thousand eight hundred and fifty-six, assembled in conference,

Considering:

That maritime law in time of war has long been the subject of deplorable disputes;

That the uncertainty of the law and of the duties in such a matter give rise to differences of opinion between neutrals and belligerents which may occasion serious difficulties, and even conflicts; that it is consequently advantageous to establish a uniform doctrine on so important a point;

That the Plenipotentiaries assembled in Congress at Paris cannot better respond to the intentions by which their Governments are animated, than by seeking to introduce into international relations fixed principles, in this respect.

The above-mentioned Plenipotentiaries, being duly authorized, resolved to concert among themselves as to the means of attaining this object; and having come to an agreement, have adopted the following solemn declaration:

1. Privateering is and remains abolished;

2. The neutral flag covers enemy's goods, with the exception of contraband of war;

3. Neutral goods, with the exception of contraband of war, are not liable to capture under enemy's flag;

4. Blockades, in order to be binding, must be effective — that is to say, maintained by a force sufficient really to prevent access to the coast of the enemy.

The Governments of the undersigned Plenipotentiaries engage to bring the present Declaration to the knowledge of the States which have not taken part in the Congress of Paris, and to invite them to accede to it.

Convinced that the maxims which they now proclaim cannot but be received with gratitude by the whole world, the undersigned Plenipotentiaries doubt not that the efforts of their Governments to obtain the general adoption thereof will be crowned with full success.

The present declaration is not and shall not be binding, except between those Powers who have acceded, or shall accede, to it.

Done at Paris, the sixteenth of April, one thousand eight hundred and fifty-six.

APPENDIX VI

THE LAWS AND USAGES OF WAR AT SEA

A NAVAL WAR CODE

GENERAL ORDERS,   NAVY DEPARTMENT,
 No. 551.   *Washington, June 27, 1900.*

The following code of naval warfare, prepared for the guidance and use of the naval service by Capt. Charles H. Stockton, United States Navy, under the direction of the Secretary of the Navy, having been approved by the President of the United States, is published for the use of the Navy and for the information of all concerned.

         JOHN D. LONG,
           Secretary.

THE LAWS AND USAGES OF WAR AT SEA

SECTION I

HOSTILITIES

ARTICLE 1. The general object of war is to procure the complete submission of the enemy at the earliest possible period, with the least expenditure of life and property.

The special objects of maritime war are: The capture or destruction of the military and naval forces of the enemy; of his fortifications, arsenals, dry docks, and dockyards; of his various military and naval establishments, and of his maritime commerce; to prevent his procuring war material from neutral sources; to aid and assist military operations on land, and to protect and defend the national territory, property, and sea-borne commerce.

ART. 2. The area of maritime warfare comprises the high

seas or other waters that are under no jurisdiction, and the territorial waters of belligerents. Neither hostilities nor any belligerent right, such as that of visitation and search, shall be exercised in the territorial waters of neutral States.

The territorial waters of a State extend seaward to the distance of a marine league from the low-water mark of its coast line. They also include, to a reasonable extent, which is in many cases determined by usage, adjacent parts of the sea, such as bays, gulfs, and estuaries inclosed within head-lands; and where the territory by which they are inclosed belongs to two or more States, the marine limits of such States are usually defined by conventional lines.

ART. 3. Military necessity permits measures that are indispensable for securing the ends of the war and that are in accordance with modern laws and usages of war.

It does not permit wanton devastation, the use of poison, or the doing of any hostile act that would make the return of peace unnecessarily difficult.

Noncombatants are to be spared in person and property during hostilities, as much as the necessities of war and the conduct of such noncombatants will permit.

The launching of projectiles and explosives from balloons, or by other new methods of a similar nature, is prohibited for a term of five years by the Declaration of the Hague, to which the United States became a party. This rule does not apply when at war with a 'noncontracting power.

ART. 4. The bombardment, by a naval force, of unfortified and undefended towns, villages, or buildings is forbidden, except when such bombardment is incidental to the destruction of military or naval establishments, public depots of munitions of war, or vessels of war in port, or unless reasonable requisitions for provisions and supplies essential, at the time, to such naval vessel or vessels are forcibly withheld, in which case due notice of bombardment shall be given.

The bombardment of unfortified and undefended towns and places for the nonpayment of ransom is forbidden.

2 D

ART. 5. The following rules are to be followed with regard to submarine telegraphic cables in time of war, irrespective of their ownership:

(a) Submarine telegraphic cables between points in the territory of an enemy, or between the territory of the United States and that of an enemy, are subject to such treatment as the necessities of war may require.

(b) Submarine telegraphic cables between the territory of an enemy and neutral territory may be interrupted within the territorial jurisdiction of the enemy.

(c) Submarine telegraphic cables between two neutral territories shall be held inviolable and free from interruption.

ART. 6. If military necessity should require it, neutral vessels found within the limits of belligerent authority may be seized and destroyed or otherwise utilized for military purposes, but in such cases the owners of neutral vessels must be fully recompensed. The amount of the indemnity should, if practicable, be agreed on in advance with the owner or master of the vessel. Due regard must be had to treaty stipulations upon these matters.

ART. 7. The use of false colors in war is forbidden, and when summoning a vessel to lie to, or before firing a gun in action, the national colors should be displayed by vessels of the United States.

ART. 8. In the event of an enemy failing to observe the laws and usages of war, if the offender is beyond reach, resort may be had to reprisals, if such action should be considered a necessity; but due regard must always be had to the duties of humanity. Reprisals should not exceed in severity the offense committed, and must not be resorted to when the injury complained of has been repaired.

If the offender is within the power of the United States he can be punished, after due trial, by a properly constituted military or naval tribunal. Such offenders are liable to the punishments specified by the criminal law.

SECTION II

BELLIGERENTS

ART. 9. In addition to the armed forces duly constituted for land warfare, the following are recognized as armed forces of the State.

(1) The officers and men of the Navy, Naval Reserve, Naval Militia, and their auxiliaries.

(2) The officers and men of all other armed vessels cruising under lawful authority.

ART. 10. In case of capture, the personnel of the armed forces or armed vessels of the enemy, whether combatants or noncombatants, are entitled to receive the humane treatment due to prisoners of war.

The personnel of all public unarmed vessels of the enemy, either owned or in his service as auxiliaries, are liable, upon capture, to detention as prisoners of war.

The personnel of merchant vessels of an enemy who, in self-defense and in protection of the vessel placed in their charge, resist an attack, are entitled, if captured, to the status of prisoners of war.

ART. 11. The personnel of a merchant vessel of an enemy captured as a prize can be held, at the discretion of the captor, as witnesses, or as prisoners of war when by training or enrollment they are immediately available for the naval service of the enemy, or they may be released from detention or confinement. They are entitled to their personal effects and to such individual property, not contraband of war, as is not held as part of the vessel, its equipment, or as money, plate, or cargo contained therein.

All passengers not in the service of the enemy, and all women and children on board such vessels should be released and landed at a convenient port, at the first opportunity.

Any person in the naval service of the United States who pillages or maltreats, in any manner, any person found on board a merchant vessel captured as a prize, shall be severely punished.

.

ART. 12. The United States of America acknowledge and protect, in hostile countries occupied by their forces, religion and morality; the persons of the inhabitants, especially those of women; and the sacredness of domestic relations. Offenses to the contrary shall be rigorously punished.

SECTION III

BELLIGERENT AND NEUTRAL VESSELS

ART. 13. All public vessels of the enemy are subject to capture, except those engaged in purely charitable or scientific pursuits, in voyages of discovery, or as hospital ships under the regulations hereinafter mentioned.

Cartel and other vessels of the enemy, furnished with a proper safe-conduct, are exempt from capture, unless engaged in trade or belligerent operations.

ART. 14. All merchant vessels of the enemy, except coast fishing vessels innocently employed, are subject to capture, unless exempt by treaty stipulations.

In case of military or other necessity, merchant vessels of an enemy may be destroyed, or they may be retained for the service of the government. Whenever captured vessels, arms, munitions of war, or other material are destroyed or taken for the use of the United States before coming into the custody of a prize court, they shall be surveyed, appraised, and inventoried by persons as competent and impartial as can be obtained; and the survey, appraisement, and inventory shall be sent to the prize court where proceedings are to be held.

ART. 15. Merchant vessels of the enemy that have sailed from a port within the jurisdiction of the United States, prior to the declaration of war, shall be allowed to proceed to their destination, unless they are engaged in carrying contraband of war or are in the military service of the enemy.

Merchant vessels of the enemy, in ports within the jurisdiction of the United States at the outbreak of war, shall be allowed thirty days after war has begun to load their cargoes and depart, and shall thereafter be permitted to proceed to their destination, unless they are engaged in carrying contraband of war or are in the military service of the enemy.

Merchant vessels of the enemy, which shall have sailed from any foreign port for any port within the jurisdiction of the United States before the declaration of war, shall be permitted to enter and discharge their cargo and thereafter to proceed to any port not blockaded.

ART. 16. Neutral vessels in the military or naval service of the enemy, or under the control of the enemy for military or naval purposes, are subject to capture or destruction.

ART. 17. Vessels of war of the United States may take shelter during war in a neutral port subject to the limitations that the authorities of the port may prescribe as to the number of belligerent vessels to be admitted into the port at any one time. This shelter, which is allowed by comity of nations, may be availed of for the purpose of evading an enemy, from stress of weather, or to obtain supplies or repairs that the vessel needs to enable her to continue her voyage in safety and to reach the nearest port of her own country.

ART. 18. Such vessel or vessels must conform to the regulations prescribed by the authorities of the neutral port with respect to the place of anchorage, the limitation of the stay of the vessel in port, and the time to elapse before sailing in pursuit or after the departure of a vessel of the enemy.

No increase in the armament, military stores, or in the number of the crew of a vessel of war of the United States shall be attempted during the stay of such vessel in a neutral port.

ART. 19. A neutral vessel carrying the goods of an enemy is, with her cargo, exempt from capture, except when carrying contraband of war or endeavoring to evade a blockade.

ART. 20. A neutral vessel carrying hostile dispatches, when sailing as a dispatch vessel practically in the service of the enemy, is liable to seizure. Mail steamers under neutral flags carrying such dispatches in the regular and customary manner, either as a part of their mail in their mail bags, or separately as a matter of accommodation and without special arrangement or remuneration, are not liable to seizure and should not be detained, except upon clear grounds of suspicion of a violation of the laws of war with respect to contraband, blockade, or unneutral service, in which case the mail bags must be forwarded with seals unbroken.

SECTION IV

HOSPITAL SHIPS — THE SHIPWRECKED, SICK, AND WOUNDED

ART. 21. Military hospital ships — that is to say, vessels constructed or fitted out by the belligerent States for the special and sole purpose of assisting the wounded, sick, or shipwrecked, and whose names have been communicated to the respective Powers at the opening or in the course of hostilities, and in any case before they are so employed, shall be respected, and are not liable to capture during the period of hostilities.

Such ships shall not be classed with warships, with respect to the matter of sojourn in a neutral port.

ART. 22. Hospital ships fitted out, in whole or in part, at the expense of private individuals, or of officially recognized relief societies, shall likewise be respected and exempt from capture, provided the belligerent Power to whom they are subject has given them an official commission and has notified the hostile Power of the names of such ships at the beginning or in the course of hostilities, and in any case before they are employed.

These ships should be furnished with a certificate, issued by the proper authorities, setting forth that they were under the control of such authorities during their equipment and at the time of their final departure.

ART. 23. The vessels mentioned in Articles 21 and 22 shall afford relief and assistance to the wounded, sick, and shipwrecked of the belligerents without distinction of nationality.

It is strictly forbidden to use these vessels for any military purpose.

These vessels must not in any way hamper the movements of the combatants.

During and immediately after engagements they act at their own risk and peril.

The belligerents have the right to control and visit such vessels; they may decline their coöperation, require them to withdraw, prescribe for them a fixed course, and place a commissioner on board; they may even detain them, if required by military necessity.

When practicable, the belligerents shall enter upon the log of hospital ships such orders as they may give them.

ART. 24. Military hospital ships shall be distinguished by being painted white outside, with a horizontal band of green about 1½ meters wide.

The ships designated in Article 22 shall be distinguished by being painted white outside, with a horizontal band of red about 1½ meters wide.

The boats of hospital ships, as well as small craft that may be devoted to hospital service, shall be distinguished by being painted in the same colors.

Hospital ships shall, in general, make themselves known by hoisting, with their national flag, the white flag with a red cross prescribed by the Geneva Convention.

ART. 25. Merchant vessels, yachts, or neutral vessels that happen to be in the vicinity of active maritime hostilities, may gather up the wounded, sick, or shipwrecked of the belligerents. Such vessels, after this servi-- formed, shall report to the belliger ling the waters thereabouts, for future directions, and while accompanying a belligerent will be, in all cases, under his orders; and if a neutral, be designated by the national flag of that belligerent carried at the foremasthead, with the red cross flag flying immediately under it.

These vessels are subject to capture for any violation of neutrality that they may commit. Any attempt to carry off such wounded, sick, and shipwrecked, without permission, is a violation of neutrality. They are also subject, in general, to the provisions of Article 23.

ART. 26. The religious, medical, and hospital personnel of any vessel captured during hostilities shall be inviolable and not subject to be made prisoners of war. They shall be permitted, upon leaving the ship, to carry with them those articles and instruments of surgery which are their private property.

Such personnel shall continue to exercise their functions as long as may be necessary, whereupon they may withdraw when the commander in chief deems it possible to do so.

The belligerents shall insure to such personnel, when falling into their hands, the free exercise of their functions, the receipt of salaries, and entire freedom of movement, unless a military necessity prevents.

ART. 27. Sailors and soldiers, embarked when sick or wounded, shall be protected and cared for by the captors, no matter to what nation they may belong.

ART. 28. The shipwrecked, wounded, or sick of the enemy, who are captured, are considered prisoners of war. The captor must decide, according to circumstances, whether it is expedient to keep them or send them to a port of his own country, to a neutral port, or even to a port of the enemy. In the last case, the prisoners thus returned to their country can not serve again during the period of the war.

ART. 29. The shipwrecked, wounded, or sick, who are landed at a neutral port with the consent of the local authorities, shall, unless there exist an agreement to the contrary between the neutral State and the belligerent States, agree that they will not again take part in the operations of war.

The expenses of hospital care and of internment shall be borne by the State to which such shipwrecked, wounded, or sick belong.

SECTION V

The Exercise of the Right of Search

Art. 30. The exercise of the right of search during war shall be confined to properly commissioned and authorized vessels of war. Convoys of neutral merchant vessels, under escort of vessels of war of their own State, are exempt from the right of search, upon proper assurances, based on thorough examination, from the commander of the convoy.

Art. 31. The object of the visit or search of a vessel is:

(1) To determine its nationality.

(2) To ascertain whether contraband of war is on board.

(3) To ascertain whether a breach of blockade is intended or has been committed.

(4) To ascertain whether the vessel is engaged in any capacity in the service of the enemy.

The right of search must be exercised in strict conformity with treaty provisions existing between the United States and other States and with proper consideration for the vessel boarded.

Art. 32. The following mode of procedure, subject to any special treaty stipulations, is to be followed by the boarding vessel, whose colors must be displayed at the time:

The vessel is brought to by firing a gun with blank charge. If this is not sufficient to cause her to lie to, a shot is fired across the bows, and in case of flight or resistance force can be used to compel the vessel to surrender.

The boarding vessel should then send one of its smaller boats alongside, with an officer in charge wearing side arms to conduct the search. Arms may be carried in the boat, but not upon the persons of the men. When the officer goes on board of the vessel he may be accompanied by not more than two men, unarmed, and he should at first examine the vessel's papers to ascertain her nationality, the nature of the cargo, and the ports of departure and destination. If the papers show contraband, an offense in respect of blockade, or enemy service, the vessel should be seized; otherwise she should be released, unless suspicious circumstances justify a further search. If the vessel be released, an entry in the log book to that effect should be made by the boarding officer.

ART. 33. Irrespective of the character of her cargo, or her purported destination, a neutral vessel should be seized if she:

(1) Attempts to avoid search by escape; but this must be clearly evident.

(2) Resists search with violence.

(3) Presents fraudulent papers.

(4) Is not supplied with the necessary papers to establish the objects of search.

(5) Destroys, defaces, or conceals papers.

The papers generally expected to be on board of a vessel are:

(1) The register.

(2) The crew and passenger list.

(3) The log book.

(4) A bill of health.

(5) The manifest of cargo.

(6) A charter party, if the vessel is chartered.

(7) Invoices and bills of lading.

SECTION VI

CONTRABAND OF WAR

ART. 34. The term "contraband of war" includes only articles having a belligerent destination and purpose. Such articles are classed under two general heads:

(1) Articles that are primarily and ordinarily used for military purposes in time of war, such as arms and munitions of war, military material, vessels of war, or instruments made for the immediate manufacture of munitions of war.

(2) Articles that may be and are used for purposes of war or peace, according to circumstances.

Articles of the first class, destined for ports of the enemy or places occupied by his forces, are always contraband of war.

Articles of the second class, when actually and especially destined for the military or naval forces of the enemy, are contraband of war.

In case of war, the articles that are conditionally and unconditionally contraband, when not specifically mentioned in treaties previously made and in force, will be duly announced in a public manner.

ART. 35. Vessels, whether neutral or otherwise, carrying contraband of war destined for the enemy, are liable to seizure and detention, unless treaty stipulations otherwise provide.

ART. 36. Until otherwise announced, the following articles are to be treated as contraband of war:

Absolutely contraband. — Ordnance; machine guns and their appliances and the parts thereof; armor plate and whatever pertains to the offensive and defensive armament of naval vessels; arms and instruments of iron, steel, brass, or copper, or of any other material, such arms and instruments being specially adapted for use in war by land or sea; torpedoes and their appurtenances; cases for mines, of whatever material; engineering and transport materials, such as gun carriages, caissons, cartridge boxes, campaigning forges, canteens, pontoons; ordnance stores; portable range finders; signal flags destined for naval use; ammunition and explosives of all kinds and their component parts; machinery for the manufacture of arms and munitions of war; saltpeter; military accouterments and equipments of all sorts; horses and mules.

Conditionally contraband. — Coal, when destined for a naval station, a port of call, or a ship or ships of the enemy; materials for the construction of railways or telegraphs; and money, when such materials or money are destined for the enemy's forces; provisions, when actually destined for the enemy's military or naval forces.

SECTION VII

BLOCKADE

ART. 37. Blockades, in order to be binding, must be effective; that is, they must be maintained by a force sufficient to render hazardous the ingress to or egress from a port.

If the blockading force be driven away by stress of weather and return without delay to its station, the continuity of the blockade is not thereby broken. If the blockading force leave its station voluntarily, except for purposes of the blockade, or is driven away by the enemy, the blockade is abandoned or broken. The abandonment or forced suspension of a blockade requires a new notification of blockade.

ART. 38. Neutral vessels of war must obtain permission to pass the blockade, either from the government of the State whose forces are blockading the port, or from the officer in general or local charge of the blockade. If necessary, these vessels should establish their identity to the satisfaction of the commander of the local blockading force. If military operations or other reasons should so require, permission to enter a blockaded port can be restricted or denied.

ART. 39. The notification of a blockade must be made before neutral vessels can be seized for its violation. This notification may be general, by proclamation, and communicated to the neutral States through diplomatic channels; or it may be local, and announced to the authorities of the blockaded port and the neutral consular officials thereof. A special notification may be made to individual vessels, which is duly indorsed upon their papers as a warning. A notification to a neutral State is a sufficient notice to the citizens or subjects of such State. If it be established that a neutral vessel has knowledge or notification of the blockade from any source, she is subject to seizure upon a violation or attempted violation of the blockade.

The notification of blockade should declare, not only the limits of the blockade, but the exact time of its commencement and the duration of time allowed a vessel to discharge, reload cargo, and leave port.

ART. 40. Vessels appearing before a blockaded port, having sailed before notification, are entitled to special notification by a blockading vessel. They should be boarded by an officer, who should enter upon the ship's log or upon its papers, over his official signature, the name of the notifying vessel, a notice of the fact and extent of the blockade, and of the date and place of the visit. After this notice, an attempt on the part of the vessel to violate the blockade makes her liable to capture.

ART. 41. Should it appear, from the papers of a vessel or otherwise, that the vessel had sailed for the blockaded port after the fact of the blockade had been communicated to the country of her port of departure, or after it had been commonly known at that port, she is liable to capture and detention as a prize. Due regard must be had in this matter to any treaties stipulating otherwise.

ART. 42. A neutral vessel may sail in good faith for a blockaded port, with an alternative destination to be decided upon by information as to the continuance of the blockade obtained at an intermediate port. In such case, she is not allowed to continue her voyage to the blockaded port in alleged quest of information as to the status of the blockade, but must obtain it and decide upon her course before she arrives in suspicious vicinity; and if the blockade has been formally established with due notification, sufficient doubt as to the good faith of the proceeding will subject her to capture.

ART. 43. Neutral vessels found in port at the time of the establishment of a blockade, unless otherwise specially ordered, will be allowed thirty days from the establishment of the blockade, to load their cargoes and depart from such port.

ART. 44. The liability of a vessel purposing to evade a blockade, to capture and condemnation, begins with her departure from the home port and lasts until her return, unless in the meantime the blockade of the port is raised.

ART. 45. The crews of neutral vessels violating or attempting to violate a blockade are not to be treated as prisoners of war, but any of the officers or crew whose testimony may be desired before the prize court should be detained as witnesses.

SECTION VIII

The Sending in of Prizes

ART. 46. Prizes should be sent in for adjudication, unless otherwise directed, to the nearest suitable port, within the territorial jurisdiction of the United States, in which a prize court may take action.

ART. 47. The prize should be delivered to the court as nearly as possible in the condition in which she was at the time of seizure, and to this end her papers should be carefully sealed at the time of seizure and kept in the custody of the prize master.

ART. 48. All witnesses whose testimony is necessary to the adjudication of the prize should be detained and sent in with her, and if circumstances permit, it is preferable that the officer making the search should act as prize master.

The laws of the United States in force concerning prizes and prize cases must be closely followed by officers and men of the United States Navy.

ART. 49. The title to property seized as prize changes only by the decision rendered by the prize court. But if the vessel or its cargo is needed for immediate public use, it may be converted to such use, a careful inventory and appraisal being made by impartial persons and certified to the prize court.

ART. 50. If there are controlling reasons why vessels that are properly captured may not be sent in for adjudication — such as unseaworthiness, the existence of infectious disease, or the lack of a prize crew — they may be appraised and sold, and if this can not be done, they may be destroyed. The imminent danger of recapture would justify destruction, if there should be no doubt that the vessel was a proper prize. But in all such cases all of the papers and other testimony should be sent to the prize court, in order that a decree may be duly entered.

SECTION IX

ARMISTICE, TRUCE, AND CAPITULATIONS, AND VIOLATIONS OF LAWS OF WAR

ART. 51. A truce or capitulation may be concluded, without special authority, by the commander of a naval force of the United States with the commander of the forces of the enemy, to be limited, however, to their respective commands.

A general armistice requires an agreement between the respective belligerent governments.

ART. 52. After agreeing upon or signing a capitulation the capitulator must neither injure nor destroy the vessels, property, or stores in his possession that he is to deliver up, unless the right to do so is expressly reserved to him in the agreement or capitulation.

ART. 53. The notice of the termination of hostilities, before being acted upon, must be officially received by a commander of a naval force.

Except where otherwise provided, acts of war done after the receipt of the official notice of the conclusion of a treaty of peace or of an armistice, are null and void.

ART. 54. When not in conflict with the foregoing the regulations respecting the laws of war on land, in force with the armies of the United States, will govern the Navy of the United States when circumstances render them applicable.

ART. 55. The foregoing regulations are issued with the approval of the President of the United States, for the government of all persons attached to the naval service, subject to all laws and treaties of the United States that are now in force or may hereafter be established.

APPENDIX VII

UNITED STATES NEUTRALITY LAWS

SEC. 5281. Every citizen of the United States, who within the territory or jurisdiction thereof, accepts and exercises a commission to serve a foreign prince, state, colony, district, or people, in war, by land or by sea, against any prince, state, colony, district, or people, with whom the United States are at peace, shall be deemed guilty of a high misdemeanor, and shall be fined not more than two thousand dollars, and imprisoned not more than three years.

SEC. 5282. Every person, who, within the territory or jurisdiction of the United States, enlists or enters himself, or hires or retains another person to enlist or enter himself, or to go beyond the limits or jurisdiction of the United States with intent to be enlisted or entered in the service of any foreign prince, state, colony, district, or people, as a soldier, or as a marine or seaman, on board of any vessel of war, letter of marque, or privateer, shall be deemed guilty of high misdemeanor, and shall be fined not more than one thousand dollars, and imprisoned not more than three years.

SEC. 5283. Every person, who, within the limits of the United States, fits out and arms, or attempts to fit out and arm, or procures to be fitted out and armed, or knowingly is concerned in the furnishing, fitting out, or arming, of any vessel, with intent that such vessel shall be employed in the service of any foreign prince or state, or of any colony, district, or people, to cruise or commit hostilities against the subjects, citizens, or property of any foreign prince or state, or of any colony, district, or people, with whom the United States are at peace, or who issues or delivers a commission within the territory or jurisdiction of the United States, for any vessel, to the intent that she may be so employed, shall be deemed guilty of a high misdemeanor, and shall be fined not more than ten thousand dollars, and imprisoned not more than three years. And every such vessel, her tackle, apparel, and furniture, together with all materials, arms, ammunition, and stores, which may have been procured for the building and equipment thereof, shall be forfeited; one half to the use of the informer, and the other half to the use of the United States.

SEC. 5284. Every citizen of the United States who, without the limits thereof, fits out and arms, or attempts to fit out and arm, or procures to be fitted out and armed, or knowingly aids or is concerned in furnishing, fitting out, or arming any private vessel of war, or privateer, with intent that such vessel shall be employed to cruise, or commit hostilities, upon the citizens of the United States, or their property, or who takes the command of, or enters on board of any such vessel, for such intent, or who purchases any interest in any such vessel, with a view to share in the profits thereof, shall be deemed guilty of a high misdemeanor, and fined not more than ten thousand dollars, and imprisoned not more than ten years. And the trial for such offense, if committed without the limits of the United States, shall be in the district in which the offender shall be apprehended or first brought.

SEC. 5285. Every person who, within the territory or jurisdiction of the United States, increases or augments, or procures to be increased or augmented, or knowingly is concerned in increasing or augmenting, the force of any ship of war, cruiser, or other armed vessel, which, at the time of her arrival within the United States, was a ship of war or cruiser or armed vessel, in the service of any foreign prince or state or of any colony, district, or people, or belonging to the subjects or citizens of any such prince or state, colony, district, or people, the same being at war with any foreign prince or state or of any colony, district, or people, with whom the United States are at peace, by adding to the number of the guns of such vessel or by changing those on board of her for guns of a larger caliber or by adding thereto any equipment solely applicable to war, shall be deemed guilty of a high misdemeanor, and shall be fined not more than one thousand dollars and be imprisoned not more than one year.

Sec. 5286. Every person, who, within the territory or jurisdiction of the United States, begins or sets on foot, or provides, or prepares the means for, any military expedition or enterprise, to be carried on from thence against the territory or dominions of any foreign prince or state, or of any colony, district, or people, with whom the United States are at peace, shall be deemed guilty of a high misdemeanor and shall be fined not exceeding three thousand dollars and imprisoned not more than three years.

Sec. 5287. The district courts shall take cognizance of all complaints, by whomsoever instituted, in cases of captures made within the waters of the United States or within a marine league of the coasts or shores thereof. [18 St. 320.]

In every case in which a vessel is fitted out and armed, or attempted to be fitted out and armed, or in which the force of any vessel of war, cruiser, or other armed vessel is increased or augmented, or in which any military expedition or enterprise is begun or set on foot, contrary to the provisions and prohibitions of this Title; and in every case of the capture of a vessel within the jurisdiction or protection of the United States as before defined ; and in every case in which any process issuing out of any court of the United States is disobeyed or resisted by any person having the custody of any vessel of war, cruiser, or other armed vessel of any foreign prince or state, or of any colony, district, or people, or of any subjects or citizens of any foreign prince or state, or of any colony, district, or people, it shall be lawful for the President, or such other person as he shall have empowered for that purpose, to employ such part of the land or naval forces of the United States or of the militia thereof, for the purpose of taking possession of and detaining any such vessel, with her prizes, if any, in order to the execution of the prohibitions and penalties of this Title, and to the restoring of such prizes in the cases in which restoration shall be adjudged; and also for the purpose of preventing the carrying on of any such expedition or enterprise from the territories or jurisdiction of the United States against the territories or dominions of any foreign princes or state, or of any colony, district, or people with whom the United States are at peace.

SEC. 5288. It shall be lawful for the President or such person as he shall empower for that purpose to employ such part of the land or naval forces of the United States or of the militia thereof, as shall be necessary to compel any foreign vessel to depart the United States in all cases in which, by the laws of nations or the treaties of the United States, she ought not to remain within the United States.

SEC. 5289. The owners or consignees of every armed vessel sailing out of the ports of the United States, belonging wholly or in part to citizens thereof, shall, before clearing out the same, give bond not to commit hostilities against any country with whom the United States are at peace.

SEC. 5290. Collectors of customs are to detain vessels built for warlike purposes and about to depart the United States until the decision of the President, or until the owner gives bond.

SEC. 5291. This applies to the construction of the Title.[1]

[1] The British Foreign Enlistment Acts of 1819 and 1870 may be found in 2 Lorimer, 476 *et seq.*

APPENDIX VIII

PROCEDURE IN PRIZE COURT

DISTRICT COURT OF THE UNITED STATES, SOUTHERN DISTRICT OF FLORIDA

The United States v. Str. **X**

PRIZE

LIBEL

To the Honorable A. B., Judge of said Court.

The libel of C. D., Attorney of the United States, for the Southern District of Florida, who libels for the United States and for all parties in interest against the steam vessel X, in a cause of prize, alleges: —

That pursuant to instructions for that purpose from the President of the United States, W. M. of the United States Navy, in and with the United States Commissioned ship of war, the N., her officers and crew, did on the 22d day of April, in the year of our Lord One thousand eight hundred and ninety-eight, subdue, seize, and capture on the high seas, as prize of war, the said steam vessel X, and the said vessel and her cargo have been brought into the port and harbor of Key West, in the state of Florida, where the same now are, within the jurisdiction of this Honorable Court, and that the same are lawful prize of war and subject to condemnation and forfeiture as such.

WHEREFORE the said Attorney prays that the usual process of attachment of Prize causes may issue against the said vessel her tackle, apparel, furniture, and cargo, that Monition may issue citing all persons, having or claiming to have any interest or property in said vessel and cargo to appear and claim the same; that the nature, amount, and value may be determined; that due and proper proofs may be taken and heard; and that all due proceedings being had, the said vessel X, together with her tackle, apparel, furniture, and cargo may, on the final hearing of this cause, by the definitive sentence of this Court, be condemned, forfeited, and sold, and the proceeds distributed according to law.

C. D.
U. S. Attorney, So. Dist. of Florida.

Key West, Fla. April 23d, 1898.
Let attachment and monition issue as prayed returnable on Monday the 9th day of May, 1898.

Entered as of course.
E. F., Clerk,
by G. H., Dy. Clerk.

ENDORSED:
Libel for Prize. — Filed Apr. 23d, 1898.   E. F., Clerk.

CLAIMANTS' PETITION

To the Honorable A. B., Judge of the District Court of the United States in and for the Southern District of Florida, in admiralty.

The United States v. The S. S. X and cargo

PRIZE

And now comes into Court, I. J., and says that he is a citizen of Mobile, Ala., and agent in the United States for the firm of P. & P. of London, England, and that about 400,000 feet of pine lumber, being about one half of the cargo, is the sole and exclusive property of the said firm of P. & P., of London, England, and of no other person or persons, and that no person or persons whomsoever, enemies of the United States, have any right, title, or interest whatever in and to said cargo or any part thereof.

That the said firm consists solely of [names] who are subjects of Great Britain, residing at London, England.

And he further denies that the said cargo is lawful prize of war as alleged and set forth in the captor's libel exhibited and filed in this cause.

Now therefore, the said I. J., comes into Court and claims the right to the possession of the said portion of the said cargo for the said firm of P. & P., and prays that upon a hearing of this cause the Court will award to them restitution thereof free from charges for costs and expenses, and of such other and further relief in the premises as is right and just, and he will ever pray, etc.

I. J. Agent for P. & P.

I. J., being duly sworn, deposes and says that he is the authorized agent in the United States of said P. & P. of London, where all the members of the firm are and reside; that he knows the contents of the foregoing claim; that the matters and allegations therein contained are true as therein set forth; and that his knowledge of said matters is absolute and acquired by means of his agency in the United States for the said P. & P. and by reason of his connection with the shipment of the said cargo.

I. J.

Sworn to and subscribed before me this 2nd day of May, 1898.

[SEAL]   K. L., Clerk of the United States District Court for the Southern District of Alabama.

M. N.
Proctor for Claimant.

ENDORSED:
Claim for one half Cargo. — Filed May 6th, 1898.

L. O., Clerk

(Another claim for the other half was filed by another claimant.)

At a stated term of the District Court of the United States, for the Southern District of Florida, held in the United States Court Rooms at Key West, on the   day of May, 1898.

Present: —

Honorable A. B., District Judge.

PETITION OF BAILEE OF OWNERS OF VESSEL

The United States v. *The Steamship X and her cargo*

And now O. P., intervening as bailee for the interest of [names] in the said Steamship X, her engines, boilers, tackle, apparel, furniture and equipment, appears before this Honorable Court and makes claim to the said steamship etc., as the same are attached by the Marshal, under process of this Court, at the instance of the United States of America, under a libel against said steamship, her cargo etc., as a prize of war, and the said O. P. avers that before and at the time of the alleged capture of said steamship, her cargo etc., the above named [names], residing in England, and [names] residing in Spain, all of whom are Spanish subjects, were true and *bona fide* owners of the said vessel, her engines, boilers, tackle, apparel and furniture; that no other person was the owner thereof, that he was in possession thereof for the said owners, and that the vessel, if restored, will belong to the said owners, and he denies that she was lawful prize.

Wherefore the said O. P., for and in behalf of the said owners, for whom he is duly authorized to make this claim, prays to be admitted to defend accordingly, and to show cause pursuant to the terms of the monition issued herein and served upon the said steamship, and upon the master thereof, as bailee, why the said steamship, her engines, etc., were not liable to be treated enemy's property at the time and place, and under the circumstances of the alleged capture, and why she should not be condemned as lawful prize of war, but should be restored with damages and costs.

O. P.

Sworn to before me this 18th day of May, 1898.
[SEAL]   G. H., *Dy. Clerk.*

Q. R.
Proctor for Claimant.

ENDORSED:

Claim to X by O. P.   Q. R., *Proctor for Claimant.* — Filed May 18th, 1898.   E. F., *Clerk.*

U.S. DISTRICT COURT, SOUTHERN DISTRICT OF FLORIDA

The United States v. *The Steamship X and her cargo*

TEST AFFIDAVIT

SOUTHERN DISTRICT OF FLORIDA, S.S.

O. P. being duly sworn, deposes and says: —

1. I am the claimant herein and have verified the claim on knowledge derived from my position as master of the vessel about three and a half years and from my official communications with the ship owners and their representatives; the names and residences of the part owners I have learned since my examination *in preparatorio*, from cables to my counsel to the said owners.

2. The X is a Spanish merchant vessel, and since I have been in command of her as aforesaid has traded between ports in England and Spain and the United States and West Indies; the vessel carries no passengers or mails, but is exclusively a cargo carrier.

3. In the ordinary course of her said business as a common carrier, the vessel, in the month of April, 1898, loaded a full cargo of lumber, at Ship Island, Miss., and on the

14th of April, 1898, the vessel and cargo were cleared at the
Custom House in Scranton, Miss. The cargo was destined
for Rotterdam, in the Kingdom of Holland, but the vessel
was cleared coastwise from Scranton for Norfolk, in the
State of Virginia, to which port the steamer was bound for
coals. In the ordinary course of such a voyage the foreign
clearance of a vessel for Rotterdam would have been obtained
and issued from the Custom House in Norfolk.

The vessel was laden at the loading port under the agency
of W. S. K. & Co., an American firm as I am informed and
believe, and conformed there in all things to the laws and
regulations of the United States and of said port. She was
detained at Ship Island by the low water on the bar until
April 19th, 1898, between 8 and 9 o'clock A.M., when she
sailed from said place and proceeded on her voyage toward
Norfolk, Va., as aforesaid.

But for her capture and detentions as heretofore set forth,
she would have reached Norfolk, and would have coaled
and sailed from said port prior to May 21st, 1898.

4. It appeared from the ship's papers delivered to the
captors, and was a fact, that her cargo was all taken on
board prior to May 21st, 1898. And as I am informed and
believe, the vessel was not otherwise excluded from the
benefits and privileges of the President's Proclamation of
April 26th, 1898.

5. At all times before the ship's seizure on April 22d,
1898, I and all my officers were ignorant that war existed
between Spain and the United States, and the vessel was
bound and following the ordinary course of her voyage.

6. While on the said voyage and in due prosecution
thereof, at about 7 or 7.30 of the clock in the morning of
April 22d, 1898, said steamship X being then about eight
or nine miles from Sand Key Light, was seized and wrong-
fully captured by the United States ship of war N.,
under the command of a line officer of the United States
Navy, and by means of a prize crew then and there placed
on board, was forcibly brought into this port of Key West.

On being stopped by said United States ship of war, N., and being informed of the existence of war, the master and officers of the X submitted without resistance to seizure and to the placing of a prize crew on board of said vessel, proceeding therewith, under her own steam, into port.

7. Deponent is informed and believes that by the existing policy of the Government of the United States, as evidenced by the repeated declarations of its Executive, and by the Proclamation of the President of the United States, issued and published April 26th, 1898, as well as upon principles in harmony with the present views of nations and sanctioned by recent practice, in accordance with which the President has directed that the war should be conducted, the steamship X, at the time and place, and in the circumstances under which she was seized, was not liable to be treated as enemy's property, but on the contrary, having sailed from a port of the United States prior to the 21st of April, 1898, and being bound to another port of the United States, which in the ordinary course of her voyage she would have reached and left, with her coals, long prior to May 21st, 1898, was exempt from capture as prize of war.

O. P.

Sworn to before me this 18th day of May, 1898.

[SEAL]   G. H., *Dy. Clerk.*

ENDORSED :

Test affidavit for X. — Filed May 16th, 1898, E. F., *Clerk.*

IN THE DISTRICT COURT OF THE UNITED STATES, SOUTHERN DISTRICT OF FLORIDA

United States v. *Spanish Steamer X and Cargo*
PRIZE.   DECREE

This cause having come on to be heard upon the allegations of the libel, the claims of the master, and testimony taken *in preparatorio*, and the same having been fully heard and considered, and it appearing to the Court that the said steamer X was enemy's property, and was upon the high seas and not in any port or place of the United States upon the outbreak of the war, and was liable to condemnation and seizure, it is ordered that the same be condemned and forfeited to the United States as lawful prize of war; but it appearing that the cargo of said steamer was the property of neutrals, and not contraband or subject to condemnation and forfeiture, it is ordered that said cargo be released and restored to the claimants for the benefit of the true and lawful owners thereof.

It is further ordered that the Marshal proceed to advertise and sell said vessel, and make deposit of the proceeds in accordance with law. A. B., *Judge.*

Key West, Florida, May 27th, 1898.

ENDORSED:

Decree. — Filed May 27th, 1898. E. F., *Clerk.*

FORM OF DECREE OF DISTRIBUTION.

DISTRICT COURT OF THE UNITED STATES, SOUTHERN DISTRICT OF FLORIDA.

The United States   PRIZE

v.

Captured, _____ 1898.

A Final Decree of Condemnation of Vessel and Cargo having been pronounced in this Case, and no Appeal being taken, and it Appearing to the Court that the Gross Proceeds of the Sales are as follows, — to-wit, —

        Vessel,
        Cargo,
        Total,

And the Costs, Expenses and Charges as taxed and allowed are as follows, —

Marshal's Fees and Charges including all expenses of Sales, Advertising, and Auctioneer's Commissions,
  District Attorney's Fees,
  Prize Commissioner's Fees and Expenses,
  Clerk's Fees,
Leaving a Net Residue of _____ ($_____)

And it appearing to the Court upon the Report of the Prize Commissioner, that the U. S. S. _____
Commanding, was the sole Capturing Vessel, and entitled to share in the Prize, and was of Superior Force to the Captured Vessel, and it appearing that the Marshal has paid and satisfied the Bills of Costs and Charges as herein taxed, and allowed, it is ORDERED that the same be paid to him out of the money on Deposit with the Assistant Treasurer of the United States subject to the Court in this case, and it is FURTHER ORDERED that the said Residue of the Gross Proceeds deposited with the Assistant Treasurer in this Case be paid into the Treasury of the United States, for Distribution, one half to the officers and crew of said ——— and one half to the United States.[1]

Judge of the District Court of the United States,
for the Southern District of Florida.

[1] See late U. S. statute cited on p. 327.

APPENDIX IX

DIGEST OF IMPORTANT CASES ARRANGED UNDER TITLES

15. PRECEDENT AND DECISIONS

Bolton v. *Gladstone*, 5 East, 155

In an action on a policy of insurance in 1804 on a Danish ship and cargo warranted neutral and captured by a French ship of war (Denmark being at peace with France), it appeared that the court in which the Danish ship was libelled declared her good and lawful prize. Held by Ellenborough C. J., "that all sentences of foreign courts of competent jurisdiction to decide questions of prize" were to be received "as conclusive evidence in actions upon policies of assurance, upon every subject immediately and properly within the jurisdiction of such foreign courts, and upon which they have professed to decide judicially."

United States v. *Rauscher*, 119 U. S. 407

The defendant was extradited from England on the charge of murder committed on an American vessel on the high seas. He was indicted in the United States Circuit Court, not for murder, but for a minor offense not included in the treaty of extradition. It was held that he could not be tried for any other offense than murder until he had had an opportunity to return to the country from which he was taken for the purpose alone of trial for the offense specified in the demand for his surrender.

21. RECOGNITION OF NEW STATES

Harcourt v. *Gaillard*, 12 Wheat. 523

This case is fully stated in the text, p. 42.

Williams v. *The Suffolk Insurance Company*, 13 Pet. 415

This case held that when the executive branch of the government, which is charged with the foreign relations of the United States shall, in its correspondence with a foreign nation, assume a fact in regard to the sovereignty of any island or country, it is conclusive on the judicial department.

State of Mississippi v. *Johnson*, 4 Wall. 475, 501

This case held that "a bill praying an injunction against the execution of an act of Congress by the incumbent of the presidential office cannot be received, whether it describes him as President or as a citizen of a state."

Jones v. *United States*, 137 U.S. 202

This case held that the determination of the President, under U.S. Rev. Sts., § 5570, that a guano island shall be considered as appertaining to the United States, may be declared through the Department of State, whose acts in this regard are in legal contemplation the acts of the President.

55. VESSELS
Wildenhus's Case, 120 U.S. 1

This case held that the Circuit Court of the United States has jurisdiction to issue a writ of *habeas corpus* to determine whether one of the crew of a foreign vessel in a port of the United States, who is in the custody of the state authorities, charged with the commission of a crime, within the port, against the laws of the state, is exempt from local jurisdiction under the provisions of a treaty between the United States and the foreign nation to which the vessel belongs. The Convention of March 9, 1880, between Belgium and the United States was considered.

64. EXTRADITION
In the Matter of Metzger, 5 How. 176, 188

This case held that the Treaty with France of 1843 provides for the mutual surrender of fugitives from justice and

that where a district judge decided that there was sufficient cause for the surrender of a person claimed by the French Government, and committed him to custody to await the order of the President of the United States, the Supreme Court had no jurisdiction to issue a *habeas corpus* for the purpose of reviewing that decision.

101. Non-Combatants
Alcinous v. *Nigreu*, 4 Ellis and Blackburn, 217

This was an action for work and labor brought by a Russian against an Englishman during the Crimean war. Lord Campbell said: "The contract having been entered into before the commencement of hostilities is valid; and, when peace is restored, the plaintiff may enforce it in our Courts. But, by the law of England, so long as hostilities prevail he cannot sue here."

104. Personal Property of Enemy Subjects
Brown v. *United States*, 8 Cr. 110

It was held that British property within the territory of the United States at the beginning of hostilities with Great Britain could not be condemned without a legislative act, and that the act of Congress declaring war was not such an act. The property in question was the cargo of an American ship and was seized as enemy's property in 1813, nearly a year after it had been discharged from the ship.

110. Privateers
United States v. *Baker*, 5 Blatchford, 6

This was an indictment in 1861 against Baker, the master of a private armed schooner, and a part of the officers and crew for piracy. They claimed to have acted under a commission from Jefferson Davis, President of the Confederate States of America. Nelson J. charged the jury at length; but they failed to agree on a verdict.

112. CAPTURE AND RANSOM
The Grotius, 9 Cr. 368

The question in this case, which was heard in 1815, was whether the capture was valid. The master, the mate, and two of the seamen swore that they did not consider the ship to have been seized as prize, and that the young man who was put on board by the captain of the privateer was received and considered as a passenger during the residue of the voyage. It was held that the validity of the capture of the vessel as a prize of war was sufficiently established by the evidence.

113. POSTLIMINIUM
The Two Friends, 1 C. Rob. 271

An American ship was taken by the French in 1799 when the relations between France and America were strained. She was recaptured by the crew, some of whom were British seamen. They were awarded salvage.

The Santa Cruz, 1 C. Rob. 49

A Portuguese vessel was taken by the French in 1796 and retaken by English cruisers a few days later. It was held that the law of England, on recapture of property of allies, is the law of reciprocity; it adopts the rule of the country to which the claimant belongs.

115. NON-HOSTILE RELATIONS OF BELLIGERENTS
The Venus, 4 C. Rob. 355

A British vessel went to Marseilles, under cartel, for the exchange of prisoners, and there took on board a cargo and was stranded and captured on a voyage to Port Mahon. Held that the penalty was confiscation.

The Sea Lion, 5 Wall. 630

This case held that a license from a "Special Agent of the Treasury Department and Acting Collector of Customs"

2 F

in 1863 to bring cotton "from beyond the United States military lines" had no warrant from the Treasury Regulations prescribed by the President conformably to the act of 13th July, 1861.

119. TERMINATION OF WAR BY TREATY OF PEACE
The Schooner Sophie, 6 C. Rob. 138

A British ship, having been captured by the French, was condemned in 1799 by a French Consular Court in Norway. Other proceedings were afterwards had, on former evidence in the case, in the regular Court of Prize in Paris and the sentence of the Consular Court was affirmed. Sir William Scott said, "I am of opinion, therefore, that the intervention of peace has put a total end to the claim of the British proprietor, and that it is no longer competent to him to look back to the enemy's title, either in his own possession, or in the hands of neutral purchasers."

126. NEUTRAL TERRITORIAL JURISDICTION
The Caroline
People v. McLeod, 25 Wendell, 483

During the Canadian rebellion of 1837–1838, a force was sent in the night by the British commander to capture the steamer Caroline, owned by an American. The steamer was engaged in transporting war material and men to Navy Island, in the Niagara River, through which runs the line separating the British from the American possessions. The vessel not being in her usual place in Canadian waters, the force went into American jurisdiction and seized and destroyed her. One Durfee, an American, was killed. To the American assertion that the proceeding was an outrage, the British Government replied that the insurgents had used American ground as the starting-point of their expeditions and as their base of supplies. The controversy was renewed by the arrest, in 1841, in the state of New York, of one McLeod, and his indictment for the murder of Durfee.

Great Britain demanded the release of McLeod, stating that as he was an agent of the British Government engaged at the time in a public duty, he could not be held amenable to the laws of any foreign jurisdiction. Mr. Webster, then Secretary of State, admitted the correctness of the British contention, but seemed powerless to obtain the release of McLeod, on account of the inherent weakness of the Federal system.[1] The Supreme Court of the state of New York held in *People* v. *McLeod*, that McLeod could be proceeded against individually on an indictment for arson and murder, though his acts had been subsequently averred by the British Government. This view was generally condemned by jurists;[2] but the difficulty soon ended by the acquittal of McLeod. The British Government's contention was that the seizure of the *Caroline* was excusable on the ground stated by Mr. Webster himself as "a necessity of self-defense, instant, overwhelming, leaving no choice of means and no moment for deliberation."

The Twee Gebroeders, 3 C. Rob. 162

This case holds that a ship within three miles of neutral territory can not send boats beyond the line of division for the purpose of capturing enemy vessels.

129. POSITIVE OBLIGATIONS OF A NEUTRAL STATE

The Alabama Cases

Up to the period of the American civil war the opinion obtained among many that a vessel of war might be sent to sea from a neutral port with the sole liability to capture as legitimate contraband, with the exception that, if she was ready to go in condition for immediate warlike use, it was the duty of the neutral to prevent her departure. In 1863 during the American civil war this view was practically

---

[1] See 1 Whart., § 67.

[2] See *ibid.*, §§ 21, 60 c., 3 *ibid.*, § 350.

taken by the British court in the case of the *Alexandra;*[1] but the vessel after her release was taken on a new complaint at Nassau and held until after the end of the war. Lawrence says that the attitude of the British Government in regard to this vessel, its purchase in 1863 of two iron-clad rams of the Messrs. Laird for the navy, the construction, destination, and intended departure of which occasioned the now famous correspondence between Lord Russell and Mr. Adams, the detention of the *Pampero*, which was seized in the Clyde, until the end of the American civil war, and the preventing the sale of "Anglo-Chinese gunboats against the advice of its own law officers," indicated that that government "had uneasy doubts as to the validity of the doctrine laid down in their law-courts and maintained in their dispatches."[2] This doctrine would admit of a ship of war going to sea from a neutral port without arms, which she might receive on the high seas from another vessel which had sailed from the same port. For example, the *Alabama* left Liverpool in 1862 ready for warlike use, but without warlike equipment. This and her crew were received on the high seas from other vessels which had cleared from Liverpool; and her career as a Confederate cruiser then began. The cases of the *Florida*, the *Georgia*, and the *Shenandoah* were almost identical. The spoliations committed by these vessels led to the *Alabama* claims, the British maintaining that the American contention that it was the duty of a neutral to prevent the departure of all vessels that could reasonably be expected as about to be used for warlike purposes was unsound.[3]

The *Alabama* case and kindred cases have produced much

[1] Attorney Gen'l *v.* Sillem *et als*, 2 Hurlstone *v.* Coltman, Exchequer Reports, 431.

[2] Page 544. For the cases of the "Pampero" and the two iron-clad rams, see Wheat., D., note p. 572 *et seq.*

[3] The American view may be found in Cushing's "Treaty of Washington," and the British in Bernard's "Historical Account of the Neutrality of Great Britain during the American Civil War."

speculation as to the establishment of a true and correct rule. After the enactment of the American neutrality statutes in 1818, there were numerous decisions of the United States courts to the effect that the intent was to govern, that is, if the purpose was to send articles of contraband, with the risk of capture, to a belligerent's country for sale, the neutral government had nothing to say, but if the purpose was to send out a vessel to prey on the commerce of a friendly power, then the neutral government should prevent her departure. It must be admitted that the rule is hardly satisfactory.[1]

Hall contends that the true test should be "the character of the ship itself." If built for warlike use, the vessel should be detained; if for commercial purposes, she should be allowed to depart. This rule has at least one element of fairness and sense. It is not always possible to get at intent, but the character of the vessel is likely to reward observation and scrutiny.[2]

Regret has been expressed by many writers that the award of the arbitrators appointed under the Treaty of Washington of 1871, upon the *Alabama* claims, has proved of so little value as a precedent upon the liability of a neutral power for the departure from its ports of vessels fitted out and equipped for the destruction of belligerent commerce.

Article VI. of the Treaty provided that the Arbitrators should be "governed by the following three rules, which are agreed upon by the high contracting parties as rules to be taken as applicable to the case, and by such principles of international law not inconsistent therewith as the Arbitrators shall determine to have been applicable to the case.

"A neutral Government is bound —

"First to use due diligence to prevent the fitting out, arming, or equipping, within its jurisdiction, of any vessel which it has reasonable ground to believe is intended to

---

[1] See Wheat., D., note p. 553 *et seq.*   [2] Hall, § 225.

cruise or to carry on war against a Power with which it is at peace; and also to use like diligence to prevent the departure from its jurisdiction of any vessel intended to cruise or carry on war as above, such vessel having been specially adapted, in whole or in part, within such jurisdiction, to warlike use.

"Secondly, not to permit or suffer either belligerent to make use of its ports or waters as the base of naval operations against the other, or for the purpose of the renewal or augmentation of military supplies or arms, or the recruitment of men.

"Thirdly, to exercise due diligence in its own ports and waters, and, as to all persons within its jurisdiction, to prevent any violation of the foregoing obligations and duties."

The British government declared that it "cannot assent to the foregoing rules as a statement of principles of international law which were in force at the time when the claims mentioned" arose but "in order to evince its desire of strengthening the friendly relations between the two countries and of making satisfactory provision for the future, agrees that in deciding the questions between the two countries arising out of those claims, the Arbitrators should assume that her Majesty's government had undertaken to act upon the principles set forth in these rules.

"And the high contracting parties agree to observe these rules as between themselves in the future, and to bring them to the knowledge of other maritime Powers, and to invite them to accede to them."[1]

The phrases "due diligence" and "base of naval operations" gave rise to a difference of opinion, as also the last part of paragraph "First" relative to preventing the departure of vessels intended to carry on war and adapted for warlike use.

The contentions and the decision relative to the last point were as follows:

[1] U. S. Treaties, 481.

1. The British Contention

This was that the only duty of Great Britain applied to the departure of the vessel originally, and that, if she escaped, and afterwards as a duly commissioned war-ship entered a British port, there was no obligation to detain her.[1] The case of the *Schooner Exchange* v. *M'Faddon*[2] was cited, in which a libel was filed in 1811 against that vessel, then in American waters, as an American vessel unlawfully in the custody of a Frenchman, the libellants contending that in December 1810, while pursuing her voyage she had been forcibly taken by a French vessel at sea. The Attorney General suggested that she was a public armed vessel of France, visiting our waters as a matter of necessity. Chief Justice Marshall decided that as a public vessel of war coming into our ports and demeaning herself in a friendly manner she was exempt from the jurisdiction of the country.

2. The American Contention

This was that if a Confederate cruiser, which had originally escaped, afterwards came into a British port, her commission was no protection, as it was given by a government whose belligerency only, not sovereignty, had been acknowledged.[3]

3. The Award of the Tribunal

This award exceeded the claim of the United States in deciding that " the effects of a violation of neutrality committed by means of the construction, equipment and armament of a vessel are not done away with by any commission which the Government of the belligerent power, benefited by the violation of neutrality, may afterwards have granted to that vessel; and the ultimate step, by which the offense

---

[1] Argument of Sir R. Palmer in the " Argument at Geneva," published by the United States at p. 426 *et seq.*

[2] 7 Cranch, 116.

[3] Argument of Mr. Evarts in " Argument at Geneva," p. 448 *et seq.*

is completed, cannot be admissible as a ground for the absolution of the offender, nor can the consummation of his fraud become the means of establishing his innocence," that "the privilege of extra-territoriality accorded to vessels of war has been admitted into the law of nations, not as an absolute right, but solely as a proceeding founded on the principles of courtesy and mutual deference between different nations, and therefore can never be appealed to for the protection of acts done in violation of neutrality," and that "the absence of a previous notice can not be regarded as a failure in any consideration required by the law of nations, in those cases in which a vessel carries with it its own condemnation." [1]

That the decision of the Tribunal has not become a precedent is quite generally conceded. Lawrence asserts that the award seems "to have been dictated more by a regard for equitable considerations than by reference to principles hitherto accepted among nations;" that other nations have refused to accede to the "three rules" and "that it has been doubted whether they bind the two powers which originally contracted to observe them." [2]

It is to be observed, however, that at the present time a cruiser is of such peculiar construction and depends for her efficiency on such a large outlay of money that an honest neutral is likely to have abundant proof of her character and hence the best reasons for detaining her.

131. CONTRABAND

The Peterhoff, 5 Wall. 28, 62

The Peterhoff, a British steamer, bound from London to Matamoras in Mexico, was seized in 1863 by a United States vessel. It was held that the mouth of the Rio Grande was not included in the blockade of the ports of the

[1] Decision and Award of the Tribunal of Arbitration in 3 Wharton, § 402 a.

[2] pp. 553, 554.

Confederate states; that neutral commerce with Matamoras, a neutral town on the Mexican side of the river, except in contraband destined to the enemy, was entirely free; and that trade between London and Matamoras, even with intent to supply, from Matamoras, goods to Texas, then an enemy of the United States, was not unlawful on the ground of such violation. Questions of contraband were also considered, and Chief Justice Chase concluded, "Considering . . . the almost certain destination of the ship to a neutral port, with a cargo, for the most part, neutral in character and destination, we shall not extend the effect of this conduct of the captain to condemnation, but we shall decree payment of costs and expenses by the ship as a condition of restitution."

The Commercen, 1 Wheat. 382

In 1814, during the war between the United States and Great Britain, a Swedish vessel bound from Limerick, Ireland, to Bilboa, Spain, with cargo of barley and oats, the property of British subjects, was seized and brought into an American port. The cargo was shipped for the sole use of the British forces in Spain. The cargo was condemned.

132. PENALTY FOR CARRYING CONTRABAND
The Jonge Tobias, 1 C. Rob. 329

This was a case of a ship taken on a voyage from Bremen to Rochelle, laden with tar. The ship was claimed by one Schraeder and others. Schraeder, who was owner of the cargo, withheld his claim, knowing it would affect the ship. The cargo and his share of the vessel were condemned in 1799, and an attestation was required of the other part owners of the vessel that they had no knowledge of the contraband goods.

The Magnus, 1 C. Rob. 31

A ship laden with coffee and sugars was taken on a voyage from Havre to Genoa. The claimant of the cargo was a

Swiss merchant. Held, that while interior countries are allowed to export and import through an enemy's ports, strict proof of property is required. The cargo was condemned.

133. UNNEUTRAL SERVICE

The Kow-Shing Affair, Takahashi, 24–51

On July 25, 1894, a Japanese war-ship stopped the *Kow-Shing*, a British transport engaged in carrying Chinese troops. After fruitless parleying, the *Kow-Shing* refusing to surrender as her British captain was overawed by the Chinese he was carrying, the *Kow-Shing* was sunk by the Japanese war ship. The affair produced great excitement in England, and there was a demand of satisfaction from Japan on the ground that war had not been declared between that country and China. The facts appearing that a declaration of war is not necessary, and that the British captain of the transport was under compulsion, the affair was referred to Mr. Choate, the American Ambassador to Great Britain, as referee.

The Friendship, 6 C. Rob. 420, 429

This was the case of an American ship bound on a voyage from Baltimore to Bordeaux, with a light cargo and ninety French mariners as passengers, shipped by direction of the French minister in America. In condemning the ship and cargo in 1807, Sir William Scott said, " It is the case of a vessel letting herself out in a distinct manner, under a contract with the enemy's government, to convey a number of persons, described as being in the service of the enemy, with their military character traveling with them, and to restore them to their own country in that character."

The Orozembo, 6 C. Rob. 430

An American vessel, having been ostensibly chartered by a merchant at Lisbon "to proceed in ballast to Macao, and

there to take a cargo to America," was afterwards, by his
directions, fitted up for three military officers and two persons in civil departments in the government of Batavia, who
had come from Holland to take their passage to Batavia,
under the appointment of the Government of Holland. The
vessel was condemned in 1807 as a transport, let out in the
service of the government of Holland.

The Atalanta, 6 C. Rob. 440

A Bremen ship and cargo were captured on a voyage from
Batavia to Bremen, in July, 1807, having come last from the
Isle of France, where a packet, containing dispatches from
the government of the Isle of France to the Minister of
Marine at Paris, was taken on board by the master and one
of the supercargoes, and was afterwards found concealed in
the possession of the second supercargo. Both ship and
cargo were condemned.

137. VIOLATION OF BLOCKADE
The Juffrow Maria Schroeder, 3 C. Rob. 147

"Where a ship has contracted the guilt by sailing with
an intention of entering a blockaded port, or by sailing out,
the offense is not purged away till the end of the voyage;
till that period is completed, it is competent to any cruisers
to seize and proceed against her for that offense." In this
case the plea of remissness in the blockading force in permitting vessels to go in or out, was held to avail, and the
ship, which was a Prussian one taken on a voyage from
Rouen to Altona and proceeded against for a breach of the
blockade of Havre, was restored.

138. CONTINUOUS VOYAGES
The Hart, 3 Wall. 559, 560

"Neutrals who place their vessels under belligerent control and engage them in belligerent trade; or permit them to
be sent with contraband cargoes under cover of false des-

tination to neutral ports, while the real destination is to belligerent ports, impress upon them the character of the belligerent in whose service they are employed, and cannot complain if they are seized and condemned as enemy property." See the preceding case, *The Bermuda*, 3 Wall. 514.

The Maria, 5 C. Rob. 365

This was a case of a continuous voyage in the colonial trade of the enemy. The Court reviewed former cases and asked for further proof on the facts. On such further proof the court decreed restitution. See *The William*, 5 C. Rob. 385.

139. PRIZE AND PRIZE COURTS
The Ship La Manche, 2 Sprague, 207

This case held that captors are not liable for damages where the vessel captured presents probable cause for the capture, even though she was led into the predicament, involuntarily, and by the mistakes of the revenue officers of the captor's own government.

APPENDIX X

CONVENTION BETWEEN THE UNITED STATES
AND CERTAIN POWERS FOR THE PACIFIC
SETTLEMENT OF INTERNATIONAL DISPUTES

Signed at The Hague, July 29, 1899
Ratification advised by the Senate February 5, 1900
Ratified by the President of the United States April 7, 1900
Ratification deposited with the Netherlands Government Sep-
    tember, 4, 1900
Proclaimed November 1, 1901

BY THE PRESIDENT OF THE UNITED STATES OF AMERICA

A PROCLAMATION

Whereas a Convention for the pacific settlement of international disputes was concluded and signed on July 29, 1899, by the Plenipotentiaries of the United States of America, Germany, Austria-Hungary, Belgium, China, Denmark, Spain, the United Mexican States, France, Great Britain and Ireland, Greece, Italy, Japan, Luxembourg, Montenegro, the Netherlands, Persia, Portugal, Roumania, Russia, Servia, Siam, Sweden and Norway, Switzerland, Turkey and Bulgaria, the original of which Convention, in the French language, is word for word as follows [French text omitted]:

[Translation]

His Majesty the Emperor of Germany, King of Prussia; His Majesty the Emperor of Austria, King of Bohemia etc. and Apostolic King of Hungary; His Maies+ ··

the Belgians; His Majesty the Emperor of China; His
Majesty the King of Denmark; His Majesty the King of
Spain and in His Name Her Majesty the Queen Regent of
the Kingdom; the President of the United States of
America; the President of the United Mexican States; the
President of the French Republic; Her Majesty the Queen
of the United Kingdom of Great Britain and Ireland, Em-
press of India; His Majesty the King of the Hellenes; His
Majesty the King of Italy; His Majesty the Emperor of
Japan; His Royal Highness the Grand Duke of Luxemburg,
Duke of Nassau; His Highness the Prince of Montenegro;
Her Majesty the Queen of the Netherlands; His Imperial
Majesty the Shah of Persia; His Majesty the King of
Portugal and of the Algarves etc.; His Majesty the King of
Roumania; His Majesty the Emperor of all the Russias;
His Majesty the King of Servia; His Majesty the King of
Siam; His Majesty the King of Sweden and Norway; the
Swiss Federal Council; His Majesty the Emperor of the
Ottomans and His Royal Highness the Prince of Bulgaria

Animated by a strong desire to concert for the maintenance of the general peace;

Resolved to second by their best efforts the friendly settlement of international disputes;

Recognizing the solidarity which unites the members of
the society of civilized nations;

Desirous of extending the empire of law, and of strengthening the appreciation of international justice;

Convinced that the permanent institution of a Court of
Arbitration, accessible to all, in the midst of the independent Powers, will contribute effectively to this result;

Having regard to the advantages attending the general
and regular organization of arbitral procedure;

Sharing the opinion of the august Initiator of the International Peace Conference that it is expedient to record in
an international Agreement the principles of equity and
right on which are based the security of States and the wel-
fare of peoples;

Being desirous of concluding a Convention to this effect, have appointed as their Plenipotentiaries, to wit:

[Here follow the names and titles of the Plenipotentiaries.]

Who, after communication of their full powers, found in good and due form, have agreed on the following provisions:

TITLE I. — ON THE MAINTENANCE OF THE GENERAL PEACE

ARTICLE 1. With a view to obviating, as far as possible, recourse to force in the relations between States, the Signatory Powers agree to use their best efforts to insure the pacific settlement of international differences.

TITLE II. — ON GOOD OFFICES AND MEDIATION

ART. 2. In case of serious disagreement or conflict, before an appeal to arms, the Signatory Powers agree to have recourse, as far as circumstances allow, to the good offices or mediation of one or more friendly Powers.

ART. 3. Independently of this recourse, the Signatory Powers recommend that one or more Powers, strangers to the dispute, should, on their own initiative, and as far as circumstances may allow, offer their good offices or mediation to the States at variance.

Powers, strangers to the dispute, have the right to offer good offices or mediation, even during the course of hostilities.

The exercise of this right can never be regarded by one or the other of the parties in conflict as an unfriendly act.

ART. 4. The part of the mediator consists in reconciling the opposing claims and appeasing the feelings of resentment which may have arisen between the States at variance.

ART. 5. The functions of the mediator are at an end when once it is declared, either by one of the parties to the dispute, or by the mediator himself, that the means of reconciliation proposed by him are not accepted.

ART. 6. Good offices and mediation, either at the request of the parties at variance, or on the initiative of Powers strangers to the dispute, have exclusively the character of advice and never having binding force.

ART. 7. The acceptance of mediation can not, unless there be an agreement to the contrary, have the effect of interrupting, delaying, or hindering mobilization or other measures of preparation for war.

If mediation occurs after the commencement of hostilities, it causes no interruption to the military operations in progress, unless there be an agreement to the contrary.

ART. 8. The Signatory Powers are agreed in recommending the application, when circumstances allow, of special mediation in the following form:

In case of a serious difference endangering the peace, the States at variance choose respectively a Power, to whom they intrust the mission of entering into direct communication with the Power chosen on the other side, with the object of preventing the rupture of pacific relations.

For the period of this mandate, the term of which, unless otherwise stipulated, cannot exceed thirty days, the States in conflict cease from all direct communication on the subject of the dispute, which is regarded as referred exclusively to the mediating Powers, who must use their best efforts to settle it.

In case of a definite rupture of pacific relations, these Powers are charged with the joint task of taking advantage of any opportunity to restore peace.

TITLE III. — ON INTERNATIONAL COMMISSIONS OF INQUIRY

ART. 9. In differences of an international nature involving neither honor nor vital interests, and arising from a difference of opinion on points of fact, the Signatory Powers recommend that the parties, who have not been able to come to an agreement by means of diplomacy, should as far as circumstances allow, institute an International Commis-

sion of Inquiry, to facilitate a solution of these differences
by elucidating the facts by means of an impartial and con-
scientious investigation.

ART. 10. The International Commissions of Inquiry are
constituted by special agreement between the parties in
conflict.

The Convention for an inquiry defines the facts to be ex-
amined and the extent of the Commissioners' powers.

It settles the procedure.

On the inquiry both sides must be heard.

The form and the periods to be observed, if not stated in
the inquiry Convention, are decided by the Commission
itself.

ART. 11. The International Commissions of Inquiry are
formed, unless otherwise stipulated, in the manner fixed by
Article 32 of the present convention.

ART. 12. The powers in dispute engage to supply the
International Commission of Inquiry, as fully as they may
think possible, with all means and facilities necessary to
enable it to be completely acquainted with and to accurately understand the facts in question.

ART. 13. The International Commission of Inquiry communicates its Report to the conflicting Powers, signed by all
the members of the Commission.

ART. 14. The Report of the International Commission of
Inquiry is limited to a statement of facts, and has in no
way the character of an Arbitral Award. It leaves the
conflicting Powers entire freedom as to the effect to be
given to this statement.

TITLE IV. — ON INTERNATIONAL ARBITRATION

CHAPTER I. *On the System of Arbitration*

ART. 15. International arbitration has for its object the
settlement of differences between States by judges of their
own choice, and on the basis of respect for law.

2 G

ART. 16. In questions of a legal nature, and especially in the interpretation or application of International Conventions, arbitration is recognized by the Signatory Powers as the most effective, and at the same time the most equitable, means of settling disputes which diplomacy has failed to settle.

ART. 17. The Arbitration Convention is concluded for questions already existing or for questions which may arise eventually.

It may embrace any dispute or only disputes of a certain category.

ART. 18. The Arbitration Convention implies the engagement to submit loyally to the Award.

ART. 19. Independently of general or private Treaties expressly stipulating recourse to arbitration as obligatory on the Signatory Powers, these Powers reserve to themselves the right of concluding, either before the ratification of the present Act or later, new Agreements, general or private, with a view to extending obligatory arbitration to all cases which they may consider it possible to submit to it.

CHAPTER II. *On the Permanent Court of Arbitration*

ART. 20. With the object of facilitating an immediate recourse to arbitration for international differences, which it has not been possible to settle by diplomacy, the Signatory Powers undertake to organize a permanent Court of Arbitration, accessible at all times and operating, unless otherwise stipulated by the parties, in accordance with the Rules of Procedure inserted in the present Convention.

ART. 21. The Permanent Court shall be competent for all arbitration cases, unless the parties agree to institute a special Tribunal.

ART. 22. An International Bureau, established at The Hague, serves as record office for the Court.

This Bureau is the channel for communications relative to the meetings of the Court.

It has the custody of the archives and conducts all the administrative business.

The Signatory Powers undertake to communicate to the International Bureau at The Hague a duly certified copy of any conditions of arbitration arrived at between them, and of any award concerning them delivered by special Tribunals.

They undertake also to communicate to the Bureau the Laws, Regulations, and documents eventually showing the execution of the awards given by the Court.

ART. 23. Within the three months following its ratification of the present Act, each Signatory Power shall select four persons at the most, of known competency in questions of international law, of the highest moral reputation, and disposed to accept the duties of Arbitrators.

The persons thus selected shall be inscribed, as members of the Court, in a list which shall be notified by the Bureau to all the Signatory Powers.

Any alteration in the list of Arbitrators is brought by the Bureau to the knowledge of the Signatory Powers.

Two or more Powers may agree on the selection in common of one or more Members.

The same person can be selected by different Powers.

The Members of the Court are appointed for a term of six years. Their appointments can be renewed.

In case of the death or retirement of a member of the Court, his place shall be filled in accordance with the method of his appointment.

ART. 24. When the Signatory Powers desire to have recourse to the Permanent Court for the settlement of a difference that has arisen between them, the Arbitrators called upon to form the competent Tribunal to decide this difference, must be chosen from the general list of members of the Court.

Failing the direct agreement of the parties on the composition of the Arbitration Tribunal, the following course shall be pursued:

Each party appoints two Arbitrators, and these together choose an Umpire.

If the votes are equal, the choice of the Umpire is intrusted to a third Power, selected by the parties by common accord.

If an agreement is not arrived at on this subject, each party selects a different Power, and the choice of the Umpire is made in concert by the Powers thus selected.

The Tribunal being thus composed, the parties notify to the Bureau their determination to have recourse to the Court and the names of the Arbitrators.

The Tribunal of Arbitration assembles on the date fixed by the parties.

The Members of the Court, in the discharge of their duties and out of their own country, enjoy diplomatic privileges and immunities.

ART. 25. The Tribunal of Arbitration has its ordinary seat at The Hague.

Except in cases of necessity, the place of session can only be altered by the Tribunal with the assent of the parties.

ART. 26. The International Bureau at The Hague is authorized to place its premises and its staff at the disposal of the Signatory Powers for the operations of any special Board of Arbitration.

The jurisdiction of the Permanent Court may, within the conditions laid down in the Regulations, be extended to disputes between non-Signatory Powers, or between Signatory Powers and non-Signatory Powers, if the parties are agreed on recourse to this Tribunal.

ART. 27. The Signatory Powers consider it their duty, if a serious dispute threatens to break out between two or more of them, to remind these latter that the Permanent Court is open to them.

Consequently, they declare that the fact of reminding the conflicting parties of the provisions of the present Convention, and the advice given to them, in the highest interests of peace, to have recourse to the Permanent Court, can only be regarded as friendly actions.

ART. 28. A Permanent Administrative Council, composed of the Diplomatic Representatives of the Signatory Powers accredited to The Hague and of the Netherland Minister for Foreign Affairs, who will act as President, shall be instituted in this town as soon as possible after the ratification of the present Act by at least nine Powers.

This Council will be charged with the establishment and organization of the International Bureau, which will be under its direction and control.

It will notify to the Powers the constitution of the Court and will provide for its installation.

It will settle its Rules of Procedure and all other necessary Regulations.

It will decide all questions of administration which may arise with regard to the operations of the Court.

It will have entire control over the appointment, suspension or dismissal of the officials and employés of the Bureau.

It will fix the payments and salaries, and control the general expenditure.

At meetings duly summoned the presence of five members is sufficient to render valid the discussions of the Council. The decisions are taken by a majority of votes.

The Council communicates to the Signatory Powers without delay the Regulations adopted by it. It furnishes them with an annual Report on the labors of the Court, the working of the administration, and the expenses.

ART. 29. The expenses of the Bureau shall be borne by the Signatory Powers in the proportion fixed for the International Bureau of the Universal Postal Union.

CHAPTER III. *On Arbitral Procedure*

ART. 30. With a view to encourage the development of arbitration, the Signatory Powers have agreed on the following Rules which shall be applicable to arbitral procedure, unless other rules have been agreed on by the parties.

ART. 31. The Powers who have recourse to arbitration sign a special Act ("Compromis"), in which the subject of the difference is clearly defined, as well as the extent of the Arbitrators' powers. This Act implies the undertaking of the parties to submit loyally to the award.

ART. 32. The duties of Arbitrator may be conferred on one Arbitrator alone or on several Arbitrators selected by the parties as they please, or chosen by them from the members of the Permanent Court of Arbitration established by the present Act.

Failing the constitution of the Tribunal by direct agreement between the parties, the following course shall be pursued:

Each party appoints two arbitrators, and these latter together choose an Umpire.

In case of equal voting, the choice of the Umpire is intrusted to a third Power, selected by the parties by common accord.

If no agreement is arrived at on this subject, each party selects a different Power, and the choice of the Umpire is made in concert by the Powers thus selected.

ART. 33. When a Sovereign or the Chief of a State is chosen as Arbitrator, the arbitral procedure is settled by him.

ART. 34. The Umpire is by right President of the Tribunal.

When the Tribunal does not include an Umpire, it appoints its own President.

ART. 35. In case of the death, retirement, or disability from any cause of one of the Arbitrators, his place shall be filled in accordance with the method of his appointment.

ART. 36. The Tribunal's place of session is selected by the parties. Failing this selection the Tribunal sits at The Hague.

The place thus fixed cannot, except in case of necessity, be changed by the Tribunal without the assent of the parties.

ART. 37. The parties have the right to appoint delegates or special agents to attend the Tribunal, for the purpose of serving as intermediaries between them and the Tribunal.

They are further authorized to retain, for the defense of their rights and interests before the Tribunal, counsel or advocates appointed by them for this purpose.

ART. 38. The Tribunal decides on the choice of languages to be used by itself, and to be authorized for use before it.

ART. 39. As a general rule the arbitral procedure comprises two distinct phases; preliminary examination and discussion.

Preliminary examination consists in the communication by the respective agents to the members of the Tribunal and to the opposite party of all printed or written Acts and of all documents containing the arguments invoked in the case. This communication shall be made in the form and within the periods fixed by the Tribunal in accordance with Article 49.

Discussion consists in the oral development before the Tribunal of the arguments of the parties.

ART. 40. Every document produced by one party must be communicated to the other party.

ART. 41. The discussions are under the direction of the President.

They are only public if it be so decided by the Tribunal, with the assent of the parties.

They are recorded in the *procès-verbaux* drawn up by the Secretaries appointed by the President. These *procès-verbaux* alone have an authentic character.

ART. 42. When the preliminary examination is concluded, the Tribunal has the right to refuse discussion of all fresh Acts or documents which one party may desire to submit to it without the consent of the other party.

ART. 43. The Tribunal is free to take into consideration fresh Acts or documents to which its attention may be drawn by the agents or counsel of the parties.

In this case, the Tribunal has the right to require the

production of these Acts or documents, but is obliged to make them known to the opposite party.

ART. 44. The Tribunal can, besides, require from the agents of the parties the production of all Acts, and can demand all necessary explanations. In case of refusal, the Tribunal takes note of it.

ART. 45. The agents and counsel of the parties are authorized to present orally to the Tribunal all the arguments they may think expedient in defense of their case.

ART. 46. They have the right to raise objections and points. The decisions of the Tribunal on those points are final, and cannot form the subject of any subsequent discussion.

ART. 47. The members of the Tribunal have the right to put questions to the agents and counsel of the parties, and to demand explanations from them on doubtful points.

Neither the questions put nor the remarks made by members of the Tribunal during the discussions can be regarded as an expression of opinion by the Tribunal in general, or by its members in particular.

ART. 48. The Tribunal is authorized to declare its competence in interpreting the "Compromis" as well as the other Treaties which may be invoked in the case, and in applying the principles of international law.

ART. 49. The Tribunal has the right to issue Rules of Procedure for the conduct of the case, to decide the forms and periods within which each party must conclude its arguments, and to arrange all the formalities required for dealing with the evidence.

ART. 50. When the agents and counsel of the parties have submitted all explanations and evidence in support of their case, the President pronounces the discussion closed.

ART. 51. The deliberations of the Tribunal take place in private. Every decision is taken by a majority of members of the Tribunal.

The refusal of a member to vote must be recorded in the *procès-verbal*.

ART. 52. The award, given by a majority of votes, is

accompanied by a statement of reasons. It is drawn up in writing and signed by each member of the Tribunal.

Those members who are in the minority may record their dissent when signing.

ART. 53. The award is read out at a public meeting of the Tribunal, the agents and counsel of the parties being present, or duly summoned to attend.

ART. 54. The award, duly pronounced and notified to the agents of the parties at variance, puts an end to the dispute definitely and without appeal.

ART. 55. The parties can reserve in the "Compromis" the right to demand the revision of the award.

In this case, and unless there be an agreement to the contrary, the demand must be addressed to the Tribunal which pronounced the award. It can only be made on the ground of the discovery of some new fact. calculated to exercise a decisive influence on the award, and which, at the time the discussion was closed, was unknown to the Tribunal and to the party demanding the revision.

Proceedings for revision can only be instituted by a decision of the Tribunal expressly recording the existence of the new fact, recognizing in it the character described in the foregoing paragraph, and declaring the demand admissible on this ground.

The "Compromis" fixes the period within which the demand for revision must be made.

ART. 56. The award is only binding on the parties who concluded the "Compromis."

When there is a question of interpreting a Convention to which Powers other than those concerned in the dispute are parties, the latter notify to the former the "Compromis" they have concluded. Each of these Powers has the right to intervene in the case. If one or more of them avail themselves of this right, the interpretation contained in the award is equally binding on them.

ART. 57. Each party pays its own expenses and an equal share of those of the Tribunal.

General Provisions

ART. 58. The present Convention shall be ratified as speedily as possible.

The ratifications shall be deposited at The Hague.

A *procès-verbal* shall be drawn up recording the receipt of each ratification, and a copy duly certified shall be sent, through the diplomatic channel, to all the Powers who were represented at the International Peace Conference at The Hague.

ART. 59. The non-Signatory Powers who were represented at the International Peace Conference can adhere to the present Convention. For this purpose they must make known their adhesion to the Contracting Powers by a written notification addressed to the Netherlands Government, and communicated by it to all the other Contracting Powers.

ART. 60. The conditions on which the Powers who were not represented at the International Peace Conference can adhere to the present Convention shall form the subject of a subsequent Agreement among the Contracting Powers.

ART. 61. In the event of one of the High Contracting Parties denouncing the present Convention, this denunciation would not take effect until a year after its notification made in writing to the Netherlands Government, and by it communicated at once to all the other Contracting Powers.

This denunciation shall only affect the notifying Power.

In faith of which the Plenipotentiaries have signed the present Convention and affixed their seals to it.

Done at The Hague, the 29th July, 1899, in a single copy, which shall remain in the archives of the Netherlands Government, and copies of it, duly certified, be sènt through the diplomatic channel to the Contracting Powers.

For Germany:
  (L.S.) MUNSTER DERNEBURG.
For Austria-Hungary:
  (L.S.) WELSERSHEIMB.
  (L.S.) OKOLICSANYI.

For Belgium:
  (L.S.) A. BEERNAERT.
  (L.S.) CTE. DE GRELLE RO-GIER.
  (L.S.) CHR. DESCAMPS.

For China:
(L.S.) YANG YU.
For Denmark:
(L.S.) F. BILLE.
For Spain:
(L.S.) EL DUQUE DE TETUAN.
(L.S.) W. R. DEVILLA UR-
RUTIA.
(L.S.) ARTURO DE BAGUER.
For the United States of Amer-
ica:
(L.S.) ANDREW D. WHITE.
(L.S.) SETH LOW.
(L.S.) STANFORD NEWEL.
(L.S.) A. T. MAHAN.
(L.S.) WILLIAM CROZIER.
Under reserve of the declaration
made at the plenary sitting of
the Conference on the 25th of
July, 1899.
For the United Mexican States:
(L.S.) A. DE MIER.
(L.S.) J. ZENIL.
For France:
(L.S.) LÉON BOURGEOIS.
(L.S.) G. BIHOURD.
(L.S.) D'ESTOURNELLES DE
CONSTANT.
For Great Britain and Ireland:
(L.S.) PAUNCEFOTE.
(L.S.) HENRY HOWARD.
For Greece:
(L.S.) N. DELYANNI.
For Italy:
(L.S.) NIGRA.
(L.S.) A. ZANNINI.
(L.S.) G. POMPILJ.
For Japan:
(L.S.) I. MOTONO.
For Luxemburg:
(L.S.) EYSCHEN.

For Montenegro:
(L.S.) STAAL.
For the Netherlands:
(L.S.) V. KARNEBEEK.
(L.S.) DEN BEER POORTU-
GAEL.
(L.S.) T. M. C. ASSER.
(L.S.) E. N. RAHUSEN.
For Persia:
(L.S.) MIRZA RIZA KHAN, Ar-
fa-ud-Dovleh.
For Portugal:
(L.S.) Conde DE MACEDO.
(L.S.) AGOSTINHO D'ORNEL-
LAS DE VASCONCEL-
LOS.
(L.S.) Conde DE SELIR.
For Roumania :
(L.S.) A. BELDIMAN.
(L.S.) J. N. PAPINIU.
Under the reserves formulated in
Articles 16, 17, and 19 of the
present Convention (15, 16,
and 18 of the project presented
the Committee on Examina-
tion) and recorded in the *pro-
cès-verbal* of the sitting of the
Third Commission of July 20,
1899.
For Russia:
(L.S.) STAAL.
(L.S.) MARTENS.
(L.S.) A. BASILY.
For Servia:
(L.S.) CHEDO MIYATOVITCH.
Under the reserves recorded in
the *procès-verbal* of the Third
Commission of July 20, 1899.
For Siam :
(L.S.) PHYA SURIYA NUVATR.
(L.S.) VISUDDHA.

For the United Kingdoms of
   Sweden and Norway:
   (L.S.) BILDT.
For Switzerland:
   (L.S.) ROTH.
For Turkey:
   (L.S.) TURKHAN.
   (L.S.) MEHEMED NOURY.
Under reserve of the declaration
made in the plenary sitting of
the Conference of July 25, 1899.

For Bulgaria:
   (L.S.) D. STANCIOFF.
   (L.S.) Major HESSAPTCHIEFF.

Certified as a true copy, The
Secretary General of the Department of Foreign Affairs,

   (L.S.) L. H. RUYSSENAERS.
     THE HAGUE,
     January 31, 1900.

And whereas the said Convention was signed by the
Plenipotentiaries of the United States of America under
reservation of the following declaration:

"Nothing contained in this convention shall be so construed as to require the United States of America to depart
from its traditional policy of not intruding upon, interfering with, or entangling itself in the political questions of
policy or internal administration of any foreign state; nor
shall anything contained in the said convention be construed
to imply a relinquishment by the United States of America of
its traditional attitude toward purely American questions;"

And whereas the said Convention was duly ratified by
the Government of the United States of America, by and
with the advice and consent of the Senate thereof, and by
the Governments of the other Powers aforesaid with the
exception of China and Turkey;

And whereas, in pursuance of the stipulations of Article
58 of the said Convention the ratifications of the said
Convention were deposited at The Hague on the 4th day of
September, 1900, by the Plenipotentiaries of the Govern-
ments of the United States of America, Germany, Austria-
Hungary, Belgium, Denmark, Spain, France, Great Britain,
Italy, the Netherlands, Persia, Portugal, Roumania, Russia,
Siam, Sweden and Norway and Bulgaria; on the 6th day of
October, 1900, by the Plenipotentiary of the Government of
Japan; on the 16th day of October, 1900, by the Plenipo-

tentiary of the Government of Montenegro; on the 29th day of December, 1900, by the Plenipotentiary of the Government of Switzerland; on the 4th day of April, 1901, by the Plenipotentiary of the Government of Greece; on the 17th day of April, 1901, by the Plenipotentiary of the Government of Mexico; on the 11th day of May, 1901, by the Plenipotentiary of the Government of Servia; and on the 12th day of July, 1901, by the Plenipotentiary of the Government of Luxembourg.

Now, therefore, be it known that I, Theodore Roosevelt, President of the United States of America, have caused the said Convention to be made public, to the end that the same and every clause thereof may be observed and fulfilled with good faith by the United States and the citizens thereof, subject to the reserve made in the aforesaid declaration of the Plenipotentiaries of the United States.

In witness whereof, I have hereunto set my hand and caused the seal of the United States to be affixed.

Done at the City of Washington this first day of November in the year of our Lord one thousand nine [L.S.] hundred and one, and of the Independence of the United States, the one hundred and twenty-sixth.

THEODORE ROOSEVELT.

By the President:
JOHN HAY,
Secretary of State.

APPENDIX XI

CONVENTION BETWEEN THE UNITED STATES
OF AMERICA AND CERTAIN POWERS WITH
RESPECT TO THE LAWS AND CUSTOMS OF
WAR ON LAND

Signed at The Hague, July 29, 1899
Ratification advised by the Senate, March 11, 1902
Ratified by the President of the United States, March 19, 1902
Ratifications deposited with the Netherlands Government, September 4, 1900
Proclaimed April 11, 1902

[Translation]

His Majesty the Emperor of Germany, King of Prussia; His Majesty the Emperor of Austria, King of Bohemia, etc., and Apostolic King of Hungary; His Majesty the King of the Belgians; His Majesty the King of Denmark; His Majesty the King of Spain, and in His Name Her Majesty the Queen Regent of the Kingdom; the President of the United States of America; the President of the United Mexican States; the President of the French Republic; Her Majesty the Queen of the United Kingdom of Great Britain and Ireland, Empress of India; His Majesty the King of the Hellenes; His Majesty the King of Italy; His Majesty the Emperor of Japan; His Royal Highness the Grand Duke of Luxemburg, Duke of Nassau; His Highness the Prince of Montenegro; Her Majesty the Queen of the Netherlands; His Imperial Majesty the Shah of Persia; His Majesty the King of Portugal and of the Algarves, etc.;

His Majesty the King of Roumania; His Majesty the Emperor of all the Russias; His Majesty the King of Servia; His Majesty the King of Siam; His Majesty the King of Sweden and Norway; His Majesty the Emperor of the Ottomans and His Royal Highness the Prince of Bulgaria

Considering that, while seeking means to preserve peace and prevent armed conflicts among nations, it is likewise necessary to have regard to cases where an appeal to arms may be caused by events which their solicitude could not avert;

Animated by the desire to serve, even in this extreme hypothesis, the interests of humanity and the ever increasing requirements of civilization;

Thinking it important, with this object, to revise the laws and general customs of war, either with the view of defining them more precisely, or of laying down certain limits for the purpose of modifying their severity as far as possible;

Inspired by these views which are enjoined at the present day, as they were twenty-five years ago at the time of the Brussels Conference in 1874, by a wise and generous foresight;

Have, in this spirit, adopted a great number of provisions, the object of which is to define and govern the usages of war on land.

In view of the High Contracting Parties, these provisions, the wording of which has been inspired by the desire to diminish the evils of war so far as military necessities permit, are destined to serve as general rules of conduct for belligerents in their relations with each other and with populations.

It has not, however, been possible to agree forthwith on provisions embracing all the circumstances which occur in practice.

On the other hand, it could not be intended by the High Contracting Parties that the cases not provided for should, for want of a written provision, be left to the arbitrary judgment of the military Commanders.

Until a more complete code of the laws of war is issued, the High Contracting Parties think it right to declare that in cases not included in the Regulations adopted by them, populations and belligerents remain under the protection and empire of the principles of international law, as they result from the usages established between civilized nations, from the laws of humanity, and the requirements of the public conscience;

They declare that it is in this sense especially that Articles 1 and 2 of the Regulations adopted must be understood;

The High Contracting Parties, desiring to conclude a Convention to this effect, have appointed as their Plenipotentiaries, to-wit: —

[Here follow the names and titles of the Plenipotentiaries who sign after Article 5 below.]

Who, after communication of their full powers, found in good and due form, have agreed on the following: —

ARTICLE 1. The High Contracting Parties shall issue instructions to their armed land forces, which shall be in conformity with the "Regulations respecting the Laws and Customs of War on Land," annexed to the present Convention.

ART. 2. The provisions contained in the Regulations mentioned in Article 1 are only binding on the Contracting Powers, in case of war between two or more of them.

These provisions shall cease to be binding from the time when, in a war between Contracting Powers, a non-Contracting Power joins one of the belligerents.

ART. 3. The present Convention shall be ratified as speedily as possible.

The ratifications shall be deposited at the Hague.

A *procès-verbal* shall be drawn up recording the receipt of each ratification, and a copy, duly certified, shall be sent through the diplomatic channel, to all the Contracting Powers.

ART. 4. Non-Signatory Powers are allowed to adhere to the present Convention.

For this purpose they must make their adhesion known to the Contracting Powers by means of a written notification, addressed to the Netherland Government, and by it communicated to all the other Contracting Powers.

ART. 5. In the event of one of the High Contracting Parties denouncing the present Convention, such denunciation would not take effect until a year after the written notification made to the Netherland Government, and by it at once communicated to all the other Contracting Powers.

This denunciation shall affect only the notifying Power.

In faith of which the Plenipotentiaries have signed the present Convention and affixed their seals thereto.

Done at The Hague the 29th July, 1899, in a single copy, which shall be kept in the archives of the Netherland Government, and copies of which, duly certified, shall be delivered to the Contracting Powers through the diplomatic channel.

For Germany:
    (Signed)   MUNSTER DERNEBURG.

For Austria-Hungary:
    (Signed)   WELSERSHEIMB.
                OKOLICSANYI.

For Belgium:
    (Signed)   A. BEERNAERT.
                CTE DE GRELLE ROGIER.
                CHR DESCAMPS.

For Denmark:
    (Signed)   F. BILLE.

For Spain:
    (Signed)   EL DUQUE DE TETUAN.
                W. R. DE VILLA URRUTIA.
                ARTURO DE BAGUER.

For the United States of America:
    (Signed)   STANFORD NEWEL.

For the United Mexican States:
    (Signed)   M. DE MIER.
                J. ZENIL.

For France:
(Signed)   LEON BOURGEOIS. •
             G. BIHOURD.
             D'ESTOURNELLES DE CONSTANT.

For Great Britain and Ireland:
(Signed)   PAUNCEFOTE.
             HENRY HOWARD.

For Greece:
(Signed)   N. DELYANNI.

For Italy:
(Signed)   NIGRA.
             A. ZANNINI.
             G. POMPILJ.

For Japan:
(Signed)   I. MOTONO.

For Luxemburg:
(Signed)   EYSCHEN.

For Montenegro:
(Signed)   STAAL.

For the Netherlands:
(Signed)   V. KARNEBEEK.
             DEN BEER POORTUGAEL.
             T. M. C. ASSER.
             E. N. RAHUSEN.

For Persia:
(Signed)   MIRZA RIZA KHAN, Arfa-ud-Dovleh.

For Portugal:
(Signed)   CONDE DE MACEDO.
             AGOSTINHO D'ORNELLAS DE VASCON-
                CELLOS.
             CONDE DE SELIR.

For Roumania:
(Signed)   A. BELDIMAN.
             J. N. PAPINIU.

For Russia:
(Signed)   STAAL.
             MARTENS.
             A. BASILY.

For Servia:
(Signed)   CHEDO MIYATOVITCH.

For Siam:
  (Signed) PHYA SURIA NUVATR.
        VISUDDHA.

For the United Kingdoms of Sweden and Norway:
  (Signed) BILDT.

For Turkey:
  (Signed) TURKHAN.
        MEHEMED NOURY.

For Bulgaria:
  (Signed) D. STANCIOFF.
        MAJOR HESSAPTCHIEFF.

ANNEX TO THE CONVENTION

REGULATIONS RESPECTING THE LAWS AND CUSTOMS OF WAR ON LAND

SECTION I

ON BELLIGERENTS

CHAPTER I. *On the Qualifications of Belligerents*

ARTICLE 1. The laws, rights and duties of war apply not only to armies, but also to militia and volunteer corps fulfilling the following conditions:

1. To be commanded by a person responsible for his subordinates;

2. To have a fixed distinctive emblem recognizable at a distance;

3. To carry arms openly; and

4. To conduct their operations in accordance with the laws and customs of war.

In countries where militia or volunteer corps constitute the army, or form part of it, they are included under the denomination "army."

ART. 2. The population of a territory which has not been occupied who, on the enemy's approach, spontaneously take up arms to resist the invading troops without having time to organize themselves in accordance with Article 1, shall be regarded a belligerent, if they respect the laws and customs of war.

ART. 3. The armed forces of the belligerent parties may consist of combatants and non-combatants. In case of capture by the enemy both have a right to be treated as prisoners of war.

CHAPTER II. *On Prisoners of War*

ART. 4. Prisoners of war are in the power of the hostile Government, but not in that of the individuals or corps who captured them.

They must be humanely treated.

All their personal belongings, except arms, horses, and military papers remain their property.

ART. 5. Prisoners of war may be interned in a town, fortress, camp, or any other locality, and bound not to go beyond certain fixed limits; but they can only be confined as an indispensable measure of safety.

ART. 6. The State may utilize the labor of prisoners of war according to their rank and aptitude. Their tasks shall not be excessive, and shall have nothing to do with the military operations.

Prisoners may be authorized to work for the Public Service, for private persons, or on their own account.

Work done for the State shall be paid for according to the tariffs in force for soldiers of the national army employed on similar tasks.

When the work is for other branches of the Public Service or for private persons, the conditions shall be settled in agreement with the military authorities.

The wages of the prisoners shall go towards improving their position, and the balance shall be paid them at the time of their release, after deducting the cost of their maintenance.

ART. 7. The Government into whose hands prisoners of war have fallen is bound to maintain them.

Failing a special agreement between the belligerents, prisoners of war shall be treated as regards food, quarters, and clothing, on the same footing as the troops of the Government which has captured them.

ART. 8. Prisoners of war shall be subject to the laws, regulations, and orders in force in the army of the State into whose hands they have fallen.

Any act of insubordination warrants the adoption, as regards them, of such measures of severity as may be necessary.

Escaped prisoners, recaptured before they have succeeded in rejoining their army or before quitting the territory occupied by the army that captured them, are liable to disciplinary punishment.

Prisoners who, after succeeding in escaping are again taken prisoners, are not liable to any punishment for the previous flight.

ART. 9. Every prisoner of war, if questioned, is bound to declare his true name and rank, and if he disregards this rule, he is liable to a curtailment of the advantages accorded to the prisoners of war of his class.

ART. 10. Prisoners of war may be set at liberty on parole if the laws of their country authorize it, and, in such a case, they are bound, on their personal honor, scrupulously to fulfill, both as regards their own Government and the Government by whom they were made prisoners, the engagements they have contracted.

In such cases, their own Government shall not require of nor accept from them any service incompatible with the parole given.

ART. 11. A prisoner of war cannot be forced to accept his liberty on parole; similarly the hostile Government is not obliged to assent to the prisoner's request to be set at liberty on parole.

ART. 12. Any prisoner of war, who is liberated on parole and recaptured, bearing arms against the Government to whom he had pledged his honor, or against the allies of that Government, forfeits his right to be treated as a prisoner of war, and can be brought before the Courts.

ART. 13. Individuals who follow an army without directly belonging to it, such as newspaper correspondents and reporters, sutlers, contractors, who fall into the enemy's hands, and whom the latter think fit to detain, have a right to be treated as prisoners of war, provided they can produce a certificate from the military authorities of the army they were accompanying.

ART. 14. A Bureau for information relative to prisoners of war is instituted, on the commencement of hostilities, in each of the belligerent States, and when necessary, in the neutral countries on whose territory belligerents have been received. This Bureau is intended to answer all inquiries about prisoners of war, and is furnished by the various services concerned with all the necessary information to enable it to keep an individual return for each prisoner of war. It is kept informed of internments and changes, as well as of admissions into hospitals and deaths.

It is also the duty of the Information Bureau to receive and collect all objects of personal use, valuables, letters, etc., found on the battlefields or left by prisoners who have died in hospital or ambulance, and to transmit them to those interested.

ART. 15. Relief Societies for prisoners of war, which are regularly constituted in accordance with the law of the country with the object of serving as the intermediary for charity, shall receive from the belligerents for themselves and their duly accredited agents every facility, within the bounds of military requirements and Administrative Regulations, for the effective accomplishment of their humane task. Delegates of these Societies may be admitted to the places of internment for the distribution of relief, as also to the halting places of repatriated prisoners, if furnished with a personal permit by the military authorities, and on giving an engagement in writing to comply with all their Regulations for order and police.

ART. 16. The Information Bureau shall have the privilege of free postage. Letters, money orders, and valuables, as well as postal parcels destined for the prisoners of war or dispatched by them, shall be free of all postal duties both in the countries of origin and destination, as well as in those they pass through.

Gifts and relief in kind for prisoners of war shall be admitted free of all duties of entry and others, as well as of payments for carriage by the Government railways.

ART. 17. Officers taken prisoners may receive, if necessary, the full pay allowed them in this position by their country's regulations, the amount to be repaid by their Government.

ART. 18. Prisoners of war shall enjoy every latitude in the exercise of their religion, including attendance at their own church services, provided only they comply with the regulations for order and police issued by the military authorities.

ART. 19. The wills of prisoners of war are received or drawn up on the same conditions as for soldiers of the National Army.

The same rules shall be observed regarding death certificates, as well as for the burial of prisoners of war, due regard being paid to their grade and rank.

ART. 20. After the conclusion of peace, the repatriation of prisoners of war shall take place as speedily as possible.

CHAPTER III. *On the Sick and Wounded*

ART. 21. The obligations of belligerents with regard to the sick and wounded are governed by the Geneva Convention of the 22d August, 1864, subject to any modifications which may be introduced into it.

SECTION II

On Hostilities

CHAPTER I. *On Means of injuring the Enemy, Sieges and Bombardments*

ART. 22. The right of belligerents to adopt means of injuring the enemy is not unlimited.

ART. 23. Besides the prohibitions provided by special Conventions, it is especially prohibited: —

(*a*) To employ poison or poisoned arms ;

(*b*) To kill or wound treacherously individuals belonging to the hostile nation or army ;

(*c*) To kill or wound an enemy who, having laid down arms, or having no longer means of defense, has surrendered at discretion ;

(*d*) To declare that no quarter will be given ;

(*e*) To employ arms, projectiles, or material of a nature to cause superfluous injury ;

(*f*) To make improper use of a flag of truce, the national flag, or military ensigns and the enemy's uniform, as well as the distinctive badges of the Geneva Convention ;

(*g*) To destroy or seize the enemy's property, unless such destruction or seizure be imperatively demanded by the necessities of war.

ART. 24. Ruses of war and the employment of methods necessary to obtain information about the enemy and the country, are considered allowable.

ART. 25. The attack or bombardment of towns, villages, habitations or buildings which are not defended, is prohibited.

ART. 26. The Commander of an attacking force, before commencing a bombardment, except in the case of an assault, should do all he can to warn the authorities.

ART. 27. In sieges and bombardments all necessary steps should be taken to spare as far as possible edifices devoted to religion, art, science, and charity, hospitals, and places where the sick and wounded are collected, provided they are not used at the same time for military purposes.

The besieged should indicate these buildings or places by some particular and visible signs, which should previously be notified to the assailants.

ART. 28. The pillage of a town or place, even when taken by assault, is prohibited.

CHAPTER II. *On Spies*

ART. 29. An individual can only be considered a spy if, acting clandestinely, or on false pretenses, he obtains, or seeks to obtain information in the zone of operations of a belligerent, with the intention of communicating it to the hostile party.

Thus, soldiers not in disguise who have penetrated into the zone of operations of a hostile army to obtain information are not considered spies. Similarly, the following are not considered spies: soldiers or civilians, carrying out their mission openly, charged with the delivery of dispatches destined either for their own army or for that of the enemy. To this class belong likewise individuals sent in balloons to deliver dispatches, and generally to maintain communication between the various parts of an army or a territory.

ART. 30. A spy taken in the act cannot be punished without previous trial.

ART. 31. A spy who, after rejoining the army to which he belongs, is subsequently captured by the enemy, is treated as a prisoner of war and incurs no responsibility for his previous acts of espionage.

CHAPTER III. *On Flags of Truce*

ART. 32. An individual is considered as bearing a flag of truce who is authorized by one of the belligerents to enter into communication with the other, and who carries a white flag. He has a right to inviolability, as well as the trumpeter, bugler, or drummer, the flag-bearer and the interpreter who may accompany him.

ART. 33. The Chief to whom a flag of truce is sent is not obliged to receive it in all circumstances.

He can take all steps necessary to prevent the envoy taking advantage of his mission to obtain information.

In case of abuse, he has the right to detain the envoy temporarily.

ART. 34. The envoy loses his rights of inviolability if it is proved beyond doubt that he has taken advantage of his privileged position to provoke or commit an act of treachery.

CHAPTER IV. *On Capitulations*

ART. 35. Capitulations agreed on between the Contracting Parties must be in accordance with the rules of military honor.

When once settled, they must be scrupulously observed by both the parties.

CHAPTER V. *On Armistices*

ART. 36. An armistice suspends military operations by mutual agreement between the belligerent parties. If its duration is not fixed, the belligerent parties can resume operations at any time, provided always the enemy is warned within the time agreed upon, in accordance with the terms of the armistice.

ART. 37. An armistice may be general or local. The first suspends all military operations of the belligerent States; the second, only those between certain fractions of the belligerent armies and in a fixed radius.

ART. 38. An armistice must be notified officially, and in good time, to the competent authorities and the troops. Hostilities are suspended immediately after the notification, or at a fixed date.

ART. 39. It is for the Contracting Parties to settle, in the terms of the armistice, what communications may be held, on the theater of war, with the population and with each other.

ART. 40. Any serious violation of the armistice by one of the parties gives the other party the right to denounce it, and even, in case of urgency, to recommence hostilities at once.

ART. 41. A violation of the terms of the armistice by private individuals acting on their own initiative, only confers the right of demanding the punishment of the offenders, and, if necessary, indemnity for the losses sustained.

SECTION III

ON MILITARY AUTHORITY OVER HOSTILE TERRITORY

ART. 42. Territory is considered occupied when it is actually placed under the authority of the hostile army.

The occupation applies only to the territory where such authority is established, and in a position to assert itself.

ART. 43. The authority of the legitimate power having actually passed into the hands of the occupant, the latter shall take all steps in his power to reëstablish and insure, as far as possible, public order and safety, while respecting, unless absolutely prevented, the laws in force in the country.

ART. 44. Any compulsion of the population of occupied territory to take part in military operations against its own country is prohibited.

ART. 45. Any pressure on the population of occupied territory to take the oath to the hostile Power is prohibited.

ART. 46. Family honor and rights, individual lives and private property, as well as religious convictions and liberty, must be respected.

Private property cannot be confiscated.

ART. 47. Pillage is formally prohibited.

ART. 48. If, in the territory occupied, the occupant collects the taxes, dues, and tolls imposed for the benefit of the State, he shall do it, as far as possible, in accordance with the rules in existence and the assessment in force, and will in consequence be bound to defray the expenses of the administration of the occupied territory on the same scale as that by which the legitimate Government was bound.

ART. 49. If, besides the taxes mentioned in the preceding Article, the occupant levies other money taxes in the occupied territory, this can only be for military necessities or the administration of such territory.

ART. 50. No general penalty, pecuniary or otherwise, can be inflicted on the population on account of the acts of individuals for which it cannot be regarded as collectively responsible.

ART. 51. No tax shall be collected except under a written order and on the responsibility of a Commander-in-Chief.

This collection shall only take place, as far as possible, in accordance with the rules in existence and the assessment of taxes in force.

For every payment a receipt shall be given to the tax-payer.

ART. 52. Neither requisition in kind nor services can be demanded from communes or inhabitants except for the necessities of the army of occupation. They must be in proportion to the resources of the country, and of such a nature as not to involve the population in the obligation of taking part in military operations against their country.

These requisitions and services shall only be demanded on the authority of the Commander in the locality occupied.

The contributions in kind shall, as far as possible, be paid for in ready money; if not, their receipt shall be acknowledged.

ART. 53. An army of occupation can only take possession of the cash, funds, and property liable to requisition belonging strictly to the State, dépôts of arms, means of transport, stores and supplies, and, generally, all movable property of the State which may be used for military operations.

Railway plant, land telegraphs, telephones, steamers, and other ships, apart from cases governed by maritime law, as well as dépôts of arms and, generally, all kinds of war material, even though belonging to Companies or to private persons, are likewise material which may serve for military operations, but they must be restored at the conclusion of peace, and indemnities paid for them.

ART. 54. The plant of railways coming from neutral States, whether the property of those States, or of Companies, or of private persons, shall be sent back to them as soon as possible.

ART. 55. The occupying State shall only be regarded as administrator and usufructuary of the public buildings, real property, forests, and agricultural works belonging to the hostile State, and situated in the occupied country. It must protect the capital of these properties, and administer it according to the rules of usufruct.

ART. 56. The property of the communes, that of religious, charitable, and educational institutions, and those of arts and science, even when State property, shall be treated as private property.

All seizure of, and destruction, or intentional damage done to such institutions, to historical monuments, works of art or science, is prohibited, and should be made the subject of proceedings.

SECTION IV

ON THE INTERNMENT OF BELLIGERENTS AND THE CARE OF THE WOUNDED IN NEUTRAL COUNTRIES

ART. 57. A neutral State which receives in its territory troops belonging to the belligerent armies shall intern them, as far as possible, at a distance from the theater of war.

It can keep them in camps, and even confine them in fortresses or locations assigned for this purpose.

It shall decide whether officers may be left at liberty on

giving their parole that they will not leave the neutral territory without authorization.

ART. 58. Failing a special Convention, the neutral State shall supply the interned with the food, clothing, and relief required by humanity.

At the conclusion of peace, the expenses caused by the internment shall be made good.

ART. 59. A neutral State may authorize the passage through its territory of wounded or sick belonging to the belligerent armies, on condition that the trains bringing them shall carry neither combatants nor war material. In such a case, the neutral State is bound to adopt such measures of safety and control as may be necessary for the purpose.

Wounded and sick brought under these conditions into neutral territory by one of the belligerents, and belonging to the hostile party, must be guarded by the neutral State, so as to insure their not taking part again in the military operations. The same duty shall devolve on the neutral State with regard to wounded or sick of the other army who may be committed to its care.

ART. 60. The Geneva Convention applies to sick and wounded interned in neutral territory.

INDEX

INDEX

21   481